THE XXL SLOW COOKER RECIPE BOOK UK

300 Affordable, Mouthwatering and Super-Amazing Family Favourites For Everyday Enjoyment I including Inspirations for Breakfast, Lunch, Dinner, Desserts & More

MARC HEMINGWAY

TABLE OF CONTENTS

BEEF

LAMB

PORK

FISH

MEAT-FREE

DUCK

RABBIT

EXCLUSIVE BONUS

40 Weight Loss Recipes

&

14 Days Meal Plan

Scan the QR-Code and receive
the FREE download:

XXL Slow Cooker Book, 300 recipes

Tips and Tricks for Cooking with a Slow Cooker

- Read the instructions for your **slow cooker** thoroughly before use.
- Cooking times may vary according to your size, style, and brand of slow cooker.
- Adapt your ingredients' quantities to suit the size of your slow cooker.
- Some recipes suggest preheating your slow cooker, and some don't. If you prefer to preheat your slow cooker before adding ingredients, err on the side of caution and begin on a **Low** setting.
- Some recipes suggest sautéing certain ingredients before adding them to the slow cooker. However, for most slow cooker recipes you can add all the ingredients for a recipe directly to the slow cooker. However, sautéing suggested ingredients first may improve the final flavour.
- Some of the modern slow cookers include a **sauté** function. This is useful if you prefer to fry some ingredients independently before adding them to your slow cooker meal, for example, meat or onions.
- In the **Desserts** section of the cookbook, you will see lots of references to a tea towel/kitchen roll/paper towel etc., being placed between the lid and the slow cooker basin. During cooking, condensation forms on the lid of the slow cooker and will typically drip back on to the food, in the case of baked goods, potentially making it wet or soggy. The tea towel absorbs the condensation and prevents it dripping onto your cakes and desserts.

EXCLUSIVE BONUS

40 Weight Loss Recipes

&

14 Days Meal Plan

Scan the QR-Code and receive
the FREE download:

STARTERS AND SIDES

OVERNIGHT BREAKFAST CASSEROLE

INGREDIENTS

- 700g of sausages cut into 1-inch pieces (you can use up any leftover cooked sausages in this recipe)
- 1 red pepper, sliced
- 60g of spring onions, sliced
- 110g of mild green chilies, finely chopped
- 25g of fresh coriander, chopped
- 850g of shredded hash browns (frozen are fine)
- 120g of grated cheddar cheese
- 12 eggs
- 235mls of milk
- Seasoning to taste

METHOD

1. Preheat the slow cooker on a low setting and spray lightly with cooking oil.
2. Cut the sausages into pieces about 1 inch thick.
3. In a separate bowl, combine the spring onions, pepper, chillies and coriander.
4. Place the ingredients into the slow cooker in layers, starting with the hash browns, the sausages, then the green onion mixture and cheese. Repeat layers twice.
5. In another bowl, whisk up the eggs, milk, and seasoning together. Pour on the casserole.
6. Put the lid on and cook on a Low setting for 8 hours.
7. Serve

NUTRITION PER PORTION:

SERVES - 12 | CALORIES - 524KCAL | PROTEIN - 23G | CARBOHYDRATES - 33G | FAT - 34G

PORK TACOS (V1)

INGREDIENTS

- 1 x 95g jar of chipotle chilli and smoked paprika paste
- 1 teaspoon of oregano
- ¼ teaspoon of chilli flakes
- 1 teaspoon of garlic salt
- 2 tablespoons of tomato purée
- 2 tablespoons of cider vinegar
- 1.4kg pork shoulder joint
- 60mls of orange juice

To serve

- 1 red onion, sliced thinly
- Juice of 1 lime
- Pack of 10 mini tortillas, plain
- ½ an iceberg lettuce, shredded
- 10g fresh coriander, chopped
- 1 red chilli, sliced into fine pieces

METHOD

1. Combine all ingredients except the pork and orange juice in a container and season to taste.
2. Cover the pork with the marinade and rub it into the flesh.
3. Put the pork and the marinade in the slow cooker, with the orange juice.
4. Close the lid and cook on a High setting for 5 hours.
5. Now make the pickle. Put the red onion into a container and cover with boiling water. Leave for 15 minutes.
6. Drain the onions and return them to the container. Add the lime juice and a bit of salt, then stir well and for 15 minutes more.

7. Once cooked through, transfer the pork to a plate, remove any excess fat and pull out any bones.
8. Shred the joint by pulling it apart with two forks. Any pork juices will add to the flavour.
9. Warm the tortillas before serving, then fill each one with lettuce and pulled pork and serve sprinkled with coriander and a side of red chilli pickle.

NUTRITION PER PORTION:

SERVES - 12 | CALORIES - 678KCAL | PROTEIN - 80G | CARBOHYDRATES - 54G | FAT - 17G

SHREDDED PORK TACOS (V2)

INGREDIENTS

- 1.9kg of pork shoulder joint
- 1 onion, chopped finely
- 2 garlic cloves, crushed
- 100mls of apple juice
- 400g can of chopped tomatoes
- 1 tablespoon of black treacle

- 1 tablespoon of runny honey
- 1 tablespoon of black treacle
- 1 tablespoon of cider vinegar
- 4 tablespoons of BBQ sauce
- 35g of taco seasoning

- 400g can of black beans, rinsed through
- 8 taco shells
- 1 iceberg lettuce, shredded
- A selection of your favourite dips

METHOD

1. Add the meat, garlic and onion, apple juice, tomatoes, honey, treacle, cider vinegar, and BBQ sauce to the slow cooker. Put the lid on the slow cooker and cook on Low for 8 hours.
2. Once cooked, transfer the pork from the slow cooker to a plate. Use two forks to shred the meat.
3. Once shredded, return the pork to the slow cooker, and add the beans and taco seasoning. Mix thoroughly and cook on low for a further 30 minutes.
4. Serve the tacos filled with pork, topped with lettuce, and your favourite dip.

NUTRITION PER PORTION:

SERVES - 8 | CALORIES - 686KCAL | PROTEIN - 78G | CARBOHYDRATES - 33G | FAT - 24G

OPEN BREAD ROLLS WITH SHREDDED TURKEY

INGREDIENTS

- 1.25kg turkey thigh joint
- 2 medium onions, thinly sliced
- 900mls of chicken stock (stock cubes are suitable)
- 1 tablespoon of English mustard

- 2 tablespoons of dijon mustard
- 300mls of apple juice
- 2 teaspoons of paprika
- 2 teaspoons of allspice
- 2 teaspoons of chilli flakes

- 2 teaspoons of cumin seeds
- 3 star anise
- 8 fresh bread rolls
- 300g of coleslaw
- 60g of rocket leaves

METHOD

1. Clean and prepare the turkey joint. Put it in the slow cooker with the onions.
2. Meanwhile, mix the stock and apple juice with the dijon and English mustard, and the spices. Pour over the turkey joint.
3. Close the slow cooker's lid and cook for 5 hours on the highest setting.

4. Once the turkey is cooked, move it to serving dish with the onions and spices. Discard the skin, bone, and the star anise, and shred the meat.
5. Plate the rolls, divide the coleslaw, and top with turkey meat, onions and rocket leaves. Split the rolls and divide the coleslaw between them, then top with the shredded turkey, onions and rocket leaves. Serve with extra mustard

NUTRITION PER PORTION:
SERVES - 8 | CALORIES - 389KCAL | PROTEIN - 27G | CARBOHYDRATES - 33G | FAT - 16G

PORK TOSTADAS WITH PINEAPPLE SALSA
INGREDIENTS

- 1 onion, thinly sliced
- Cooking oil
- 2 garlic cloves, grated
- 1kg of pork shoulder joint, cut into two 500g pieces
- 1 tablespoon of Mexican spice blend
- 6 plain tortilla wraps
- 150g of pineapple, skinned and finely diced
- 50g of red onion, finely diced
- ½ of a red chilli, seeds removed, finely diced
- Juice of ½ a lime
- 200g of iceberg lettuce, shredded
- 3 tablespoons of coriander, roughly chopped
- 60g of soured cream

METHOD
1. Preheat the slow cooker on low and lightly spray with oil. Add the garlic and onion.
2. Rub the Mexican spice blend all over the pork pieces and add to the slow cooker with 100mls of cold water.
3. Put the lid on and cook for 4 hours on a High setting.
4. In a separate bowl, mix up the pineapple, chilli, red onion and lime juice. Add 2 tablespoons of coriander and stir.
5. 30 minutes before the pork is due to finish cooking, place the tortillas on a greased baking tray and bake at 180C for 8 minutes until crisp and golden.
6. Once cooked, take the from the slow cooker to a plate and shred with two forks. Discard any large fat bits. Add some of the onions and meat juices to the pork to taste.
7. Serve the tortillas topped with lettuce, pork and pineapple salsa, with a coriander garnish.

NUTRITION PER PORTION:
SERVES - 6 | CALORIES - 416KCAL | PROTEIN - 40G | CARBOHYDRATES - 36G | FAT - 12G

BEEF BRISKET TACOS
INGREDIENTS

- 1kg joint of beef brisket
- 1 red onion, chopped
- 2 tablespoons of vegetable oil
- 5 garlic cloves, chopped
- 1 teaspoon of chilli flakes
- 2 teaspoons of cumin seeds
- ½ teaspoon of ground cloves
- 1 teaspoon of chipotle chilli flakes
- 2 bay leaves
- ½ teaspoon of dried oregano
- 1½ tablespoons of cider vinegar
- 200mls of beef stock (fresh or from cubes)

To Serve
- 2 avocados, diced
- ½ jar of pickled jalapeño chillies, drained
- 150mls of soured cream
- 1 red onion, sliced
- 30g of fresh coriander, chopped
- 18 taco shells
- Juice of 1 lime
- 3 limes, quartered

METHOD

1. Season the beef thoroughly.
2. Add 1 tablespoon of oil to a pan and sear the beef all over for about 6-7 minutes. Set to one side in a shallow bowl.
3. Using the same pan, add the rest of the oil and the onion, and cook for about 15 minutes, stirring regularly. Add the garlic and fry for a further minute.
4. Add the cumin, chilli flakes, cloves, oregano, bay leaves and vinegar to the onion and garlic, stirring to mix.
5. Finally, place the seared beef over the onions, add any meat juices that have collected while standing, then pour in the beef stock.
6. Bring the beef and stock to the boil, then transfer them to the slow cooker. Cook on Low for 8 hours.
7. Once cooked, take the beef out of the slow cooker, transfer to a plate, and shred the meat. It should be tender enough to fall apart easily. Cover with foil and keep warm in the oven on a low heat.
8. Spoon any meat juices into a jug and keep warm.
9. Finally, mix the red onion in a separate jug with the lime juice.
10. Serve the beef in tacos topped with avocado, onion, and jalapeno. Add a drizzle of sauce, a dollop of sour cream, and garnish with coriander.
11. Finish with an extra squeeze of lime.

NUTRITION PER PORTION:
SERVES - 6 | CALORIES - 617KCAL | PROTEIN - 39G | CARBOHYDRATES - 27G | FAT - 38G

VEGETARIAN SLOPPY JOES
● ●

INGREDIENTS

- 1 garlic clove, crushed
- ½ courgette, finely sliced
- 1 pepper, finely sliced
- 1 red onion, chopped
- 1 sweet potato, peeled and chopped
- 400g of chopped tomatoes
- 1 teaspoon of hot mustard

To Serve

- 6 fresh bread rolls
- 6 lettuce leaves
- 50g of mature cheddar cheese, grated
- 2 spring onions, sliced (optional)
- Extra mustard for serving

METHOD

1. Put all the vegetables and the mustard into the slow cooker. Cook on High for 5 hours.
2. Cut the bread rolls in half.
3. On the bottom half of each roll, add some lettuce, cooked vegetables, and a large pinch of grated cheese. Serve.
4. Optional: top with spring onions and spread a little mustard on the top half of the roll before closing the sandwich.

NUTRITIONAL INFORMATION PER SERVING (EXCLUDING OPTIONAL EXTRAS):
SERVES - 6 | CALORIES - 315KCAL | PROTEIN - 7G | CARBOHYDRATES - 50G | FAT - 10G

(BOOZY) HOT CHOCOLATE

INGREDIENTS

- 1litre of milk
- 300mls of double cream
- 200g of dark chocolate pieces
- 100g of milk chocolate pieces

To Serve

- Optional: scorched marshmallows
- Optional: softly whipped cream
- Optional: grated chocolate
- Optional: 25mls of liqueur/spirit to taste

METHOD

1. Pour the double cream and milk into the slow cooker and add all the chocolate.
2. Cover and cook on a Low setting for 2 ½ hours, stirring at intervals during cooking.
3. Once cooked, ladle into mugs and top with your favourite treats.
4. Serve immediately.

NUTRITIONAL INFORMATION PER SERVING (WITHOUT LIQUEUR OR SPIRITS):

SERVES - 8-10 | CALORIES - 337KCAL | PROTEIN - 6G | CARBOHYDRATES - 19G | FAT - 30G

EASY LOAF OF BREAD

INGREDIENTS

- 500g of bread flour (use granary, white or wholemeal flour, or even mix them up!)
- 7g of dried yeast
- 350mls of warm water
- 1 teaspoon of sea salt

METHOD

1. Mix up the flour, yeast, and salt in a large bowl.
2. Pour about 300mls of lukewarm water.
3. Begin mixing the flour and water together with your hands to form a wet but soft, workable dough. Use your hands or a wooden spoon until combined into a slightly wet, workable dough. Add a bit more water if necessary.
4. On a clean, lightly floured surface, place your dough and knead for at least 10 minutes until smooth and elastic.
5. Create your desired bread shape with the dough, and place on a square of baking parchment.
6. Lift your dough using the parchment and put in the slow cooker.
7. Cover and cook on high for 2 hours.
8. After 2 hours, check your bread. It should have a crusty bottom and be springy on top. If it's not quite ready, return to the slow cooker for a further 15-30 minutes.
9. Bread cooked in the slow cooker doesn't have much crust or colour to it, so if you prefer, pop it in the oven at 220C for 5-10 minutes.

NUTRITION PER PORTION:

SERVES - 1 LOAF | CALORIES - 179KCAL | PROTEIN - 8G | CARBOHYDRATES - 32G | FAT - 1G

LIGHT AUBERGINE LUNCHEON

INGREDIENTS

- 4 tablespoons of olive oil
- 1 red onion, sliced thinly
- 2 garlic cloves, crushed

- 500g of aubergines, sliced lengthways into 1cm pieces
- 300g of ripe tomatoes cut into quarters

- 50g of sundried tomatoes
- 1 fennel bulb, sliced
- 1 teaspoon of coriander seeds
- Seasoning to taste

For the dressing

- Fresh parsley, chopped
- 2 tablespoons of olive oil

- Fresh basil, chopped
- Fresh chives, chopped

- Juice 1 lemon
- 2 teaspoons of capers

For the topping

- 100g of feta cheese

- 50g of toasted flaked almonds

To serve

- crusty bread

METHOD

1. Place two tablespoons of olive oil in the slow cooker and add the onions and garlic.
2. Brush some olive oil on the aubergine slices and layer them on the onion and garlic mixture.
3. Put the tomatoes, fennel slices, and sundried tomatoes in the spaces around the aubergines, and sprinkle all over with the coriander seeds.
4. Add seasoning to taste.
5. Turn the slow cooker to Low and cook for 8 hours until the aubergines are soft.
6. Meanwhile, blend all the dressing ingredients in a container with a food processor until smooth.
7. Put the vegetable mixture on warmed plates, drizzle with the dressing and top with flaked almonds and crumbled feta. Serve with slices of crusty bread.

NUTRITION PER PORTION:

SERVES - 6 | CALORIES - 269KCAL | PROTEIN - 8G | CARBOHYDRATES - 11G | FAT - 20G

MULLED WINE

INGREDIENTS

- 2 x 750mls bottles of red wine
- 100mls of Cointreau
- pared zest of 1 lemon zest

- Juice of 2 large oranges
- 120g of golden caster sugar
- 3 star anise

- 2 cinnamon sticks
- 4 cloves

To Serve

- Optional: slices of orange

METHOD

1. Mix everything in the slow cooker.
2. Use a Low setting to cook for 2 hours until hot.
3. Turn the setting to Keep Warm.
4. Pour into heatproof glasses. Serve with orange slices

NUTRITION PER PORTION:

SERVES - 10 | CALORIES - 191KCAL | PROTEIN - 0G | CARBOHYDRATES - 13G | FAT - 0G

MULLED CIDER

INGREDIENTS

- 1.5 litres of dry cider
- 500mls of apple juice
- 75g of soft, light brown sugar
- 1 orange, sliced
- zest of ½ lemon, pared into strips
- 5 cloves
- 10 allspice berries
- 3 cardamom pods, bruised
- 2 bay leaves
- 2 cinnamon sticks
- 100mls of (apple or brandy) calvados

METHOD

1. Mix everything except the calvados in a slow cooker.
2. Either -
   - Cook on High for 1 hour
   - Cook on Low for up to 4 hours
3. Just before serving, stir in the Calvados.
4. Turn the setting to Keep Warm.
5. Pour into heatproof glasses and serve.

NUTRITION PER PORTION:

SERVES - 10 | CALORIES - 130KCAL | PROTEIN - 0.2G | CARBOHYDRATES - 17G | FAT - 0.1G

BIO-YOGHURT

INGREDIENTS

- 2litres of whole milk
- 100mls of live yoghurt (shop-bought or made previously)

NOTE: you will need a thermometer to check the temperature of the milk

METHOD

1. Allow at least 24 hours to complete the process.
2. Pour the milk into the slow cooker and Put the lid on.
3. Heat the milk on a High setting until the temperature reaches 82C.
4. Once the milk reaches 82C, turn off the slow cooker and leave to cool to 43C.
5. Scoop out a mug of warm milk and mix it with the yoghurt.
6. Pour the mixture back into the slow cooker with the rest of the milk and mix well
7. Put the lid on and wrap the slow cooker in a cloth or towel.
8. Leave for 9-12 hours until the mixture sets.
9. The yoghurt mixture can be stored in a sealed container in the fridge for up to 2 weeks.
10. The yoghurt has a multitude of uses. Serve with cereal or porridge, or top with fresh fruit. Use in marinades, dips and smoothies.

NOTE: For thicker yoghurt strain it through a sieve lined with muslin. The whey will drain leaving a thicker mixture. Adjust to your own preference.

NUTRITION PER PORTION:

SERVES - MAKES 2 LITRES | CALORIES - 120KCAL | PROTEIN - 8G | CARBOHYDRATES - 11G | FAT - 5G

TURKISH BREAKFAST EGGS

INGREDIENTS

- 15mls of olive oil
- 2 onions, sliced
- 1 small red chilli, finely sliced
- 8 cherry tomatoes
- 1 red pepper, sliced
- 30mls of skimmed milk
- 4 eggs
- 1 slice of sourdough bread, cubed
- small bunch of parsley, chopped
- Optional: 60mls of natural yoghurt, to serve

METHOD

1. Preheat the slow cooker on Low and spray the inside with oil.
2. Add the onions, pepper, and chilli to the oil and allow to soften a little in the oil.
3. Add the cherry tomatoes, bread and seasoning. Stir thoroughly.
4. Whisk up the milk and eggs with the parsley and pour into the slow cooker making sure the breakfast ingredients are coated.
5. Cook on a Low setting for 6 hours.
6. Serve immediately, with the yoghurt.

NUTRITION PER PORTION:
SERVES - 4 | CALORIES - 165KCAL | PROTEIN - 9G | CARBOHYDRATES - 13G | FAT - 8G

HIGH PROTEIN BREAKFAST BEANS

INGREDIENTS

- 2 garlic cloves, chopped
- 1 tablespoon of olive oil
- 1 onion, thinly sliced
- 1 tablespoon of white or red wine vinegar
- 1 heaped tablespoon of soft brown sugar
- 400g can of pinto beans, rinsed through
- 200mls of passata
- Fresh coriander, chopped

METHOD

1. Preheat the slow cooker on a High setting and spray lightly with oil.
2. Add the garlic and onion to the oil and allow to soften.
3. Add the sugar and wine vinegar and leave to come to a simmer, then stir in the beans and passata. Add black pepper to taste.
4. Turn the setting to Low and leave to cook for 5 hours.
5. Check after 5 hours and if the sauce seems a little thin, turn the heat setting to High and cook for a bit longer.
6. Stir the coriander through the breakfast beans and serve.

NUTRITION PER PORTION:
SERVES - 4 | CALORIES - 149KCAL | PROTEIN - 6G | CARBOHYDRATES - 21G | FAT - 3G

OVERNIGHT PORRIDGE

INGREDIENTS

- 184g of jumbo oats
- 950mls of milk, plus a little extra to serve
- Optional: 32g of mixed dried fruits

To serve

- Flavoured toppings – e.g., sugar, honey fruit, cinnamon, yoghurt etc.

METHOD

1. Preheat the slow cooker on a Low setting.
2. Add the oats, milk, dried fruit (if using) and a pinch of salt.
3. Turn the slow cooker to its lowest setting and leave to cook (overnight) for 8 hours.
4. Give the porridge a good stir before you go to bed (and again if you are up in the night)
5. In the morning, stir the porridge, and mix in a little extra warm milk if required.
6. Serve with your favourite topping.

NUTRITION PER PORTION:

SERVES - 4 | CALORIES - 264KCAL | PROTEIN - 15G | CARBOHYDRATES - 33G | FAT - 7G

GOAN SHREDDED PORK

INGREDIENTS

- 1-inch piece of fresh ginger, sliced thinly
- 2 tablespoons of olive oil
- 1 whole garlic bulb with individual cloves peeled
- 1 large onion, sliced
- 2 tablespoons of smoked paprika
- 2 tablespoons of ground coriander
- ½-1 teaspoon cayenne pepper (depending on how hot you like it)
- 1 tablespoon of ground cumin
- 225mls of cider vinegar
- 2kg of pork leg or shoulder, bone removed

For the salad

- 3 carrots, sliced thinly (julienne pieces)
- 1 red onion, finely chopped
- 3 tomatoes, chopped
- large handful of fresh coriander
- 1 tablespoon of olive oil
- Juice of 1 lemon

To serve

- 12 warm chapatis or small wraps
- chunky cucumber raita and mango chutney

METHOD

1. Preheat the slow cooker on a Low setting. Add the onion, garlic and ginger and leave to soften.
2. Add the spices and vinegar and stir well—season with Seasoning to taste.
3. Put the pork joint into the slow cooker and turn in the mixture to coat it.
4. Turn the pork joint so that it rests in the slow cooker rind side down.
5. Cover and cook on a Low setting for 7-8 hours.
6. Meanwhile, prepare the salad. Mix the onion, garlic, carrot, tomatoes, and coriander in a container and set to one side until you are ready to serve.

7. Transfer the pork joint and its juices onto a large serving plate. Discard any rind or excess fat, then shred the meat into the juices.
8. Toss the salad with lemon juice and oil just before serving.
9. Take a chapati and add meat and salad on one side, top with raita and chutney, fold and enjoy.

NUTRITION PER PORTION:

SERVES - 6 | CALORIES - 529KCAL | PROTEIN - 65G | CARBOHYDRATES - 11G | FAT - 24G

COLD NIGHTS, HOT TODDY!

INGREDIENTS

- 1 lemon, thinly sliced, plus more for garnish
- 100g of demerara sugar
- 1 litre of water
- 600mls of Scotch whiskey
- Freshly grated nutmeg

METHOD
1. Pour the lemon, sugar, and water into your slow cooker. Turn the setting to High.
2. Cover and heat for 20-30 minutes, stirring occasionally until the sugar has dissolved.
3. Stir in the whiskey and turn the slow cooker setting to Low.
4. Serve warm with lemon slices and freshly grated nutmeg.

NUTRITION PER PORTION:

SERVES - 12 | CALORIES - 145KCAL | PROTEIN - 0.1G | CARBOHYDRATES - 8.7G | FAT - 0.1G

SODA BREAD WITH CRANBERRIES AND ROSEMARY

INGREDIENTS

- 200g of plain white flour
- 1½ teaspoons of salt
- 250g of plain wholemeal flour
- 1 teaspoon of bicarbonate of soda
- 1 teaspoon of caster sugar
- 100g of dried cranberries
- 1 tablespoon of fresh chopped rosemary
- 50g of butter, melted
- 200mls of milk
- 200g of plain Greek-style yoghurt

METHOD
1. Preheat the slow cooker on low, and lightly spritz with cooking oil. Use a piece of baking parchment to line the slow cooker.
2. In a large container, combine the both the flours, salt, bicarbonate of soda and sugar. Mix in the dried cranberries and rosemary.
3. In a separate bowl, blend the milk, melted butter and yoghurt. Make a dip in the middle of the flour mixture and pour in the liquid.
4. Combine with your hands to form a soft dough.
5. On a clean, floured surface, lightly knead the dough for about 1 minute. Don't over the dough, as soda bread differs from your usual loaf of bread.
6. Shape your dough into an oval/round loaf that will fit into your slow cooker and cut a deep slash across the top with a sharp knife.
7. Put your loaf into the slow cooker and set to High. Cover and cook for 2-2½ hours.

8. Check the loaf at 2 hours. Insert a skewer or cocktail stick into the loaf; if it comes out clean, it is ready. Otherwise, cook for a further half hour if necessary.
9. Optional: You can vary your loaf by adding different ingredients instead of the cranberries and rosemary. For example, add some sultanas or raisins, or just make a plain loaf.

NUTRITION PER PORTION:
SERVES - 6 | CALORIES - 397KCAL | PROTEIN - 13G | CARBOHYDRATES - 64G | FAT - 9G

LOADED CHORIZO POTATOES

INGREDIENTS

- 500g of small potatoes, washed, peeled, and chopped
- 50g of chopped chorizo
- Seasoning to taste
- 100g of cheddar cheese, grated
- 2 teaspoons of smoked paprika
- 3 garlic cloves, finely chopped

METHOD

1. Line the slow cooker with enough kitchen foil to fold over the top of your food, and spray with cooking oil.
2. First lay the potatoes on the foil in the slow cooker.
3. Then sprinkle the seasoning, garlic cloves, and chopped chorizo evenly over the top of the potatoes, followed by the cheddar cheese.
4. Fold the kitchen foil over the food, cover it with the lid and cook on High for 5 hours.
5. Serve hot!

NUTRITION PER PORTION:
SERVES - 3 | CALORIES - 334KCAL | PROTEIN - 16G | CARBOHYDRATES - 29G | FAT - 18G

SLOW-COOKED CABBAGE WITH LEMON

INGREDIENTS

- 1kg of white cabbage, core discarded and sliced into 1cm wide strips
- Juice and zest of 1 lemon (pare the zest in wide strips)
- 75g of lightly salted butter
- 2 teaspoons of sugar
- Seasoning to taste

METHOD

1. Preheat the slow cooker on a Low setting and let the butter melt in the bottom.
2. Add the cabbage, lemon zest, sugar, seasoning, and mix thoroughly so the cabbage is coated.
3. Cover and cook on a High setting for 2 hours, occasionally stirring, until all the liquid is gone.
4. Add the lemon juice, then cover and cook for a few minutes longer. Adjust seasoning to taste.
5. Serve hot.

   NOTE: add strips of cooked bacon or ham for extra colour and flavour.

NUTRITION PER PORTION:
SERVES - 5 | CALORIES - 167KCAL | PROTEIN - 3G | CARBOHYDRATES - 14G | FAT - 12G

SOUPS

MINESTRONE SOUP

INGREDIENTS

- 2 garlic cloves, crushed
- 2 onions, chopped
- Optional: 3 bacon rashers, chopped
- 2 small courgettes, chopped
- 3 celery sticks, chopped
- 3 carrots, chopped
- 2 tins of 400g tomatoes
- ½ teaspoon of dried oregano
- 2 bay leaves
- 1 litre of chicken or vegetable stock (from stock cubes)
- 100g of small pasta suitable for soup (for example, Orzo, small shells, Ditalini etc.)
- A large handful of spinach
- Seasoning to taste

METHOD

1. Preheat the slow cooker on High and spray a little oil into the pot.
2. Add everything to the slow cooker, except the pasta and spinach.
3. Cover and cook on a Low setting for 6 - 8 hours (alternatively, cook on High for 3 to 4 hours, depending on the time you have available).
4. Open the lid and stir in the spinach and pasta. Cover and cook for a further 10-20 minutes to soften the pasta.
5. When finished, gently stir and add extra seasoning if required.
6. Optional: Add a pinch of grated cheese on top.
7. Serve with a side of fresh crusty bread.

NUTRITION PER PORTION:
SERVES - 8 | CALORIES - 389KCAL | PROTEIN - 27G | CARBOHYDRATES - 33G | FAT - 16G

LEEK AND POTATO SOUP

INGREDIENTS

- 8 potatoes, chopped to equal sizes
- 3 leeks, chopped
- 1 onion, chopped
- 30g of butter
- 1litre of vegetable stock (from 2 stock pots/cubes)
- Seasoning to taste
- Optional: single cream, cooked bacon and/or Stilton cheese

METHOD

1. Preheat the slow cooker on a High setting, and grease with a little spray oil.
2. Add the chopped potatoes, leeks, onions, and butter.
3. Prepare the vegetable stock according to the packet instructions and add to the slow cooker to cover the ingredients.
4. Season to taste and stir.
5. Cook on a High setting for 4 hours or Low for 6 - 8 hours.
6. Once cooked, the ingredients should be soft enough to blend.
7. For a smooth soup, blend out all the lumps. For a chunkier soup, either blend on a pulse setting or use a potato masher.

8. Optional: add a dash of cream, cooked bacon and/or cheese.
9. Serve with fresh crusty bread.

NUTRITION PER PORTION:

SERVES - 4-6 | CALORIES - 512KCAL | PROTEIN - 15G | CARBOHYDRATES - 85G | FAT - 14G

TUSCAN CHICKEN TORTELLINI SOUP

INGREDIENTS

- 2 onions, peeled and finely chopped
- 3 stalks of celery, finely chopped
- 350g of carrots, peeled and finely chopped
- 3 garlic cloves, thinly sliced
- 2 tablespoons of olive oil
- 1 tablespoon of dried mixed herbs
- 3 tablespoons of tomato purée
- ½ tablespoon of caster sugar
- 1 x 400g tin of chopped tomatoes
- 2 skinless chicken breast fillets
- 25g grated parmesan, plus the rind
- 1.5 litres of chicken stock (made with 2 stock cubes/pots)
- 1 x 400g tin of haricot beans, rinsed and drained
- 200g of kale (cabbage or spinach can be used)
- 1 x 300g pack of your favourite tortellini

METHOD

1. Add the oil to your slow cooker and preheat on a High setting.
2. Add the onion, carrots, celery, and seasoning. Stir and cover until the onions start to soften.
3. Stir in the garlic, sugar, tomato purée and dried herbs and sugar, by the tinned tomatoes and the parmesan rind.
4. Place the chicken thighs carefully into the mixture, cover and leave to cook on a Low setting for 3 hours.
5. Once the vegetables are cooked and tender, put the chicken on a plate and shred with two forks. Leave to rest in its meat juices and set to one side.
6. Transfer about 400mls of the soup mixture with the softened cheese rind to a large jug or liquidiser and add half of the tin of beans and 15g of grated parmesan.
7. Puree the jug's contents and return to the slow cooker.
8. Stir in the kale, the remaining beans, and the tortellini.
9. Cover, turn to a High setting and cook for a further 20-30 minutes then add the shredded chicken and the tortellini. Cover and cook for an extra 10-15 minutes until the pasta is cooked and tender.
10. Serve hot in bowls and sprinkle the rest of the parmesan over the top.

NUTRITION PER PORTION:

SERVES - 6 | CALORIES - 335KCAL | PROTEIN - 23G | CARBOHYDRATES - 32G | FAT - 11G

CARROT AND LENTIL SOUP

INGREDIENTS

- 2 teaspoons of cumin seeds
- A pinch of chilli flakes
- 2 tablespoons of olive oil
- 140g of split red lentils
- 600g of carrots, washed and coarsely grated
- 1litre of hot vegetable stock (from a cube is fine)
- 125mls of milk
- plain yoghurt and naan bread/ crusty bread, to serve

METHOD

1. In a saucepan, dry fry (no oil) the cumin seeds and chilli flakes for about 1 minute to toast them and release their aromas.
2. Scoop out the dry-cooked seed mixture and divide it into two.
3. Place half of the seed mixture into a preheated slow cooker with the olive oil, grated carrot, and lentils.
4. Add all of the hot vegetable stock and 125mls milk to the slow cooker, cover and cook on a Low setting for about 4 hours. The lentils should swell and soften.
5. If you prefer your soup chunky, then serve as it is. If you prefer a smooth soup, then blend until all the lumps have gone.
6. Season to taste and serve with a spoonful of yoghurt and a topping of the remaining toasted spices, with naan or fresh crusty bread on the side.

NUTRITION PER PORTION:

SERVES - 4 | CALORIES - 238KCAL | PROTEIN - 11G | CARBOHYDRATES - 34G | FAT - 7G

BEAN AND PASTA SOUP

INGREDIENTS

- 200g of dried borlotti or cannellini beans,
- 2 onions, cut into small chunks, about 1cm
- 3 celery stalks, cut into small chunks, about 1cm
- 2 tablespoons of olive oil, plus extra to serve
- 2 carrots, cut into small chunks, about 1cm
- 1 litre of vegetable stock, either fresh or from stock cubes
- 4 garlic cloves, crushed
- 400g can of plum tomatoes
- 2 tablespoons of brown rice miso
- 6 rosemary sprigs
- 4 bay leaves
- 150g of small pasta shapes (ditalini, small shells or orzo for example)
- 200g kale, leaves torn, and stalks chopped small
- Optional: 30g of grated parmesan cheese to serve
- Optional: extra olive oil to serve

METHOD

1. Soak the dried beans for 6-8 hours before use, or alternatively, use canned beans.
2. Drain the beans and add to a pan of salted water. Bring them to the boil and simmer for 10 minutes: then drain, rinse and add to the slow cooker with the carrots, the onions, and the celery.
3. Stir in the olive oil, garlic, tomatoes, half a can of water, stock and the brown rice miso.
4. Tie the herbs together with kitchen string and add these to the slow cooker.
5. Season to taste, then cover and cook on a Low for 6-8 hours, until the beans are cooked through and the veg is tender.
6. Remove and the tied herbs from the soup mix and discard.
7. Add the pasta to the slow cooker and stir thorough. Cover and cook on a High setting for a further 30 minutes.
8. Finally, add the kale and cook for another 30-40 minutes.
9. Serve the soup in bowls, add a pinch of grated cheese and drizzle with a bit of olive oil.

NUTRITION PER PORTION:

SERVES - 6-8 | CALORIES - 225KCAL | PROTEIN - 10G | CARBOHYDRATES - 29G | FAT - 6G

ASIAN-STYLE TURKEY PHO

INGREDIENTS

For the stock

- 50g piece of fresh ginger, thickly sliced
- 2 onions, halved
- 3 star anise
- 2 cinnamon sticks
- ½ tablespoons of coriander seeds
- 2 cloves
- 1 turkey or chicken carcass, with all meat removed
- 2 tablespoons of sugar
- 2-3 tablespoons of fish sauce

For the phon

- 200g of flat rice noodles
- 400g of cooked and sliced turkey or chicken
- 100g of beansprouts
- 1 lime, cut into wedges
- A handful of Thai basil, mint and coriander leaves
- 2 red chillies, finely sliced
- Hoisin sauce and sriracha sauce, to serve

METHOD

1. In a pan, dry fry (no oil) the ginger and onion until it changes colour. Put in the slow cooker and heat on a Low setting.
2. Put the rest of the spices (star anise, cinnamon sticks, coriander seeds and cloves) into the slow cooker and add the meat carcass.
3. Pour 3-4 litres of boiling water into the cooker until the carcass is just about covered.
4. Cover and cook on a Low setting for 8-10 hours.
5. Once cooked, strain the stock and discard the spices and bones. Season with the fish sauce and sugar.
6. Return the stock mixture to the slow cooker and keep warm. Prepare the rest of the ingredients.
7. Cook the rice noodles according to the pack instructions and drain.
8. Divide the noodles evenly between 4 bowls and add turkey, beansprouts (and any other vegetables that you might be using).
9. Transfer the heated stock from the slow cooker to a jug and pour over the filled bowls. Sprinkle with herbs and red chilli and serve with the lime wedges and sauces.

NUTRITION PER PORTION:
SERVES - 4 | CALORIES - 334KCAL | PROTEIN - 33G | CARBOHYDRATES - 36G | FAT - 6G

CHICKEN SOUP

INGREDIENTS

- 1 tablespoon of olive oil
- 2 onions, chopped
- 3 medium carrots, chopped
- 3g of thyme leaves, chopped
- 1litre of chicken stock (prepared from stock cubes)
- 200g of frozen peas
- 300g of leftover roast chicken, shredded and skin removed
- 3 tablespoons of Greek yoghurt
- 1 garlic clove, crushed
- A squeeze of lemon juice

METHOD

1. Gently fry the onions, carrots and thyme leaves in a pan of heated oil until they are softened. Transfer to the slow cooker and pour in the chicken stock.
2. Cover, and cook for 3 hours on a High setting.
3. Add the leftover roast chicken and frozen peas. Stir through. Cook for another 30 minutes on High.
4. Scoop half the mixture into a separate container and blend to a puree.

5. Return the pureed mixture to the slow cooker and mix thoroughly. Season with Seasoning to taste, stir again and cook for another 30 minutes.
6. In a separate bowl mix up the Greek yoghurt, lemon juice and garlic.
7. Pour the soup into bowls and serve with a swirl of seasoned yoghurt.

NUTRITION PER PORTION:

SERVES - 4 | CALORIES - 339KCAL | PROTEIN - 39G | CARBOHYDRATES - 18G | FAT - 13G

HEARTY BROTH

● ●

INGREDIENTS

- Beef, veal or chicken bones
- 2 carrots, roughly chopped
- 1 celery stick, roughly chopped
- 1 leek, roughly chopped
- 1 bay leaf
- Juice of 1 lemon

METHOD

1. Spread the bones on a baking sheet and place in the oven preheated to 180C/gas mark 4.
2. Roast the bones for 1 hour, turning after 30 minutes.
3. Preheat the slow cooker on a Low setting.
4. Put the veg into the slow cooker with the roasted bones and pour over enough water to fill the pot to within 2cm of the top.
5. Add the bay leaves and lemon juice.
6. Cover and cook on a Low setting for 18-36 hours.
7. When it's ready, scoop the bones out of the slow cooker into a colander which is placed over a bowl. Return any drained liquid to the slow cooker and discard the bones.
8. Use a sieve to strain the broth into a separate pan and leave to cool.
9. Once cool, scoop out and discard any fat that has formed on the top, and season if necessary.
10. The finished broth can be stored in a fridge for up to 3 days or placed in freezer bags and frozen once cooled.

NUTRITION PER PORTION:

SERVES - 4 | CALORIES - 45KCAL | PROTEIN - 6G | CARBOHYDRATES - 4G | FAT - 0.3G

SWEET POTATO SOUP

● ●

INGREDIENTS

- 3 garlic cloves, crushed
- 1 onion, chopped
- 750g of sweet potatoes, cut into large pieces
- 1.25cm of fresh root ginger, peeled and chopped finely
- 1 teaspoon of ground coriander
- 1 red chilli, finely chopped
- 2 teaspoons of ground cumin
- 1 x 400mls tin of coconut milk
- 500ml of vegetable stock (fresh or stock cubes)
- Finely grated zest and juice of 1 lime
- 75g of crème fraiche

METHOD

1. Preheat the slow cooker on a Low and spray lightly with cooking oil.
2. Add everything, except the lime juice and creme fraiche and Put the lid on.
3. Cook on a High setting for 3 hours.
4. Transfer to a jug or blender and blend until completely smooth.

5. Season and add the lime juice.
6. Serve with a swirl of creme fraiche.

NUTRITION PER PORTION:

SERVES - 4 | CALORIES - 51KCAL | PROTEIN - 5G | CARBOHYDRATES - 46G | FAT - 26G

TOMATO SOUP

INGREDIENTS

- 15g of fresh basil, leaves removed, and stalks chopped
- 1 kg of tomatoes, chopped roughly
- 1 carrot, chopped
- 40g of butter
- 1 onion, chopped
- 3 garlic cloves, finely chopped
- 3 tablespoons of tomato puree
- 400mls of vegetable stock (fresh or from stock cubes)
- 3 tablespoons of crème fraiche

METHOD

1. Preheat the slow cooker on a Low setting.
2. Set the basil leaves and creme fraiche to one side.
3. Put all the remaining ingredients including the chopped basil stalks into the slow cooker, Put the lid on and cook on High for 3 hours.
4. Stir in the reserved crème fraiche and basil leaves.
5. Transfer the cooked soup mixture to a blender and mix until smooth. Thin with a little more water if necessary.
6. Season to taste and serve.

NUTRITION PER PORTION:

SERVES - 4 | CALORIES - 206KCAL | PROTEIN - 3G | CARBOHYDRATES - 15G | FAT - 14G

HAM, LENTIL AND KALE SOUP

INGREDIENTS

- 2 celery sticks, finely chopped
- 1 onion, finely chopped
- 1 tablespoon of olive oil
- 2 garlic cloves, crushed
- 200g of red lentils, washed
- ¼-½ teaspoon of dried chilli flakes, to taste
- 200g of kale, roughly chopped
- 1litre of chicken stock (fresh or from stock cubes)
- 180g of cooked ham hock, cut into pieces
- Zest of 1/2 a lemon, finely grated
- Handful of curly parsley, roughly chopped

METHOD

1. Preheat your slow cooker on a low setting and spritz lightly with oil.
2. Add the olive oil, onion, celery, garlic, chilli flakes and washed lentils into the slow cooker.
3. Put in the kale and stock. Season to taste.
4. Cover and cook on Low for 3-4 hours until the lentils are swollen and tender.
5. Stir in the ham, lemon zest and parsley. Season, and add a little more stock if too thick.
6. Serve in warmed bowls and drizzled with extra oil.

NUTRITION PER PORTION:

SERVES - 4 | CALORIES - 249KCAL | PROTEIN - 24G | CARBOHYDRATES - 32G | FAT - 4G

FRENCH ONION SOUP

INGREDIENTS

- 75g of butter
- 3 garlic cloves, crushed
- 700g of onions, sliced thinly
- 1 tablespoon of plain flour
- 200mls of dry white wine
- 1litre of hot vegetable stock (fresh or from stock cubes)
- Bouquet garni
- Baguette, cut into slices
- 50g of gruyere or cheddar cheese, grated or cubed

METHOD

1. Cook the garlic and onion in a pan of melted butter until soft. Add the flour and cook for a minute, stirring continuously.
2. Add the wine, and simmer to reduce, then add the stock and the bouquet garni. Bring to the boil then pour into the slow cooker.
3. Cover and cook on Low for 4 hours.
4. Before serving the soup, toast the slices of baguette on both sides and serve with the bowls of soup, topped with grated cheese.

NUTRITION PER PORTION:

SERVES - 4 | CALORIES - 438KCAL | PROTEIN - 11G | CARBOHYDRATES - 45G | FAT - 48G

CARROT AND CORIANDER SOUP

INGREDIENTS

- 700g carrots, chopped
- 1 potato, peeled and diced
- 1 white onion, peeled and diced
- 1 garlic clove, peeled
- 1litre of vegetable stock (fresh or from stock cubes)
- 1 tablespoon of creme fraiche (double cream or natural yoghurt are a suitable alternative)
- ¼ teaspoon of nutmeg
- ½ teaspoon of turmeric
- 1½ teaspoons of ground coriander
- 1 teaspoon of butter
- Seasoning to taste
- Fresh coriander, chopped

METHOD

1. Preheat the slow cooker on a Low setting and spritz lightly with cooking oil.
2. Put all the vegetables into the slow cooker with the garlic clove.
3. Add the spices, butter, Seasoning to taste to the vegetables. Pour over the stock, making sure all the vegetables are covered.
4. Cook on a Low setting for 3-4 hours until the vegetables are tender.
5. Transfer the cooked mixture to a jug or blender and blitz. If the soup is too thick, add a little more water.
6. Add the creme fraiche (or alternatives), and blend again until smooth.
7. Serve in bowls, sprinkled generously with coriander.

NUTRITION PER PORTION:

SERVES - 4 | CALORIES - 123KCAL | PROTEIN - 3G | CARBOHYDRATES - 25G | FAT - 2G

APPLE AND CELERIAC SOUP

INGREDIENTS

- 1 celery stalk, roughly chopped
- 4 tablespoons of olive oil
- 2 onions, sliced
- 1 celeriac, shopped
- 4 eating apples, cored and cut into quarters
- Fresh thyme
- 2 litres of vegetable or chicken stock (fresh or from cubes)
- 200mls of crème fraiche
- Sage leaves

METHOD

1. Preheat the slow cooker on High setting and add two tablespoons of olive oil.
2. Add the celery and onion and allow to soften before adding the celeriac, apples and thyme.
3. Add the stock to the slow cooker mixture and cook on Low for 3-4 hours until the vegetables are tender.
4. Transfer the soup mixture to a large jug or bowl and blend until smooth. Stir in half the crème fraiche.
5. Heat the remaining of olive oil and quick fry the sage leaves until crispy.
6. Serve the soup in bowls. Top with a little more creme fraiche, and crispy sage leaves.

NUTRITION PER PORTION:
SERVES - 8 | CALORIES - 237KCAL | PROTEIN - 7G | CARBOHYDRATES - 15G | FAT - 17G

CREAM OF CELERIAC SOUP

INGREDIENTS

- 3 garlic cloves, crushed
- 2kg of celeriac, chopped
- 1 onion, chopped
- 1 stalk of celery, trimmed and coarsely chopped
- 1.5litres of water
- 1 litre of chicken stock
- 125mls of single cream
- 4 tablespoons of fresh chervil leaves
- 4 tablespoons of olive oil

METHOD

1. Preheat the slow cooker on a Low setting and spritz lightly with oil.
2. Add the celeriac, onion, garlic, celery, water and stock, Put the lid on and cook on a Low setting for 8 hours.
3. Once cooked, leave standing for about 10 minutes before putting in a jug and blending until smooth.
4. Return the soup to the slow cooker and stir in the cream. Warm through once again.
5. Serve in bowls, sprinkled with chervil and drizzled with olive oil.

NUTRITION PER PORTION:
SERVES - 6 | CALORIES - 277KCAL | PROTEIN - 7G | CARBOHYDRATES - 35G | FAT - 15G

SPICED LENTIL SOUP

INGREDIENTS

- 100g of dried red lentils, rinsed
- 1 litre of chicken or vegetable stock (fresh or from stock cubes)
- 3 garlic cloves, crushed
- 2 dried bay leaves
- 100g of mild curry paste
- 2 small carrots, peeled and coarsely chopped
- 1 celery stalk, trimmed and thinly sliced
- 400g tin of chopped tomatoes
- 2 potatoes, peeled and chopped

To serve
- 140g of natural Greek yoghurt
- Seasoning to taste
- 6 tablespoons of fresh coriander finely chopped

METHOD
1. Preheat the slow cooker on a low setting and spritz lightly with oil.
2. Add everything to the slow cooker except the toppings.
3. Cover the slow cooker with the lid and cook on Low for 6 hours.
4. Season to taste and serve in bowls, topped with Greek yoghurt, coriander and black pepper.

NUTRITION PER PORTION:

SERVES - 6 | CALORIES - 364KCAL | PROTEIN - 36G | CARBOHYDRATES - 30G | FAT - 10G

SCOTCH BROTH

INGREDIENTS
- Olive oil
- 600g of leftover roast lamb
- 1 leek, washed, trimmed and chopped roughly
- 2 carrots, peeled and chopped
- 2 sticks of celery, washed, trimmed and chopped
- 2 onions, finely sliced
- 3 litres of lamb stock (fresh or from vegetable stock cubes)
- 1 small swede, peeled and diced
- 1 potato, peeled and diced
- 80 g pearl barley (soaked overnight beforehand)
- 15g of fresh flat-leaf parsley, chopped
- 1 loaf of crusty bread
- Optional: Scotch whisky

METHOD
1. Preheat your slow cooker on a High setting and spritz lightly with cooking oil.
2. Put 1 tablespoon of olive oil into the slow cooker, then add the leek, celery, onions and carrots.
3. Pour in the stock and cook on a High setting for about 2 hours.
4. Add pearl barley, swede and potato to the slow cooker and cook on High for a further 2 hours.
5. Once cooked, whisk the soup quite vigorously to break up some of the bigger pieces of vegetables, then stir in the cooked lamb.
6. Allow the lamb to heat through for about 30 minutes, then taste and season.
7. Serve the soup in bowls, with a topping of chopped parsley, and served with chunks of fresh crusty bread.

NUTRITION PER PORTION:

SERVES - 6 | CALORIES - 444KCAL | PROTEIN - 24G | CARBOHYDRATES - 31G | FAT - 29G

MUSHROOM SOUP

INGREDIENTS
- Olive oil
- 1 red onion, peeled and finely chopped
- 20-25g of dried porcini mushrooms
- 600g of mixed fresh mushrooms cleaned and sliced
- Fresh thyme leaves
- 2 garlic cloves, peeled and finely sliced
- 1 litre of vegetable stock (fresh or from stock cubes)
- 1 tablespoon of mascarpone cheese
- Fresh flat-leaf parsley, chopped
- Seasoning to taste
- Optional: Zest and juice of 1 lemon

METHOD

1. Preheat your slow cooker on a High setting and spritz lightly with oil.
2. Put the porcini mushrooms to soak in a container of boiling.
3. Add 2 tablespoons of olive oil to the preheated slow cooker and add the mushrooms. Leave to soften before adding the garlic, onion, and thyme leaves. Season to taste.
4. Drain the mushrooms through a sieve and stir the strained mushroom stock into the slow cooker.
5. Chop half of the porcini mushrooms and leave the other half whole, then add it all to the slow cooker.
6. Turn the slow cooker to a High setting and cook for about 1 hour.
7. Season the mushroom mixture and add the vegetable stock. Leave to cook on High for another 2 hours.
8. Remove the soup from the slow cooker to a jug and blend until smooth.
9. Return the blended soup to the slow cooker, stirring in the parsley and mascarpone, and adding any further seasoning to taste.
10. Serve the soup hot in a container, with finely chopped parsley and/or raw mushrooms.

NUTRITION PER PORTION:
SERVES - 6 | CALORIES - 107KCAL | PROTEIN - 4G | CARBOHYDRATES - 4G | FAT - 9G

WILD GARLIC AND POTATO SOUP

INGREDIENTS

- 2 tablespoons of cooking oil
- 600g of potatoes, peeled and diced
- 1.2 litres of vegetable stock (fresh or made with stock cubes)
- 50g of wild garlic leaves, shredded
- 1 onion, chopped
- Optional: wild garlic flowers
- Optional: crème fraiche or double cream
- Seasoning to taste

METHOD

1. Preheat the slow cooker on a High setting and add the cooking oil.
2. Add the onion and soften for a few minutes.
3. Add the potatoes and stock.
4. Put the lid on and cook on a High setting for 4 hours.
5. Add the garlic leaves but keep a few back to garnish.
6. Transfer to a large jug or blender and blitz until smooth then return to the slow cooker to reheat, and season to taste
7. Serve with crème fraiche/double cream, a few save garlic leaves and some wild garlic flowers.

NUTRITION PER PORTION:
SERVES - 4 | CALORIES - 193KCAL | PROTEIN - 3G | CARBOHYDRATES - 31G | FAT - 7G

POTATO AND MARROW SOUP WITH SAGE

INGREDIENTS

- 1 garlic clove, chopped
- 40g of butter
- 1 onion, chopped
- 750g of marrow, peeled and diced
- 350g of potato, peeled and diced
- 4 fresh sage leaves
- 1.2 litres of vegetable stock (fresh or using stock cubes)
- 2 teaspoons of sugar
- 150mls of single cream
- Optional: fresh parsley or sage leaves, chopped
- Seasoning to taste

METHOD

1. Preheat the slow cooker on a High setting and spritz with cooking oil.
2. Melt the butter in the slow cooker, then add the garlic and onion and allow to soften for a few minutes.
3. Add the potatoes, marrow and 4 sage leaves. Stir to coat in the butter.
4. Turn the slow cooker to a Low setting, cover and leave to 'sweat' for about 30-45 minutes.
5. Pour in the vegetable stock and add the sugar and seasoning. Cook on a High setting for 4 hours, or until the potatoes are cooked through.
6. Remove and discard the sage leaves, transfer to a large jug and blend until the mixture is smooth.
7. Return to the slow cooker. Stir in an extra stock or water if the soup is too thick and adjust the seasoning to taste. Leave to reheat.
8. Now turn off the heat and stir in the single cream.
9. Serve in bowls, topped with chopped parsley or sage leaves.

NUTRITION PER PORTION:

SERVES - 4 | CALORIES - 349KCAL | PROTEIN - 7G | CARBOHYDRATES - 40G | FAT - 20G

ROASTED RED PEPPER SOUP

INGREDIENTS

- 4 red peppers
- 1 onion, sliced
- 4 garlic cloves, chopped
- 2 tablespoons of olive oil
- 1 leek, chopped
- 1 red chilli, chopped (or 1 teaspoon of dried chilli flakes)
- 1 bay leaf
- 1 teaspoon of sugar
- 400g tin of chopped tomatoes
- 1 tablespoon of balsamic vinegar
- 1 tablespoon of sweet chilli sauce

METHOD

1. Preheat your oven to 200°C/Gas 6. Roast the peppers on a baking tray in the oven, turning them at intervals until the skin is slightly charred and blistering.
2. Put the peppers into a container immediately, cover and leave until cool. Peel off the skin, discard the seeds and chop.
3. Preheat the slow cooker on a High setting and spritz with cooking oil.
4. Add the garlic with the onion and leave to soften for a few minutes before adding the leek, chilli and bay leaf.
5. Add the whole tin of tomatoes with the sugar and cook on a High setting for about 2 hours. Stir occasionally.
6. Put in the red peppers, vinegar, sweet chilli sauce and 300mls of water. Allow to cook on High for another 2 hours.
7. Transfer the soup mix to a large jug or blender and blitz until smooth.
8. Season to taste, adding more vinegar or chilli sauce if required.

NUTRITION PER PORTION:

SERVES - 4 | CALORIES - 144KCAL | PROTEIN - 3G | CARBOHYDRATES - 16G | FAT - 7G

ASPARAGUS SOUP

INGREDIENTS

- 175g of trimmed, boiled asparagus (save the water after cooking)
- 1 garlic clove, chopped
- 40g of butter
- 1 onion, chopped
- 1 handful of sorrel, shredded (use spinach as an alternative)
- 600mls asparagus water with a vegetable stock cube added (make up to 600mls with water if required)
- Optional: 1 tablespoon of plain flour
- Optional: 50mls whipping or double cream
- Optional: 1 tablespoon of fresh, chopped chives
- Seasoning to taste

METHOD

1. Preheat the slow cooker on a High setting and spritz with cooking oil.
2. Melt the butter in the slow cooker, then add the garlic and onion and allow to soften for a few minutes.
3. Add the shredded sorrel (or spinach) and stir until it softens and becomes limp.
4. Pour in the asparagus water/stock, add the cooked asparagus and season to taste.
5. Scoop out a cup of stock, add the tablespoon of flour and blend until a smooth paste. Stir slowly into the asparagus soup mixture.
6. Cover with a lid and cook on a High setting for 4 hours.
7. Transfer to a jug and blitz with a blender until smooth.
8. Return the blended soup to the slow cooker, stir in the cream and leave to reheat.
9. Serve hot, in bowls, sprinkled with chopped chives.

NUTRITION PER PORTION:

SERVES - 5 | CALORIES - 84KCAL | PROTEIN - 2G | CARBOHYDRATES - 5G | FAT - 8G

SHIN BEEF AND VEGETABLE SOUP WITH NOODLES

INGREDIENTS

- 1kg shin of beef (on the bone, if possible), in 2 or 3 large chunks
- 1 red chilli, thinly sliced
- 2 inches of ginger root, peeled and sliced thinly
- 2 onions, sliced
- 3 star anise
- 1 garlic bulb, cut in half lengthways
- 1 beef stock cube
- 1 tablespoon of soy sauce
- 400g assorted, prepared vegetables – pick your favourites!
- 100g rice noodles, soaked
- in boiling water per packet instructions
- 1 tablespoon of fresh, chopped coriander

METHOD

1. Preheat the slow cooker on the High setting.
2. Put in the beef shin bone with everything except the assorted vegetables, rice noodles and coriander.
3. Cover with water to about 3cms above the beef, turn to Low and cook for 8.
4. Add the assorted vegetables to the slow cooker and cook on Low for a further 4 hours, then turn off the heat.
5. Optional: remove the beef shin from the slow cooker, discard the bones, and break the meat up into smaller pieces before returning it to the rest of the soup.

6. Add the rice noodles, and sprinkle with chopped coriander or basil. Turn the slow cooker to a Low setting and leave to reheat as the noodles soften.
7. Serve hot with chunks of crusty bread.

NUTRITION PER PORTION:

SERVES - 6 | CALORIES - 316KCAL | PROTEIN - 34G | CARBOHYDRATES - 14G | FAT - 13G

THAI NOODLE SOUP
• •

INGREDIENTS

- 300g of chicken thighs, bones discarded, and meat cut into small strips
- Vegetable oil for frying
- 2cm piece of ginger, grated
- ½ a small onion, peeled and diced
- 2 garlic cloves, peeled & chopped small
- 400mls of coconut milk
- 1 tablespoon of Thai red curry paste
- 400mls of vegetable or chicken stock (fresh or from stock cubes)
- 1 teaspoon of fish sauce
- 200g of rice noodles
- Fresh coriander, chopped
- 1 lime

METHOD

1. Add seasoning to the chicken pieces thoroughly, heat some oil in a frying pan and sear the chicken pieces to seal. Remove from the pan and put to one side.
2. Preheat the slow cooker on a High setting, add 2 tablespoons of oil and add the onion, garlic, ginger and curry paste. Stir and leave to soften for a few minutes.
3. Next, stir in the coconut milk, stock, fish sauce and chicken thigh meat. Add more curry paste to taste if required.
4. Cover and cook on High for 4 hours.
5. Cook the noodles per packet directions, then drain and rinse under cold water.
6. Serve the noodles in bowls with the chicken soup spooned over the top, a squeeze of lime and a garnish of coriander.

NUTRITION PER PORTION:

SERVES - 2 | CALORIES - 852KCAL | PROTEIN - 47G | CARBOHYDRATES - 35G | FAT - 63G

MOROCCAN LAMB SOUP
• •

INGREDIENTS

- 20g of butter
- 2 onions, chopped
- 3 celery stalks, diced
- 1 tablespoon of olive oil
- 3 carrots, diced
- 1 leek, diced
- 4 turnips, diced
- A pinch of saffron
- 250g shoulder of lamb, bone removed and diced into 1cm pieces
- 3 garlic cloves, crushed
- ½ teaspoon of ground cinnamon
- 1 teaspoon of ground coriander
- 1 teaspoon of ground turmeric
- 200g of red lentils (alternatively use yellow split peas or a mixture)
- 400g of tomatoes
- 1 litre of chicken stock (fresh or made from stock cubes)
- 425g tin of chickpeas, drained
- Optional: 1 tablespoon fresh coriander or mint, roughly chopped
- Seasoning to taste

METHOD

1. Season the diced lamb. Heat a little oil in a frying pan and sear the lamb pieces to seal. Remove from the heat and set aside.
2. Preheat the slow cooker on a High setting, add the butter, oil, garlic, spices, vegetables and saffron. Stir thoroughly then leave to soften for a few minutes.
3. Pour in the stock and canned tomatoes, then add the lentils and/or split peas.
4. Cook on a High setting for about 4 hours, or a Low setting for 8 hours, stirring occasionally.
5. Stir in the drained chickpeas and season well. Allow to heat through thoroughly.
6. Serve in bowls sprinkled with a coriander or mint garnish.

NUTRITION PER PORTION:

SERVES - 4 | CALORIES - 650KCAL | PROTEIN - 34G | CARBOHYDRATES - 70G | FAT - 26G

PARMESAN BRUSSEL'S SPROUTS SOUP

INGREDIENTS

- 50g of onion, chopped
- 110g of salted butter
- 1kg of Brussels sprouts, washed, trimmed, and chopped
- 1litre of whole milk
- 220g of cream cheese
- 140 of parmesan cheese, grated
- 1 tablespoon of fresh rosemary, chopped
- 2 teaspoons of garlic salt

METHOD

1. Add all of the ingredients into the slow cooker.
2. Cover and cook for 8 hours.
3. If it seems a little thick add a splash of water and heat through for another 15 minutes; if it seems a little thin, cook for a short while with the lid off until it thickens as required.
4. Serve garnished with a sprinkle of rosemary and grated parmesan.

NUTRITION PER PORTION:

SERVES - 4 | CALORIES - 797KCAL | PROTEIN - 35G | CARBOHYDRATES - 40G | FAT - 60G

WILD RICE AND MUSHROOM SOUP

INGREDIENTS

- 200g of wild rice, uncooked
- 6 carrots, chopped
- 1/2 sweet onion, diced
- 230ml of dry white wine
- 1 litre of vegetable or chicken stock (fresh or from stock cubes)
- 1 tablespoon of chopped fresh thyme
- 1/2 teaspoon of crushed red pepper flakes
- 2 bay leaves
- 1 teaspoon of paprika
- 1 parmesan rind, plus 45g of grated parmesan, and extra to serve
- 230ml of milk or single cream
- Seasoning to taste

For the mushroom mix

- 900g of mixed mushrooms chopped
- 4 cloves garlic, crushed
- 110g of butter
- Zest from 1 lemon
- Fresh thyme

METHOD

1. Add the rice and all the ingredients, except for the mushroom mix see step 5.
2. Cover and cook on low for 8 hours.

3. 30 minutes before the end of the cooking cycle, add the parmesan and milk. Recover and reheat until warmed through.
4. Lift out the bay leaves and discard.
5. For the mushrooms: An hour before serving, preheat the oven to 220C//gas7.
6. Combine the mushroom mixture all together in a baking tin with a pinch of Seasoning to taste.
7. Roast the mushrooms in the oven for 40-45 minutes. Stir halfway through cooking.
8. Use a fork to mash up the garlic and stir through the cooked mushrooms and any butter left into the soup.
9. Serve in bowls topped with the fresh thyme and parmesan.

NUTRITION PER PORTION:
SERVES - 6 | CALORIES - 411KCAL | PROTEIN - 14G | CARBOHYDRATES - 45G | FAT - 19G

SAUSAGE AND KALE SOUP

● ●

INGREDIENTS

- 500g of hot Italian sausage
- 2 x 400g cans of chopped tomatoes
- 3 garlic cloves, minced
- 2 x 400g cans white beans, rinsed and drained
- 67g of fresh kale, chopped
- 4 large carrots, finely chopped
- 1 onion, chopped
- 1 teaspoon of dried oregano
- Seasoning to taste
- 1 litre of chicken stock (fresh or from stock cubes)
- Grated parmesan cheese

METHOD

1. Heat some oil in a frying pan and cook the sausage for 6-8 minutes until no longer pink. Use a metal spoon to break it up into pieces and transfer to a slow cooker.
2. Add the kale, beans, garlic, tomatoes, carrots, onion, seasonings, and stock to the slow cooker.
3. Cover the slow cooker and cook for 8 hours.
4. Serve topped with grated parmesan cheese.

NUTRITION PER PORTION:
SERVES - 8 | CALORIES - 297KCAL | PROTEIN - 16G | CARBOHYDRATES - 31G | FAT - 13G

SAUSAGE AND PIZZA SOUP

● ●

INGREDIENTS

- 500g of Italian turkey sausage links (casing removed)
- 2 mixed peppers, seeds removed and cut into strips
- 1 x 400g can of cannellini beans, rinsed and drained
- 1 x 400g jar of pizza sauce
- 1 onion, chopped
- 1 x 400g can of chopped tomatoes, undrained
- 2 garlic cloves, minced
- 2 teaspoons of Italian seasoning
- 800ml of vegetable stock
- Crispy salad croutons
- Optional: 140g of shredded mozzarella cheese

METHOD

1. Heat some oil in a frying pan and cook the sausage-meat (removed from the casings) until no longer pink. Break up the sausage meat with a spoon.
2. Add the onion and peppers and cook until softened - about 5-8 minutes.

3. Transfer to the slow cooker.
4. Add the canned beans and tomatoes, pizza sauce, Italian seasoning and garlic cloves, then pour in broth and mix thoroughly.
5. Cover and cook on a low setting for 8 hours. Serve with croutons and mozzarella cheese.

NUTRITION PER PORTION:

SERVES - 6 | CALORIES - 158KCAL | PROTEIN - 9G | CARBOHYDRATES - 19G | FAT - 5G

CHICKEN NOODLE SOUP

INGREDIENTS

- 680g of chicken breasts, no bone or skin
- Seasoning to taste
- 1 onion, diced
- 2 litres of chicken stock
- 4 garlic cloves, minced
- 3 stalks of celery, diced
- 3 carrots, peeled and diced
- 1/2 teaspoon of dried thyme
- 2 bay leaves
- 1/2 teaspoon of dried rosemary
- 220g of dried spaghetti, broken into thirds
- Juice of 1 lemon
- 2 tablespoons of fresh chopped parsley

METHOD

1. Season the chicken to taste and put in the slow cooker.
2. Next, stir in everything except the spaghetti, lemon and parsley.
3. Cover and cook on a Low heat for 8 hours.
4. Take the chicken out of from the slow cooker and use forks to shred, then return the meat to the slow cooker. Stir in the pasta.
5. Cover again and cook on a Low heat for further 30-40 minutes.
6. Stir in the lemon juice and chopped parsley.
7. Serve immediately.

NUTRITION PER PORTION:

SERVES - 8 | CALORIES - 272KCAL | PROTEIN - 29G | CARBOHYDRATES - 21G | FAT - 8G

EASY POTATO SOUP

INGREDIENTS

- 900g of russet potatoes, peeled and diced
- 900g of gold potatoes, peeled and diced
- 1 small onion, diced
- 110g of pancetta, cubed
- 1.8 litres of chicken or vegetable stock
- 4 garlic cloves, chopped
- 1/2 teaspoon of dried thyme
- 340ml can of evaporated milk
- Seasoning to taste
- 30g of plain flour

To Serve:

- Spring onions, slice
- Bacon bits
- Grated cheddar cheese
- Cheddar cheese crackers, crumbled or croutons

METHOD

1. Preheat the slow cooker on a Low setting and spritz with cooking oil spray.
2. Put the potatoes, pancetta, onion, and garlic directly into the slow cooker.
3. Pour in the stock. Season to taste and add the thyme. Give it all a good stir.

4. Cover and cook for 4 hours on High, or 8 hours on Low.
5. Whisk together the evaporated milk and flour in a jug to form a smooth paste and pour into the slow cooker.
6. Cover and cook again for about 30 minutes until the soup thickens.
7. Use a blender to whizz to a smooth soup if necessary and serve with your choice of toppings.

NUTRITION PER PORTION:
SERVES - 8 | CALORIES - 220KCAL | PROTEIN - 7G | CARBOHYDRATES - 33G | FAT - 7G

SWEET POTATO SOUP WITH PEANUTS AND GINGER

INGREDIENTS

- 3 garlic cloves, chopped
- 1 kg of sweet potatoes, peeled and chopped
- 1 onion, chopped
- 1 litre of vegetable stock (fresh or from stock cubes)
- 1 teaspoon of ground cumin
- 1 x 400g can of chopped tomatoes
- 2-inch piece fresh ginger, cut into 4 equal sized pieces
- Optional: 1 teaspoon of ground cinnamon
- Seasoning to taste
- 70g of smooth peanut butter
- 15g of fresh coriander, shopped
- Chopped roasted salted peanuts, for garnish

METHOD

1. Combine the sweet potatoes, onion, garlic, ginger, stock, tomatoes, cumin, (optional) cinnamon, and 250ml of water in the slow cooker and season to taste.
2. Cover and cook on a Low setting for 8 hours or High for 4-5 hours, until the potatoes are tender.
3. Remove the pieces of ginger from the soup.
4. Stir in the peanut butter and coriander until well combined.
5. Blend to a smooth consistency with a blender.
6. Season serve, topped with coriander and chopped peanuts with a side of pitta chips.

NUTRITION PER PORTION:
SERVES - 6 | CALORIES - 394KCAL | PROTEIN - 11G | CARBOHYDRATES - 56G | FAT -15G

MAINS

CHICKEN AND TURKEY

CHICKEN CASSEROLE

INGREDIENTS

- 3 garlic cloves, crushed
- 50g of butter
- ½ tablespoon of olive oil
- 1 large onion, finely chopped
- 1 ½ tablespoons of plain flour
- 650g boneless, skinless chicken thighs
- 400g of baby new potatoes, halved
- 2 sticks celery, diced
- 2 carrots, diced
- 250g mushrooms quartered
- 15g dried porcini mushrooms, soaked in 50ml boiling water (save the water)
- 500ml stock (fresh or from stock cubes
- 2 bay leaves
- 2 teaspoons of dijon mustard, plus extra to serve

METHOD

1. Melt the butter and heat with the olive oil in a large frying pan. Fry the onion for 8-10 minutes until it softens.
2. Put the flour and seasoning in a shallow bowl and toss in the chicken so it's coated.
3. Add the chicken and garlic to the pan and stir fry about 5 minutes more until the chicken starts to brown.
4. Transfer the contents of the pan to the slow cooker with all the prepared vegetables. Pour in the chicken stock and the water remaining from soaking the porcini. Stir in the dijon mustard and bay leaves.
5. Cover the slow cooker with the lid and cook on a Low setting for 7 hours or High setting for 4 hours.
6. Serve with wedges of crusty bread and a little dijon mustard.

NUTRITION PER PORTION:

SERVES - 4 | CALORIES - 382KCAL | PROTEIN - 41G | CARBOHYDRATES - 30G | FAT - 9G

CHICKEN CHILLI CON CARNE

INGREDIENTS

- 2 tablespoons of olive oil
- 1 onion, sliced
- 2 peppers, sliced (use mixed colours)
- 2 garlic cloves, crushed
- 1 tablespoon of ground cumin
- 1 small bunch of coriander, chopped
- ½ tablespoon of ground coriander
- 1-2 teaspoons of chipotle paste
- 1 tablespoon of tomato purée
- 400g can of chopped tomatoes
- 300ml of chicken stock
- 1 small cinnamon stick
- 4 skinless chicken thighs, bone-in
- 400g can of black beans with liquid
- 400g can of kidney beans, drained
- 1 tablespoon of red wine vinegar
- 20g of 70% dark chocolate, broken into pieces
- Cooked rice to serve 6
- Optional: soured cream

METHOD

1. Heat the oil in a frying and cook the onion and peppers for a few minutes until softened. Add the garlic, coriander stalks, ground coriander, cumin and chipotle paste, and stir fry for a couple of minutes. Transfer to the slow cooker.
2. Add the canned tomatoes and tomato pureé. Wash a little chicken stock around the frying pan to collect the flavours and pour into the slow cooker with the rest of the stock. Add the cinnamon stick.
3. Place the chicken thighs into the mixture in the slow cooker.
4. Cover the slow cooker with the lid and cook on a Low setting for 6 hours or High setting for 3 hours.
5. Remove the chicken thighs to a chopping board to shred the meat and discard any bones and return the shredded meat to the slow cooker.
6. Add the black beans along with their liquid, the drained kidney beans, vinegar and chocolate. Cook on the same setting for a further hour.
7. Once cooked, remove the cinnamon stick, season to taste and stir the coriander leaves.
8. Serve with rice and a dollop of sour cream, scattered with chopped coriander if available.

NUTRITION PER PORTION:

SERVES - 6 | CALORIES - 346KCAL | PROTEIN - 23G | CARBOHYDRATES - 22G | FAT - 16G

ITALIAN CHICKEN (SERVED WITH RICE OR PASTA)

INGREDIENTS

- 600g chicken thighs skin and bone removed
- 2 red onions, each cut into 6 even pieces
- 5 Chestnut mushrooms sliced
- 1 pepper, chopped (preferably red or yellow)
- 16 pitted Kalamata olives
- 1 x 400g tin of chopped tomatoes
- 4 tablespoons of tomato paste
- 150ml chicken stock (fresh or made with 1 stock cube)
- 5 garlic cloves, crushed
- 3-4 teaspoons of dried Italian mixed herbs
- Seasoning to taste

METHOD

1. Preheat the slow cooker on a Low setting and spritz lightly with cooking oil.
2. Put the chicken thighs in the slow cooker first, then spread the chopped vegetables and olives in an even layer on top.
3. In a separate container, combine the chicken stock with the chopped tomatoes and garlic, then the herbs and seasoning and stir well to mix. Pour over the chicken.
4. Cover and cook on High for 4 hours or Low for 6 hours.
5. Serve on a bed of rice, or in a container with wedges of crusty bread.

   NOTE: Before serving, either shred the meat and return to the slow cooker; or serve the thighs intact.

NUTRITION PER PORTION:

SERVES - 4 | CALORIES - 797KCAL | PROTEIN - 77G | CARBOHYDRATES - 87G | FAT - 26G

CHICKEN CACCIATORE

INGREDIENTS

- 1 tablespoon of olive oil plus 2 further teaspoons
- 3 garlic cloves, minced
- Seasoning to taste
- 900g of boneless skinless chicken breasts
- 1 medium onion, chopped
- 1 tablespoon balsamic vinegar plus 1/2 teaspoon extra
- 2 x 400g tins of chopped tomatoes
- 1 medium green pepper, chopped
- 225g of fresh mushrooms sliced in half
- 2 teaspoons of Italian seasoning

METHOD

1. Preheat your slow cooker on a Low setting and lightly spray with cooking oil.
2. Heat 1 tablespoon of oil in a frying pan on a medium heat. Season the chicken then cook each side for about 3-4 minutes until browned, then transfer to the slow cooker.
3. Heat the extra oil in the same frying pan, add the onion and stir fry until softened. Add the garlic and 1 tablespoon balsamic vinegar and stir fry for another minute. Transfer the onion mix and juices to the slow cooker.
4. Pour in the tomatoes with the chopped pepper, mushrooms and Italian seasoning. Give it all a good stir.
5. Cover and cook on High for 1 1/2 to 2 1/2 hours or Low for 4 to 5 hours.
6. Optional: keep the chicken pieces whole, or transfer the chicken to a chopping board, shred it and return it to the slow cooker.
7. Now, take the lid off the slow cooker and cook on for a further 1 hour on High. The sauce will thicken and develop in flavour. Just before serving, stir in the extra half a spoon of balsamic vinegar, taste and season as preferred.
8. Serve the chicken Cacciatore with pasta, rice or polenta, topped with fresh, chopped parsley and grated parmesan.

NUTRITION PER PORTION:

SERVES - 4 | CALORIES - 228KCAL | PROTEIN - 32G | CARBOHYDRATES - 10G | FAT - 8G

CHICKEN CURRY

INGREDIENTS

Horrible.

- 1 tablespoon of olive oil
- 2 red peppers, thinly sliced
- 1 large, sweet potato, cleaned and diced into 1/2-inch pieces
- 60ml of water
- Juice of 2 limes, freshly squeezed
- 1 teaspoon of ground cumin
- 2 tablespoons of curry powder
- 2 teaspoons of smoked paprika
- 1 teaspoon of ground chilli powder
- Seasoning to taste
- 700g of boneless, skinless chicken thighs
- 400g can of coconut milk
- 2 tablespoons of cornflour mixed with 3 tablespoons water
- Optional: brown or white rice or quinoa and fresh chopped coriander

METHOD

1. Put the prepared sweet potatoes and peppers into the slow cooker and pour the water and lime juice over the top.
2. Combine the curry powder, smoked paprika, cumin, chilli powder, and salt in a shallow bowl. Use roughly ⅔ of the spice mix to season and rub into the chicken thighs. Save the remaining ⅓ of the spices.
3. Heat the oil in a frying pan and briefly sear the chicken on each side until nicely browned and put straight into the slow cooker on top of the vegetables.

4. Sprinkle with the remaining spice mix, cover and cook on a low setting for 4 to 5 hours or High for 2 to 3 hours.
5. Remove the chicken from the slow cooker carefully, place on a cutting board and shred the meat with two forks, discarding any bones. Set to one side momentarily.
6. Pour the coconut milk and cornflour mix into the slow cooker and stir into the mixture.
7. Cover and cook for a further 15 minutes on High.
8. Stir in the shredded chicken; cover and cook for a final 15 minutes on High.
9. Serve warm over rice or quinoa topped with fresh chopped coriander.

NUTRITION PER PORTION:
SERVES - 4 | CALORIES - 425KCAL | PROTEIN - 35G | CARBOHYDRATES - 29G | FAT - 18G

CHICKEN CURRY, JAMAICAN
• •

INGREDIENTS

- 1 teaspoon of salt
- 1 onion, finely chopped
- 650g of chicken breast cut into 1-inch pieces
- 2 tablespoons of olive oil
- 2 jalapeno peppers, very finely chopped
- 1 red pepper, finely chopped
- 1-inch of fresh ginger, minced

- 3 garlic cloves, minced
- 1 teaspoon of turmeric
- 1/4 teaspoon of cayenne pepper plus additional to taste
- 3/4 teaspoon of allspice
- 1 red pepper, finely chopped
- 2 medium potatoes, peeled, diced and rinsed in cold water
- 1 x 400g can of coconut milk

- 1 tablespoon of Worcestershire sauce
- 1½ teaspoons of white wine vinegar
- 1 teaspoon of hot sauce plus additional to taste
- Chopped fresh coriander

METHOD

1. Sprinkle the chicken with salt and set to one side.
2. Heat some oil in a frying pan and cook the onions, stirring occasionally, until the onions begin to soften.
3. Add the pepper, jalapeños, garlic, and ginger and stir fry for a couple of minutes to release the flavours.
4. Next, stir in the spices, curry powder, turmeric, cayenne, and allspice. Cook and stir constantly, until the spices become golden and fragrant.
5. Finally, add the chicken and stir fry for about 5 minutes until browned.
6. Transfer the chicken mixture to the slow cooker. Stir a little coconut milk around the frying pan to collect the juices and flavours that have accumulated. Add to the slow cooker with the rest of the coconut milk followed by the diced potatoes.
7. Stir in Worcestershire sauce, vinegar, and hot sauce.
8. Cover and cook on a Low setting for 4 to 5 hours or High for 2 to 3 hours.
9. Remove the chicken from the slow cooker carefully, place on a cutting board and shred the meat with two forks, discarding any bones. Return the meat to the slow cooker, cover, and cook on High for a further 15 minutes.
10. Taste and add any further seasoning as required and serve with rice, scattered with chopped coriander.

NUTRITION PER PORTION:
SERVES - 4 | CALORIES - 428KCAL | PROTEIN - 33G | CARBOHYDRATES - 29G | FAT - 19G

SLOW COOKER BUTTER CHICKEN

INGREDIENTS

- 900g of boneless, skinless chicken breasts
- 1 tablespoon of coconut oil
- 1-inch of fresh ginger, peeled and grated
- 1 small onion, diced
- 4 garlic cloves, minced
- 1 1/2 tablespoons of curry powder
- 1 ½ teaspoons of chilli powder
- 1 tablespoon of garam masala
- Seasoning to taste
- 170g of tomato paste
- 1 small cauliflower, trimmed and divided into florets
- 30g of cold butter, diced
- 250ml of coconut milk
- 140ml of Greek yoghurt
- Optional garnish: chopped coriander

METHOD

1. In a frying pan on a medium heat, cook the onion until it begins to soften. Add the ginger, garlic, curry, chilli powder, garam masala, salt, and tomato paste and stir fry for about 30 seconds until fragrant.
2. Put the onion and spice mixture into a slow cooker and add in layers, the chicken, the cauliflower florets and finally the tomato sauce. Combine the florets and sauce a little, but don't disturb the chicken underneath.
3. Scatter the cubes of butter over the top.
4. Cover and cook on a High setting for about 2 hours or on Low for about 5 hours until the chicken is cooked through.
5. Remove the chicken to a chopping board and allow to cool slightly.
6. Meanwhile, stir the contents of the slow cooker, recover, and leave to cook on High for about 30 minutes more to tenderise the florets.
7. Cut the chicken into pieces and return to the slow cooker.
8. Stir in the coconut milk, then add the Greek yoghurt gradually.

   NOTE: Don't stir in the yoghurt right away when the butter chicken is too hot, or it will curdle.
9. Serve with rice or quinoa, topped with roughly chopped fresh coriander.

NUTRITION PER PORTION:
SERVES - 6 | CALORIES - 346KCAL | PROTEIN - 39G | CARBOHYDRATES - 19G | FAT - 13G

THAI GREEN CHICKEN CURRY

INGREDIENTS

- 8 boneless chicken thighs
- Optional: 1 stick of lemongrass
- 400ml can of coconut milk
- 4 - 6 tablespoons of Thai Green Curry Paste
- 2 green chillies, sliced
- 2 kaffir lime leaves or juice of 1 lime
- 1 green pepper, sliced
- 1 tablespoon of fish sauce
- 100g of baby corn
- 100g of mange tout

METHOD

1. Warm the coconut milk gently in a saucepan over a low heat, and blend in the Thai green curry paste.
2. Remove the saucepan from the heat and stir in the brown sugar, lime juice/kaffir lime leaves, fish sauce, (optional) lemongrass and fresh green chillies.
3. Layer the chicken in the bottom of the slow cooker and pour the Thai Green curry sauce over the top.
4. Cover the slow cooker and cook on Low for 4 to 5 hours or High for 3 to 4 hours.
5. About half an hour before the end of the cooking program add the green peppers, mange tout and baby corn, so they remain crunchy.

NOTE: the peppers, mange tout and baby corn can be added with the chicken at the beginning, but they will be softer.

6. Serve with rice or noodles.

NUTRITION PER PORTION:

SERVES - 4 | CALORIES - 699KCAL | PROTEIN - 61G | CARBOHYDRATES - 34G | FAT - 39G

CHICKEN-STUFFED PEPPERS

INGREDIENTS

- 500g of turkey mince
- 1 onion, finely sliced
- 2 garlic cloves, crushed
- 2 teaspoons of dried mixed herbs
- 2 tablespoons of tomato puree
- 1 tablespoon of Worcestershire sauce
- Optional: 100g of cooked rice
- 100g of grated cheddar

METHOD

1. In a container, mix the turkey, onion, garlic, herbs, tomato puree, Worcestershire sauce, cooked rice and half of the grated cheese.
2. Scoop the mixture into the peppers.
3. Pour the chicken stock or passata into the base of the slow cooker.
4. Place the peppers in the slow cooker in an upright position.
5. Place the lid on top and set off on low for 4 to 5 hours or high for 3 hours.
6. Top the peppers with the remaining grated cheese and replace the lid for a further 5 to 10 minutes, or until the cheese melts.

NUTRITION PER PORTION:

SERVES - 6 | CALORIES - 122KCAL | PROTEIN - 17G | CARBOHYDRATES - 3G | FAT - 5G

SWEET AND SOUR CHICKEN

INGREDIENTS

- 8 boneless chicken thighs
- 1 onion, chopped
- 2 mixed peppers, deseeded and sliced
- 2 carrots, chopped
- 1 garlic clove, crushed

For the Sweet and Sour Sauce

- 1 x 250ml can of pineapple pieces
- 3 tablespoons of tomato ketchup
- 2 tablespoons of cornflour
- 150ml of apple cider vinegar
- 1 tablespoon of soy sauce
- 100g of brown sugar

METHOD

1. Mix everything for the sweet and sour sauce in a container together until they are thoroughly combined.
   NOTE: Adjust the apple cider vinegar measurement depending on how tangy you like your sweet and sour sauce.
2. Layer the chicken pieces into the slow cooker, and add the garlic, peppers, onions, and carrots on top.
   NOTE: if you prefer your peppers to be a little crunchier, put them to one side and add them about half an hour/30 minutes before the end of cooking.
3. Pour the sweet and sour sauce over the top of the chicken and Put the lid on.

4. Cook on Low for 5 to 6 hours, or High for 4 hours.
5. Serve over rice with prawn crackers on the side.

NUTRITION PER PORTION:
SERVES - 4 | CALORIES - 378KCAL | PROTEIN - 21G | CARBOHYDRATES - 33G | FAT - 17G

CHICKEN STEW - PERSIAN STYLE

INGREDIENTS

- 750g chicken thighs, bone in
- ½ teaspoons of ground ginger
- ½ teaspoons of turmeric
- ½ teaspoon of ground cinnamon
- 1 onion, peeled and sliced into rings
- 1 tablespoon of olive oil
- 100g of dried dates
- 25g of walnut halves
- 550g of new potatoes, cut into halves
- 150ml of chicken stock (fresh or from stock cubes)
- 2 tablespoons of harissa paste
- 150g of natural yoghurt
- Optional: mixed cooked greens

METHOD

1. Put the spices in a shallow bowl and toss in the chicken thighs. Coat thoroughly with the seasoning.
2. Fry the onion with the olive oil until it softens. Add the walnuts and fry briefly.
3. Layer the potatoes in a slow cooker followed by the chicken thighs. Spoon the onion and walnuts over the top, then add the dates.
4. Finally, pour the stock in over everything.
5. Put the lid on and cook on Low for about 5 hours until the meat no longer shows up any pink.
6. In a separate bowl, blend the harissa paste into the yoghurt.
7. Serve the chicken with mixed greens and the spiced yoghurt on the side.

NUTRITION PER PORTION:
SERVES - 4 | CALORIES - 523KCAL | PROTEIN - 28G | CARBOHYDRATES - 37G | FAT - 30G

CHICKEN STEW - THAI STYLE

INGREDIENTS

- 5 chicken thighs
- 5 chicken drumsticks
- 1 tablespoons of vegetable oil
- 4 tablespoons of red curry paste
- 2 tablespoons of soft brown sugar
- Juice of half a lemon
- 1 tablespoon of Worcestershire sauce
- 2 tablespoons of fish sauce
- Juice and zest of 2 limes
- 125ml of vegetable or chicken stock (fresh or from stock cubes)
- 1 x 400g tin of coconut milk
- Optional: chopped fresh coriander to serve
- Optional: red chillies, sliced finely

METHOD

1. Preheat the slow cooker on a Low setting and spritz lightly with cooking oil
2. Heat some oil in a large pan, then season the chicken pieces and sear in the oil until they turn brown on all sides. Place into the heated slow cooker.
3. Use the same frying pan to sauté the curry paste for 2 minutes. Add the sugar with the lemon juice and Worcestershire sauce and keep stirring while the sugar melts.
4. Stir in the coconut milk, stock, lime zest and juice and the fish sauce. Blend together then pour into the slow cooker over the chicken.

5. Cover and cook on a High setting for 4 hours or Slow for 8 hours. The chicken should be cooked through with no pink showing.
6. Serve with rice and scattered with fresh chopped coriander and sliced red chillies.

NUTRITION PER PORTION:

SERVES - 4-6 | CALORIES - 276KCAL | PROTEIN - 30G | CARBOHYDRATES - 9G | FAT - 13G

SLOW-COOKED CHICKEN STROGANOFF
• •

INGREDIENTS

- 2 tablespoons of olive oil
- 1 onion, peeled and chopped
- 4 large skinless chicken breasts
- 300g of closed cup mushrooms halved
- 150m of chicken stock (fresh or made with stock cubes)
- 1 x 294g can of condensed chicken soup
- 100ml of soured cream
- 1 teaspoon of paprika
- 15g of chopped chives
- Tagliatelle

METHOD

1. Heat the oil in a large frying, then add the chicken breasts and the onion. Cook for a few minutes until the onion has softened and the chicken is browned on both sides.
2. Move the onion and chicken over to the slow cooker.
3. Put the chopped mushrooms chicken stock, condensed soup, paprika and soured cream on top and mix well. The chicken should be well-coated coated in the ingredients.
4. Cover and cook on a Low setting for 5–6 hours.
5. When the meat is cooked through with no pink showing, serve with tagliatelle, scattered with the chopped chives.

NUTRITION PER PORTION:

SERVES - 4 | CALORIES - 347KCAL | PROTEIN - 40G | CARBOHYDRATES - 9G | FAT - 17G

CHICKEN TERIYAKI
• •

INGREDIENT

In the slow cooker

- 615g of chicken thighs without skin or bone
- 75ml of rice wine vinegar
- 1-inch piece of ginger, finely grated
- 100ml of light soy sauce
- 3 tablespoons of runny honey
- 2 garlic cloves, chopped
- 100ml of water
- 1 tablespoon of cornflour (plus water to mix)

For the stir fry

- 1 clove garlic, chopped
- 1 red chilli, sliced
- 1-inch piece of fresh ginger, sliced
- 200g pak choi, shredded
- Optional: 2 tablespoons of toasted sesame seeds
- Optional: 4 spring onions, sliced

METHOD

1. Heat some oil in a large frying pan. Season the chicken then cook briefly in the oil so it is brown on all sides. Put the browned chicken into the slow cooker.
2. In a jug, blend the soy sauce, rice vinegar, ginger, garlic and honey and pour into the slow cooker over the chicken. in the slow cooker.
3. Add about 100ml of water so that the chicken is nearly, but not quite submerged.
4. Cover and cook on a High setting for about 3 hours, until the chicken is tender and falling apart.
5. Cook the rice per the pack directions.
6. Carefully lift the chicken pieces from the slow cooker to a plate and set to one side. Transfer the sauce from the slow cooker to a saucepan.
7. Blend the cornflour with 2 tablespoons of water and mix until smooth. Add the mix to the sauce and bring to the boil. Simmer for 3-5 minutes until it thickens.
8. Meanwhile, using two forks, shred the chicken and discard the bones.
9. Now, heat a wok and spray with cooking oil. When it's hot, flash fry the garlic, ginger and chilli. Then add the pak choi and flash fry for about a minute. Add a splash of water and cook for a further 1 minute, until the vegetables have about softened.
10. Put the shredded chicken into the saucepan with the sauce and bring to a gentle simmer again.
11. Serve the chicken and stir fry vegetables on a bed of rice. Top with a sprinkle of sliced spring onion and sesame seeds.

NUTRITION PER PORTION:

SERVES - 4 | CALORIES - 357KCAL | PROTEIN - 33G | CARBOHYDRATES - 21G | FAT - 15G

SEASONED SLOW-COOKED CHICKEN WITH HERBED BABY POTATOES

INGREDIENTS

- 2 fennel bulbs, trimmed and sliced thinly
- 4 teaspoons of olive oil
- 500g baby carrots, cut in two lengthways

- 1 medium whole chicken
- 2 garlic cloves, lightly crushed
- 1 lemon, cut into quarters
- Fresh thyme
- 175g of baby leeks

- 1kg of baby potatoes
- Fresh chopped parsley

METHOD

1. Preheat the slow cooker on a Low setting and spritz lightly with cooking oil.
2. Place the chopped carrots and fennel in the bottom.
3. Next, rub the chicken all over with 1 teaspoon of oil and the crushed garlic. Place the lemon, thyme, and garlic inside the chicken.
4. Season the outside of the chicken and place it in the slow cooker on the vegetable layer. Adjust the vegetables if necessary to make sure the lid fits snuggly on the slow cooker.
5. Cover and cook on High for 2 ½ hours, then add the leeks.
6. Cover again and cook for a further 1 ½ hours on High.
7. Cook the baby potatoes for 20-30 minutes in a pan of boiling water and drain immediately. Season to taste and toss with any leftover olive oil and chopped parsley.
8. Serve the chicken in thick slices accompanied by the meat juice and vegetables.

NUTRITION PER PORTION:

SERVES - 6 | CALORIES - 501KCAL | PROTEIN - 43G | CARBOHYDRATES - 30G | FAT - 21G

EASY JERK CHICKEN

INGREDIENTS

For the chicken

- 515g of boneless chicken thigh fillets
- 2 tablespoons of Jerk Seasoning
- 1 red onion, sliced
- 1 green pepper, seeds removed and diced
- 1 tablespoon of tomato purée
- 2 garlic cloves, crushed
- 1 peeled mango, cut into 1cm cubes

For the slaw

- 300g of crunchy coleslaw (homemade or bought)
- 2 tablespoons of chopped cashew nuts
- 2 spring onions, finely chopped
- 2 tablespoons mint leaves
- Juice of 1 lime

To serve

- 450g white rice, cooked according to packet instructions
- Optional: chopped red chilli

METHOD

1. Put the all the chicken ingredients directly into the slow cooker and mix well.
2. Add 250ml water and cook on High for 6 hours until the chicken is cooked through.
3. Cook the rice according to the pack instructions about 20 minutes before the chicken is ready.
4. Finally, combine the coleslaw with the spring onions, cashew nuts, mint leaves and lime juice, and place all together in a separate bowl.
5. Serve the chicken with rice and a side of slaw, garnished with chopped red chilli.

NUTRITION PER PORTION:

SERVES - 6 | CALORIES - 687KCAL | PROTEIN - 36G | CARBOHYDRATES - 100G | FAT - 16G

CHICKEN AND TARRAGON CASSEROLE

INGREDIENTS

- 600g of boneless chicken thigh fillets
- 1 garlic clove, crushed
- 220g tin of cannellini beans, rinsed through
- 4 shallots, peeled and halved
- 150g of baby carrots
- 1 teaspoon of dried tarragon
- 300ml white wine (or chicken stock if preferred)
- 1 teaspoon of cornflour
- 180g of french beans
- Optional: 100ml of creme fraiche
- Optional: chopped parsley to serve

METHOD

1. Preheat the slow cooker on a Low setting and spritz lightly with cooking oil.
2. Layer the chicken fillets in the slow cooker with the crushed garlic and season with freshly ground black pepper. Add the shallots, carrots, cannellini beans and dried tarragon over the top.
3. Pour over the white wine (or chicken stock). Stir, cover, and cook on High for 4 hours.

4. Blend the cornflour in a small jug with 1 teaspoon of cold water and mix to a paste. Stir into the casserole in the slow cooker. Add the fine beans and give it all a good stir. Replace the lid and cook for a further 1 hour.
5. Just before serving, pour the crème fraiche over the chicken and stir through the casserole. One plated, sprinkle with chopped parsley.

NUTRITIONAL INFORMATION PER SERVING (INCLUDING THE CREME FRAICHE):
SERVES - 4 | CALORIES - 506CAL | PROTEIN - 33G | CARBOHYDRATES - 15G | FAT - 28G

WHOLE CHICKEN WITH BACON GRAVY

INGREDIENTS

- 2 tablespoons of rapeseed oil
- 1.35kg whole chicken
- 8 shallots, peeled and halved
- 6 garlic cloves, crushed
- 4 bacon rashers, chopped
- Fresh thyme
- 1 tablespoon of chopped sage
- 200ml of chicken stock (fresh or made from cubes)
- 100ml of white wine (or water if preferred)
- 3 tablespoons of chicken gravy granules

METHOD

1. Heat the oil in a large frying pan and when hot, fry the whole chicken on all sides until golden. Place into the slow cooker.
2. Using the frying pan, fry the shallots for a couple of minutes until they soften, then add the bacon and garlic. Stir fry for about 2 minutes until they start to brown, then place in the slow cooker with the chicken.
3. Wash a little chicken stock around the frying pan to collect the flavours of the onion and bacon and pour into the slow cooker with the rest of the stock.
4. Pour in the white wine (or water), the sage and thyme, then Put the lid on and cook on Low for 5 hours,
5. Lift the chicken out onto a plate and keep warm. Remove the thyme sprigs and discard. Stir the gravy granules into the sauce in the slow cooker.
6. Finally, carve the chicken, divide between 4 plates and spoon over the bacon gravy. Serve with mash and spring greens.

NUTRITION PER PORTION:
SERVES - 6 | CALORIES - 586KCAL | PROTEIN - 69G | CARBOHYDRATES - 8G | FAT - 27G

MISO CHICKEN RAMEN

INGREDIENTS

- 3 garlic cloves, chopped
- Whites of 6 spring onions, sliced
- 1-inch piece of ginger, chopped
- Optional: 50ml of cream sherry
- 2 tablespoon of miso paste
- 1 teaspoon of red chilli flakes
- 1 tablespoon of olive oil
- 300ml of milk
- 1.2 litres of chicken stock
- 4 skinless, boneless chicken thighs, cut into pieces
- 100g of shiitake mushrooms sliced
- 300g of easy-cook noodles
- Optional: 15g of fresh coriander, roughly chopped
- Optional: 1 spring onion, sliced
- Optional: 3 medium eggs, soft boiled and halved
- Optional: 1 red chilli, thinly sliced

METHOD

1. Use a blender to blitz together the spring onions, garlic, ginger, (optional) sherry, miso paste, chilli flakes and oil until smooth.
2. Tip the mixture into the slow cooker, mix in the stock and milk then put the chicken and mushrooms in too.
3. Cover and cook on Low for 5 hours.
4. When the chicken is ready, cook your noodles according to packet instructions and put into bowls.
5. Spoon the chicken and broth over the bowls of noodles, and serve garnished with chopped coriander, spring onion, chilli, and top with cooked egg.

NUTRITION PER PORTION:

SERVES - 6 | CALORIES - 418KCAL | PROTEIN - 17G | CARBOHYDRATES - 23G | FAT - 29G

CATALAN CHICKEN

INGREDIENTS

- 1 teaspoon of paprika
- 2 tablespoon of olive oil
- 1.35kg whole chicken
- 2 red onions, roughly chopped
- 1 garlic clove, finely sliced
- 2 mixed peppers, seeds removed, roughly chopped

- 1 bay leaf
- 6 medium tomatoes, cut into quarters
- 150ml of dry white wine
- 200ml of chicken stock
- Pinch of saffron, steeped in 2 tablespoons of warm water

- Optional: 1 tablespoon of finely chopped flat-leaf parsley
- Optional: 20g toasted and flaked almonds, chopped

METHOD

1. In a small bowl, blend the olive oil and paprika, then massage all over the chicken. Set to one side.
2. Heat the remaining oil in a large frying pan. First lightly fry the onions until they begin to soften, then the peppers and garlic. Once softened and beginning to brown, remove from the heat and set to one side.
3. First, put the chicken into the slow cooker. Mix the fried pepper and onion mixture with the bay leaf and tomatoes and put in with the chicken.
4. Pour in the wine and stock and the saffron, including the 2 tablespoons of water it steeped in. The chicken should be about covered, but the slow cooker shouldn't be more than ¾ full of liquid.
5. Cook in two stages. Cook first a High setting for 1 hour, then turn Low and cook for another 5 hours. The meat juices should be clear.
6. Serve sprinkled with parsley and almonds.

NUTRITION PER PORTION:

SERVES - 4 | CALORIES - 543KCAL | PROTEIN - 67G | CARBOHYDRATES - 13G | FAT - 22G

EASY TURMERIC CHICKEN CURRY

INGREDIENTS

- 100ml of water
- 400ml tin of coconut milk
- 2 garlic cloves, crushed
- 1 tablespoon of tomato purée
- 2 onions, chopped
- 2 tablespoons of ground almonds

- 2 teaspoons of chilli powder
- 1 tablespoon of ground turmeric
- 1 tablespoon of garam masala
- 650g chicken breast fillets, diced
- Juice of 1 lime

To Serve

- 200g of steamed basmati or jasmine rice
- 2 tablespoons of chopped coriander
- 4 tablespoons of plain yoghurt
- 2 tablespoons of toasted flaked almonds

METHOD

1. Pour the coconut milk into the slow cooker, followed by 100ml of water.
2. Stir in the onions, tomato purée, ground almonds, garlic, spices and chicken until combined.
3. Cover and cook on Low for 6 hours.
4. Just before serving, prepare the rice per the directions on the packet then drain. Add the lime juice and mix.
5. Serve the curry over a bed of jasmine rice, drizzled with yoghurt and topped with flaked almonds and coriander.

NUTRITION PER PORTION:

SERVES - 6 | CALORIES - 424KCAL | PROTEIN - 35G | CARBOHYDRATES - 16G | FAT - 26G

CHICKEN CHASSEUR

INGREDIENTS

- 2 tablespoons of olive oil
- 1 onion, chopped
- 4 chicken thighs
- 200g of halved mushrooms halved
- 2 garlic cloves, crushed
- 200ml of white wine
- 200g of tinned chopped tomatoes
- 1 tablespoons of tomato purée
- Fresh thyme
- 1 bay leaf
- 400ml of chicken stock (fresh or from stock cubes)
- Optional: 20-30g of parsley, finely

METHOD

1. Preheat the slow cooker on a Low setting and heat the oil in a frying pan on a medium cooker hob.
2. Season the chicken thoroughly, then fry all over for a few minutes until golden all over. Set to one side.
3. In the same pan, fry the shallots, then add and fry the garlic and mushrooms until softened and turning golden. Pour in the wine and leave to bubble for a few minutes until it has reduced by half.
4. Stir in the tomato purée, chopped tomatoes and herbs. Season well and bring to a simmer.
5. Pour the sauce into the slow cooker and add the chicken thighs. Next add the chicken stock. You may need to add more water to ensure the chicken is covered.
6. Cover and cook on Low for 8 hours.
7. Transfer the chicken to a plate. If you prefer a thicker sauce, then leave it to bubble for a few minutes more with the lid off, (or pour the sauce into a pan and simmer until reduced).
8. Serve, sprinkled with parsley and accompanied with roast potatoes, mash, rice or pasta.

NUTRITION PER PORTION:

SERVES - 2 | CALORIES - 485KCAL | PROTEIN - 29G | CARBOHYDRATES - 15G | FAT - 26G

CHICKEN AND DUMPLINGS IN RED WINE GRAVY

INGREDIENTS

For the casserole

- 6 chicken breasts, bones removed
- 3 tablespoons of olive oil
- 3 tablespoons of plain flour
- 3 onions, each cut into 8 pieces
- 200g of smoked bacon lardons
- 3 garlic cloves, peeled and grated
- 300g large flat mushrooms chopped
- 2 tablespoons of redcurrant sauce
- 2 bay leaves
- Zest of 1 orange, peeled in 3 strips
- 300ml of red wine
- 300ml of chicken stock

For the dumplings

- 100g of self-raising flour
- 140g butter, cold and cut into cubes
- 1 tablespoon of wholegrain mustard
- 100g of fresh white breadcrumbs
- 2 tablespoons of fresh parsley, chopped
- 2 teaspoons of fresh thyme leaves
- 2 eggs, beaten

METHOD

1. Coat the chicken breasts in seasoned flour. Add the chicken to some heated oil in a pan and brown the meat on all sides.
2. Transfer the chicken breast to the slow cooker, add all the remaining casserole and season to taste.
3. Cover and cook on High for 4 hours.
4. For the dumplings: Use a blender to blend the flour, breadcrumbs, mustard and butter to a very fine crumb consistency.
5. Transfer to a bowl and add the thyme, parsley, eggs and seasoning and using floured hands, bind to create a moist dough. Create 6 large even-sized balls.
6. When the slow cooker cycle has ended, drop in the dumplings so that they sit on the surface of the casserole.
7. Cover the slow cooker again and cook for a further 25-30 minutes on a High setting. The dumplings will have expanded and be light and fluffy.
8. Serve with roast or mashed potatoes with seasonal greens.

NUTRITION PER PORTION:

SERVES - 6 | CALORIES - 701KCAL | PROTEIN - 47G | CARBOHYDRATES - 38G | FAT - 37G

CHRISTMAS ALTERNATIVE: TURKEY BREASTS IN BACON AND WINE GRAVY

INGREDIENTS

- 2 turkey breast fillets, approx. 800-900g each
- 16 smoked streaky bacon rashers, (8 for each turkey breast)
- 2 tablespoons of fresh thyme leaves
- 1 tablespoon of sunflower oil
- 2 carrots, sliced
- 15g of dried porcini mushrooms
- 1 onion, thickly sliced
- 2 bay leaves
- 500ml of chicken stock (fresh or from stock cubes)
- 150ml of dry white wine
- 2 tablespoons of plain flour

METHOD

1. Lay two 'crosshatches' of bacon rashers across a large chopping board. Scatter with 1 tablespoon of thyme leaves and ground black pepper.
2. Put the turkey fillet on each bacon 'crosshatch,' and wrap the bacon around it. Secure the bacon with skewers or string so it won't come unwrapped during cooking.
3. Heat the oil in a large frying pan and fry the fillets on all sides until browned. Set to one side.
4. In the same pan, fry the onions and carrots until they soften and begin to colour slightly, then tip into the slow cooker, adding the bay leaves and mushrooms too.
5. Put the turkey fillets in a layer on top.
6. Pour the wine and stock into the pan, boil then pour straight into the slow cooker.
7. Cover and cook on Low for 3-4 hours.
8. Transfer the turkey pieces to a plate and keep warm with some foil.
9. Combine the flour with 4 tablespoons of water to make a smooth paste.
10. Strain the cooking juices into a pan on a low heat on the hob and add the flour paste. Whisk continuously while the gravy comes to the boil and simmer until it thickens a little.
11. Serve sliced turkey breasts with traditional Christmas dinner vegetables and accompaniments.

NUTRITION PER PORTION:

SERVES - 8 | CALORIES - 297KCAL | PROTEIN - 35G | CARBOHYDRATES - 7G | FAT - 12G

CHIPOTLE CHICKEN

INGREDIENTS

- 1 tablespoon of cooking oil
- 2 red onions, sliced
- 3 garlic cloves, crushed
- 2 teaspoons of ground coriander
- 1-2 tablespoons of chipotle paste, to taste
- 1 teaspoon of smoked paprika
- 2 tablespoons of tomato purée
- 400g tin of black beans, rinsed through
- 2 peppers, finely sliced (mixed colours)
- 400g tin of chopped tomatoes
- 4 tablespoons of chicken stock or water
- 800g of chicken thigh fillets
- Juice of 2 limes
- Optional: a large handful fresh coriander, roughly chopped (optional)

METHOD

1. Heat the oil in a frying pan and add the onions with a large pinch of salt. Fry until the onions start to soften, then add the garlic and cook briefly until fragrant.
2. Add the paprika, coriander, tomato purée and chipotle paste. Fry for another minute.
3. Transfer the fried onion mixture to the slow cooker and add everything else except the chicken and lime juice.
4. Season the chicken pieces to taste and add as a top layer in the slow cooker.
5. Put the lid on and cook on a Low setting for 6hours. The chicken should be tender enough to pull apart.
6. Remove the chicken thighs very carefully to a chopping board and shred the chicken with two forks. Stir the shredded meat back into the sauce giving it time to heat up again before serving.
7. Serve on a bed of rice, with guacamole on the side and sprinkled with fresh, chopped coriander.

NUTRITION PER PORTION:

SERVES - 6 | CALORIES - 338KCAL | PROTEIN - 29G | CARBOHYDRATES - 18G | FAT - 16G

CHICKEN PICCATA

INGREDIENTS

- 1 tablespoon of vegetable oil
- 500g of chicken breast
- 3 lemons (1 sliced into pieces; juice from the other 2)
- 250ml of chicken stock
- 125g of unsalted butter
- 200ml of white wine
- Optional: 20-30g of parsley, chopped
- 2 tablespoons of capers, rinsed

METHOD

1. Heat the oil in a large non-stick pan and fry the chicken breasts briefly on both sides until they are browned. Place in the slow cooker.
2. Put the sliced lemon in the slow cooker along with the chicken stock. Add seasoning to taste, cover and cook on High for 1 hour until the chicken is cooked thoroughly.
3. Melt 75g of butter into a saucepan, and once melted, stir in the wine, 60ml of lemon juice, the capers and a large splash of the chicken juices. Bring to the boil and simmer on a high heat until reduced by half.
4. Turn off the heat and stir in the remaining butter, season to taste and stir in the parsley.
5. Serve the chicken breast with mashed potato and a big drizzle of sauce.

NUTRITION PER PORTION:
SERVES - 4 | CALORIES - 425KCAL | PROTEIN - 30G | CARBOHYDRATES - 1G | FAT - 31G

CHICKEN KORMA

INGREDIENTS

- 2 garlic cloves, crushed
- 2 teaspoons of vegetable oil
- 1 onion, chopped
- 3cm piece fresh root ginger, peeled and grated
- 1 red chilli, seeds removed and chopped finely
- 2 teaspoons of garam masala
- 1 teaspoon of ground turmeric
- 200ml of creamed coconut
- 650g chicken thigh fillets, cut into pieces
- 50g of ground almonds
- 3 tablespoons of double cream
- Optional: a large handful of fresh, chopped coriander

METHOD

1. Heat the oil in a pan and cook the onion until soft. Add the ginger, chilli and garlic and fry for a few more minutes until fragrant. Add the spices to the mixture and repeat. Now transfer the mixture to the slow cooker.
2. Add the chicken, the coconut cream and season to taste. Add a little water if the sauce is too thick.
3. Cover, and cook on a Low setting for 6 hours.
4. Stir in the almonds and double cream and serve on a bed of fluffy rice, topped with fresh coriander.

NUTRITION PER PORTION:
SERVES - 4 | CALORIES - 467KCAL | PROTEIN - 39G | CARBOHYDRATES - 10G | FAT - 30G

FRUIT AND SPICE CHICKEN STEW

INGREDIENTS

- 1 tablespoon of olive oil
- 400g of peeled butternut squash, diced into 2 ½cm pieces.
- 1 large onion, finely sliced
- 1 teaspoon of ground ginger
- 550g pack of chicken thigh fillets, cut into bite-sized pieces
- Few pinches saffron
- 1/2 teaspoons of ground turmeric
- 1 cinnamon stick
- 50g of blanched almonds, roughly chopped
- 400ml of chicken stock (fresh or from stock cubes)
- 400g tin of chickpeas, rinsed through
- 75g apricots, chopped
- 200g cherry tomatoes

METHOD

1. Preheat the slow cooker and spritz lightly with a little cooking oil.
2. Add everything except the tomatoes into the slow cooker.
3. Cover and cook on High for 4 hours.
4. Reduce the heat to a Low setting, stir in the tomatoes and seasoning, cover again and cook on low for a further 30 minutes.
5. Season to taste and serve with couscous, garnished with chopped parsley, feta and pomegranate seeds.

NUTRITION PER PORTION:
SERVES - 6 | CALORIES - 433KCAL | PROTEIN - 29G | CARBOHYDRATES - 24G | FAT - 25G

SUMMER CHICKEN CASSEROLE WITH TENDERSTEM BROCCOLI

INGREDIENTS

- 1 teaspoon of dried chilli flakes
- 2 garlic cloves, crushed
- 8 chicken thighs, keep skin and bone on
- 1 teaspoon of olive oil
- 750ml hot chicken stock (fresh or from stock cubes)
- 3 x 400g tins of butter beans, rinsed through
- 400g of tenderstem broccoli
- Zest of 1 lemon, finely grated
- 25 g parsley, leaves picked and roughly chopped

METHOD

1. In a large container, mix up the garlic, chilli flakes and seasoning to taste. Toss in the chicken to coat thoroughly.
2. Heat the oil in a pan and fry the chicken until evenly browned all over. Put on a plate and set to one side.
3. Place the butter beans and stock in the slow cooker and give it a stir. Layer the chicken thighs on the top and Put the lid on.
4. Cook on a Low setting for 6 hours, until the chicken is cooked through.
5. Next press the broccoli into the stock ensuring it's all covered.
6. Put the lid back on the slow cooker and cook for a further 15 minutes on Low.
7. Stir in the lemon zest and parsley, check the seasoning, and serve.

NUTRITION PER PORTION:
SERVES - 4 | CALORIES - 501KCAL | PROTEIN - 58G | CARBOHYDRATES - 30G | FAT - 12G

SPANISH CHICKEN

INGREDIENTS

- 1.1 litres of hot chicken stock (fresh or from stock cubes)
- 1 teaspoon of ground turmeric
- 2 tablespoons of vegetable oil
- 4 skinless, boneless chicken thigh fillets, roughly diced
- 2 garlic cloves, crushed
- 1 onion, chopped
- 50g of chorizo, diced
- 1 red pepper, deseeded and sliced
- 300g of long-grain rice
- 125g of frozen peas
- Optional: Freshly chopped parsley leaves to garnish

METHOD

1. Mix the ground turmeric and the stock in a jug and leave to infuse.
2. Meanwhile, heat the oil in a large pan and fry the chicken all over until golden. Transfer to the slow cooker.
3. Using the same pan, add the onion and fry until soft. Add the red pepper and chorizo and cook for a few minutes, then add the garlic and cook for a further minute.
4. Add the rice to the pan and stir well, then pour in the turmeric-infused stock with the peas and season to taste.
5. Cover and cook on Low for 3 hours.
6. Serve on a plate, garnished with parsley, and with crusty wedges of bread.

NUTRITION PER PORTION:
SERVES - 4 | CALORIES - 671KCAL | PROTEIN - 23G | CARBOHYDRATES - 70G | FAT - 28G

CHICKEN AND PEANUT STEW

INGREDIENTS

- 8 chicken thighs, skinned
- Seasoning to taste
- 2cm piece ginger, skin on finely grated
- 1 large onion, finely chopped
- 4 tablespoons of vegetable oil
- 1-2 teaspoons of dried chilli flakes
- 2cm piece ginger, skin on finely grated
- 2 tablespoons of tomato purée
- 1 teaspoon of cumin seeds, toasted and ground
- 1 teaspoon of ground coriander
- 1 teaspoon of ground turmeric
- 400g tin of plum tomatoes
- 200g of peanut butter (no added sugar if possible)
- 500mls of boiling water
- 1 red chilli, finely sliced
- 50g of roasted salted peanuts, chopped
- Optional: fresh coriander, chopped

METHOD

1. Preheat the slow cooker as required and spritz lightly with cooking oil.
2. Season the chicken ready for cooking.
3. Heat the oil in a large pan and fry the ginger, onion and chilli flakes for about 10 minutes until it softens. Stir in the tomato puree and spices, then add the chicken, mixing well to coat. Leave to cook for 5 minutes then add the tinned tomatoes.
4. Stir well and then gently transfer the contents of the pan into the slow cooker.
5. Stir in the peanut butter and 500ml of boiling water.
6. Season, Mix, cover and cook for 4 hours on High or 8 hours on Low.
7. Serve with steamed rice, sprinkled with sliced chilli, peanuts and coriander.

NUTRITION PER PORTION:
SERVES - 4 | CALORIES - 818KCAL | PROTEIN - 44G | CARBOHYDRATES - 16G | FAT - 63G

EASY CHICKEN SALSA

INGREDIENTS

- 750g - 1kg of boneless chicken thighs
- 300g of salsa (shop-bought or homemade)
- 1 teaspoon of paprika
- 8 garlic cloves, crushed
- 2 red onions, sliced

METHOD

1. Put the chicken thighs in the slow cooker, and add the salsa, garlic, paprika and sliced red onion.
2. Stir everything together, cover and cook on a Low setting for 6 to 8 hours, or High for 4 hours.
3. Serve with tortilla chips, guacamole and soured cream.

NUTRITION PER PORTION:
SERVES - 4 | CALORIES - 473KCAL | PROTEIN - 37G | CARBOHYDRATES - 12G | FAT - 30G

HUNTERS CHICKEN

INGREDIENTS

For the chicken

- 750g of chicken breasts
- 200g of smoked bacon rashers
- 150g of mature cheddar
- 100g of mozzarella cheese
- Seasoning to taste
- Optional: Fresh chopped parsley

For the BBQ sauce - or alternatively use shop-bought BBQ sauce

- 400g of tomato passata
- 4 tablespoons of muscovado sugar
- 3 tablespoons of maple syrup
- 2 teaspoons of paprika
- 2 teaspoons of garlic granules
- 3½ tablespoons of apple cider vinegar
- 1½ teaspoons of mustard powder
- ½ teaspoon of chilli powder
- 1 teaspoons of liquid smoke flavouring
- ¼ teaspoons of celery salt
- Seasoning to taste

METHOD

1. Combine all the BBQ sauce ingredients into the slow cooker and stir well.
2. Season each of the chicken breasts lightly with Seasoning to taste, wrap each piece in a bacon rasher, then put into the slow cooker, pushing gently down into the sauce ingredients.
3. Make sure to spoon the BBQ sauce over the chicken so it's lightly coated.
4. Cover and cook on High for 2 hours.
5. After 2 hours, check the chicken is cooked and sprinkle over the grated cheddar and mozzarella cheeses. Turn the slow cooker off.
6. Place some kitchen roll and place it between the chicken and the lid - this will stop any condensation from dropping into the sauce and spoiling it.
7. Cover again and leave to stand for a further 20 minutes until the cheese melts.
8. Serve immediately topped with freshly chopped parsley.

NUTRITION PER PORTION:
SERVES - 4 | CALORIES - 580KCAL | PROTEIN - 56G | CARBOHYDRATES - 34G | FAT - 24G

SLOW COOKER WHOLE CHRISTMAS TURKEY

INGREDIENTS

- 1.38kg fresh turkey crown
- 250g of large whole shallots, peeled only
- 2 garlic cloves, peeled and crushed
- 250g baby topped carrots, cleaned but unpeeled with green tops left on
- 200ml of boiling beef stock (fresh or made with stock cubes)
- 1 red wine stockpot
- 3 tablespoons of redcurrant jelly
- 1 tablespoon of balsamic vinegar
- 1 tablespoon of tomato puree
- 1 tablespoon of dijon mustard
- Fresh rosemary thyme
- Fresh thyme
- 2 bay leaves
- 2 tablespoons of water
- 2 tablespoons of cornflour
- Seasoning to taste

For the glaze

- 2 tablespoons redcurrant jelly
- 1 teaspoons dijon mustard

To garnish

- Fresh rosemary and thyme to garnish

METHOD

1. Put the shallots, carrots and crushed garlic into the slow cooker.
2. Heat a little oil in a large frying pan, then seal and brown the turkey crown all over, including each end.
3. Put the browned turkey crown in the slow cooker on top of the vegetables.
4. In a jug, mix the stock with the red wine stockpot, and stir in the redcurrant jelly, balsamic vinegar, dijon mustard and tomato puree. Stir until everything is dissolved and combined.
5. Pour the stock mixture into the slow cooker over the turkey. Add the thyme and rosemary sprigs and bay leaves.
6. Close the lid of the slow cooker and cook on a High setting for 3 1/2 hours. Lift the lid and baste the turkey in its juices ONCE ONLY.
7. When the turkey is cooked, the juices should run clear and there shouldn't be any sign of pink meat. If you're not sure, continue cooking for another 30 minutes, then repeat the checks until you are sure that the turkey is properly cooked.
8. Once cooked, transfer the turkey to a serving plate, place the shallots and carrots around the bottom of the joint, cover with foil and keep warm.
9. To make the gravy: use a sieve to strain the cooking liquid from the slow cooker, into a medium saucepan, and discard the herbs.
10. Mix the cornflour with a little water to create a smooth runny paste. Put the saucepan of cooking juices onto the stove and add the cornflour paste, stirring continuously. Bring to the boil, reduce the heat and simmer, stirring well, for 4-5 minutes or until thickened. Season according to taste.

    NOTE: you can adjust the amount of cornflour to use depending on how thick - or not - you like your gravy.

For the redcurrant glaze

11. Heat the redcurrant jelly and mustard in a small saucepan until just melted and stir until smooth. Brush the mixture over the turkey just before serving and garnish the plate with a few sprigs of fresh thyme and rosemary.
12. Pour the gravy into a gravy boat and serve immediately with the glazed turkey joint and vegetable garnish.

NUTRITION PER PORTION:

SERVES - 6 | CALORIES - 519KCAL | PROTEIN - 85G | CARBOHYDRATES - 25G | FAT - 5G

CHICKEN CHOW MEIN

INGREDIENTS

- 2½ teaspoons Chinese 5 spice seasoning
- 1 teaspoons garlic powder
- ¼ teaspoon white pepper
- ½ teaspoon mild chilli powder
- 1 large onion, sliced
- 150g of mushrooms. Sliced
- 4 tablespoons honey runny
- 1½ tablespoons mirin rice wine vinegar
- 3 tablespoons soy sauce
- 1½ tablespoons sesame oil
- 1 teaspoons of ground ginger (or equivalent in ground or grated fresh)
- 3 garlic cloves, minced
- 500g of chicken thighs skinless and boneless
- 1 carrot large, peeled and cut into fine ribbons
- 150g of fresh, crisp beansprouts
- 100g of mange tout
- 2 tablespoon cornflour
- 175mls of chicken stock (fresh or from a stock cube)
- 200 g (7 oz) egg noodles dried, medium thickness

METHOD

1. Mix the garlic powder, 5 spice, white pepper and chilli powder together to make a spice blend.
2. Add the onion and mushrooms to the slow cooker along with the minced garlic and ginger. Place the chicken thighs on top of the onions and mushrooms then sprinkle the spice blend over everything. Give it a good stir.
3. Stir in the sesame oil, soy sauce, honey and mirin.
4. Cover and cook on High for 3 hours. Add the mange tout, carrot ribbons, and beansprouts, and cover with the cornflour. Mix everything together.
5. Finally, add the 175ml of stock and submerge the dried noodles in the liquid entirely.
6. Cook for a further 1 hour on High.
7. Before serving, toss everything together and serve immediately on warmed plates.

NUTRITION PER PORTION:
SERVES - 4 | CALORIES - 422KCAL | PROTEIN - 31G | CARBOHYDRATES - 50G | FAT - 12G

TARRAGON CHICKEN

INGREDIENTS

- 1 onion, diced
- 150 grams chestnut mushrooms sliced
- 1 green pepper, diced
- 2 small leeks, sliced
- 500g of chicken thighs
- 3 garlic cloves, crushed
- Tarragon with stalks removed and leaves chopped roughly
- 1 teaspoons of dried thyme
- 1 teaspoon of wholegrain mustard
- 2 tablespoons of cornflour
- 3 bay leaves
- 200ml of chicken stock (fresh or from stock cubes)
- Seasoning to taste
- 100ml of double cream
- 3 tablespoons of natural yoghurt
- 2 tablespoons of cooking oil

METHOD

1. Line the bottom of the slow cooker with the onions, green pepper, leeks and mushrooms; then add the crushed garlic, mustard, tarragon and thyme. Stir the flour thoroughly to coat the vegetables.
2. Season the chicken thighs with Seasoning to taste. Heat some oil in a frying pan and fry the chicken thighs until they are brown all over. Put in the slow cooker with the vegetables.
3. Pour over the chicken stock and add the bay leaves.
4. Cover the slow cooker with the lid and leave on a Low setting for 10-15 minutes.
5. Now, stir the yoghurt and double cream through the meat and vegetables ensuring a good coating of sauce. Adjust seasoning to taste.

6. Cook on Low for 6 hours.
7. Serve.

CHICKEN TIKKA MASALA

• •

INGREDIENTS

For the Marinade

- 1 teaspoon of ginger ground
- 1 teaspoon of cumin
- Seasoning to taste
- 4 garlic cloves crushed
- 1 teaspoon of dried coriander
- 1 teaspoon of garam masala
- 1 teaspoon of smoked paprika
- 1 teaspoon of mild ground chilli powder
- Juice of 1 lemon
- 3 tablespoons of natural yoghurt
- 500g of chicken thighs cut into large chunks

For the Sauce

- 2 tablespoons of oil
- 1 large onion, chopped
- 3 garlic cloves, crushed
- 3 tablespoons of tomato paste
- 2 red peppers, chopped
- 400g of tomato passata
- 1 tablespoon of ground, sweet paprika
- 1 teaspoons of salt
- 1½ teaspoons of sugar
- 1 tablespoon of ground ginger
- 1 teaspoon of turmeric
- 1 teaspoon of garam masala
- 1 tablespoon of cumin
- 1 teaspoon of mild ground chilli powder
- ½ teaspoon of cayenne pepper
- 1 tablespoon of dried coriander
- 5 tablespoons of natural yoghurt
- 75ml of single or double cream

METHOD

1. Marinade the chicken
2. Blend all the marinade ingredients in a container and mix.
3. Turn the chopped chicken thighs in the marinade mixture so they are coated thoroughly. Cover the bowl and refrigerate for about 3 hours.

Cook chicken and sauce

4. Heat the oil in a frying pan and briefly fry the marinated chicken pieces until a golden brown colour all over.
5. Add the chicken to the slow cooker, along with any marinade left in the bowl, followed by the onion, garlic and pepper.
6. Now combine all the ingredients for the sauce in another bowl and mix thoroughly.
7. Pour the sauce over the meat and vegetables in the slow cooker, coating all the ingredients with the mixture.
8. Cover and cook for 4 hours on a High setting, or for 6 hours on Low, stirring occasionally.
9. Serve with rice and a sprinkle of freshly chopped coriander.

CHICKEN PIE (PIE FILLING)

INGREDIENTS

- 500g of skinless and boneless chicken thighs cut into 3-4cm chunks
- 1 leek, sliced
- 1 carrot, sliced
- 1 onion, sliced
- 125g of mushrooms sliced
- 3 garlic cloves, crushed
- 3 tablespoons of flour
- 200ml of chicken stock
- 150ml of white wine
- 100ml of single or double cream, or creme fraiche
- 1 tablespoon of thyme
- 3 bay leaves
- Seasoning to taste
- 1/2 teaspoon of sugar
- 550g of puff pastry
- 1 egg, beaten

METHOD

For the Pie Filling

1. Heat some oil in a frying pan and lightly brown the chopped onions, leeks and carrots for a few minutes, then transfer to the slow cooker.
2. Add the mushrooms crushed garlic and chicken pieces to the slow cooker.
3. Season with salt, pepper and thyme, then sprinkle the flour over the top so it coats everything evenly.
4. Using the same pan, add the white wine and cook on a high heat for 2-3 minutes. Pour in the chicken stock and hot water and stir, then pour the liquid into the slow cooker.
5. Stir in the cream, sugar and bay leaves making sure the cream blends in with the stock, and the meat and vegetables are completely covered in the sauce.
6. Cover and cook on Low for 8 hours or High for 4 hours.
7. Once cooked through, turn off the heat and allow to cool before making your pie.

Constructing the pie

NOTE: Whether you make several small pies or one big one, the method is the same. However, you may need to adjust cooking times accordingly. This method makes one large pie.

8. Spoon the pie filling into your pie dish up to 1cm below the rim. Spread the mixture evenly.
9. Prepare your pastry (shop bought or homemade) to fit your pie dish and also set aside 1 long strip about 1cm wide.
10. Brush the rim of the pie dish with egg, then press the long strip along the rim. This will help create a seal for the pastry 'lid.' Brush again with egg.
11. Lay your sheet of pastry over the dish, lightly pressing down on the edges to seal, and trim the excess off with a sharp knife.
12. Brush the top of the pie with egg in the centre area only.
13. Cook your pie in the middle of the oven either according to the instructions on your ready-made packet, or for 25-30 minutes at 204C//Gas 6.
14. Remove from the oven and serve immediately.

NUTRITION PER PORTION:

SERVES - 6 | CALORIES - 738KCAL | PROTEIN - 26G | CARBOHYDRATES - 52G | FAT - 46G

CHICKEN MARINARA

INGREDIENTS

- 500g skinless, boneless chicken thighs
- 400g can of chopped tomatoes
- 350g of tomato passata
- 4 tablespoons of tomato paste
- 3 garlic cloves, crushed
- 1 onion, diced
- 50ml of chicken stock (either fresh or made from stock cubes)
- 2 tablespoons of dried oregano
- 2 teaspoons of sugar
- 2 tablespoons of dried basil
- Seasoning to taste
- Optional: 100g of parmesan cheese to serve
- 200g of pasta (tagliatelle, linguine, spaghetti etc.)
- 2 tablespoons of fresh basil chopped
- 75g pitted black olives, finely sliced

METHOD

1. Put the chicken thighs in the slow cooker and season to taste.
2. Add the onions, garlic and olives followed by the dried basil, oregano and sugar.
3. Pour over the chopped tomatoes, passata, and the chicken stock. Stir in the tomato paste.
4. Mix everything together well, then cover the slow cooker and cook on a Low setting for 8 hours or High for 4 hours.
5. About 15-20 minutes before the cooking time is complete, put the pasta on to cook as the packet instructs.
6. Remove the lid from the slow cooker and roughly shred the chicken in the pot using two forks and stir through the basil leaves.
7. Return the lid to the slow cooker and leave to finish cooking.
8. Finally, add the cooked pasta to the slow cooker and mix well to coat the pasta completely.
9. Serve immediately, sprinkled with fresh grated parmesan cheese.

NUTRITION PER PORTION:

SERVES - 4 | CALORIES - 559KCAL | PROTEIN - 44G | CARBOHYDRATES - 62G | FAT - 16G

LEFTOVER CHRISTMAS TURKEY CURRY

INGREDIENTS

- 2 tablespoons of vegetable oil
- 2cm piece of fresh ginger, peeled and grated
- 1 onion, peeled and sliced
- 1 tablespoon of dried (or fresh, chopped) coriander
- 1 teaspoon of turmeric
- 4 garlic cloves, minced
- 1½ teaspoons of garam masala
- 1 teaspoon of sweet paprika
- 1 teaspoon of ground hot chilli pepper
- ½ teaspoon of ground cinnamon
- ½ teaspoon of smoked paprika powder
- 1 x 400g can of coconut milk
- 4 tablespoons of tomato puree
- ½ teaspoon of sugar
- Seasoning to taste
- 1 stock cube chicken
- 400g of cooked turkey, cut into large pieces
- 2 mixed peppers, seeds removed, thick slices
- 2½ tablespoons of cornflour
- 6 tablespoons of water

METHOD

1. Heat the oil in a frying pan on the hob and sauté the onion until it softens.
2. Add the garlic and all the spices to the pan with the onions and cook for a further 1-2 minutes stirring continuously. Add a little water to the pan to stop it drying out but take care because it will spit a bit.
3. Put the cooked onion, garlic and spice mix in the slow cooker and add the tomato puree, sugar, stock cube, salt, chopped turkey and peppers.
4. Sprinkle the cornflour into the slow cooker evenly over everything and pour in the coconut milk. Give it a good stir.
5. Cover and cook on a Low setting for 4 hours.
6. Serve with rice.

NUTRITION PER PORTION:

SERVES - 4 | CALORIES - 366KCAL | PROTEIN - 19G | CARBOHYDRATES - 18G | FAT - 26G

CHICKEN BHUNA

INGREDIENTS

- 500g of chicken thighs, each cut into 3 pieces
- 1 onion, sliced
- 400g tin of chopped tomatoes
- 100ml of water
- Juice of ½ lemon
- 3 tablespoons of tomato paste
- 3 garlic cloves, minced
- 2 green chillies, seeds removed and sliced
- 2 teaspoons of dried or fresh chopped coriander
- 2 teaspoons of turmeric
- 2 teaspoons of garam masala
- 2 teaspoons of cumin
- 1.5 teaspoons of ground fenugreek
- A 1-inch piece of ginger root, chopped
- 1 chicken stock cube crumbled
- 2 tablespoons of corn flour
- 1 teaspoons of sugar
- Seasoning to taste

METHOD

1. Place the chicken pieces and the sliced onion in the slow cooker together.
2. In a separate bowl, combine the garam masala, turmeric, fenugreek, coriander, salt, and cumin.
3. Add the spice mix to the slow cooker with the sliced green chillies, garlic, ginger, sugar and tomato paste.
4. Crumble the stock cube over the rest of the ingredients and stir everything well.
5. Sprinkle the cornflour into the slow cooker in an even layer. Stir again.
6. Finally, stir in the water, lemon juice and chopped tomatoes and mix thoroughly.
7. Cover and cook on a Low setting for 5 hours or High for 3 hours.
8. Serve with rice and a garnish of fresh chopped coriander.

NUTRITION PER PORTION:

SERVES - 4 | CALORIES - 240KCAL | PROTEIN - 27G | CARBOHYDRATES - 20G | FAT - 6G

CHICKEN DHANSAK

INGREDIENTS

- 1 large onion, peeled and diced
- 500g of chicken thighs skinless and boneless, each cut into 3 pieces
- 1 medium sized potato, peeled, diced and rinsed
- 280g butternut squash, peeled and diced

- 1 x 400g tin of chopped tomatoes
- Juice of ½ lemon
- 4 garlic cloves, minced
- 1 x 435g tin of pineapple chunks (fruit and juice)
- 180g of dried chana dal
- 1 chicken stock cube
- 4 tablespoons of tomato puree

- 2 tablespoons of vegetable oil
- 1 teaspoon of soft brown sugar
- 425ml of water
- Seasoning to taste
- 1½ tablespoons of green cardamom pods, bruised

Spice mix

- 1 tablespoon of dried coriander
- 1 tablespoon of garam masala
- 1½ teaspoons of ground ginger
- 2 teaspoons of cumin

- 2½ teaspoons of chilli powder
- ½ teaspoon of garlic powder
- 1½ teaspoons of fenugreek
- ½ teaspoon of celery salt

- 1 teaspoon of onion powder

METHOD

1. Heat the oil in a large frying pan and gently sauté the onion, potato and squash for 2-3 minutes.
2. Add the spice mix and garlic and stir the mixture thoroughly to coat the vegetables in the flavours.
3. Pour 75ml of the water into the frying pan with the vegetables for a few minutes until the water absorbs and the vegetables have softened.
4. Transfer the mixture to the slow cooker.
5. Add the chicken thigh pieces, the remaining water, the chana dal, and all of the other ingredients except for the lemon into the slow cooker. Stir gently ensuring that everything is combined, and the vegetables are submerged in the liquid.
6. Cover and cook on High for 6 hours or Low for 7-8 hours.
7. Squeeze the lemon juice into the curry and stir thoroughly once again.
8. Serve with rice and naan, garnished with chopped coriander.

NUTRITION PER PORTION:

SERVES - 4 | CALORIES - 534KCAL | PROTEIN - 35G | CARBOHYDRATES - 61G | FAT - 18G

CHICKEN SATAY

INGREDIENTS

- 1kg of chicken thighs, skinless, boneless and each cut into 3 pieces
- 5 garlic cloves, minced
- 2 red onions, finely sliced
- 1-inch piece of fresh ginger, finely grated
- Juice of 1 lime
- 400ml can of coconut milk
- 6 tablespoons of peanut butter, crunchy or smooth as preferred
- 1 tablespoon of rice wine vinegar

- 1 chicken stock cube
- 1½ teaspoons of brown sugar
- 1 tablespoon of soy sauce
- 2 teaspoons of fresh coriander, finely chopped
- 1½ teaspoons of mild curry powder
- 1½ teaspoons of ground turmeric
- 1 teaspoon of mild chilli powder
- ½ teaspoon of chilli flakes
- ½ teaspoon of ground cinnamon
- 1½ tablespoons of cornflour

- 1 red pepper, thickly sliced
- Optional: Sugar snap peas

METHOD

1. Start heating the slow cooker on a Low setting and spray lightly with cooking oil.
2. Add the onions, garlic, and ginger to the slow cooker, then add the chicken thigh pieces on top.
3. Now evenly crumble the chicken stock cube into the slow cooker, then add all the spices - coriander, curry powder, turmeric, chilli flakes, cinnamon, chilli powder - and the sugar. Give everything a good stir to mix up the ingredients and coat the chicken and onions.
4. Pour in the lime juice, rice wine vinegar and soy sauce.
5. Sprinkle the cornflour evenly over everything in the slow cooker, followed by the coconut milk and peanut butter. Stir thoroughly again.
6. Finally, add the thickly sliced red peppers and (optional) sugar snap peas.
7. Give everything one final good mix, cover the slow cooker and cook on a Low setting for 18 hours.
8. Serve with rice, garnished with chopped coriander and red chilli peppers, accompanied by fresh, warm naan.

NUTRITION PER PORTION:
SERVES - 4 | CALORIES - 629KCAL | PROTEIN - 57G | CARBOHYDRATES - 21G | FAT - 27G

CHICKEN DAAL
● ●

INGREDIENTS

- Spray cooking oil
- 400g tin of chopped tomatoes
- 1 large onion, sliced
- 2 chicken breasts, diced, or 4 skinless, boneless chicken thighs, diced
- 1 tablespoon of mild chilli powder
- 2 garlic cloves, crushed
- 1 tablespoons of mild curry powder
- 2 tablespoons of fresh coriander
- 1-inch piece of ginger, grated
- 1 tablespoon of turmeric
- 1 tablespoon of garam masala
- 500g of fresh, washed spinach
- Optional: 1 tablespoon of cornflour
- Optional: 3 tablespoons of water

METHOD

1. Start heating the slow cooker and spray a little oil inside.
2. Add all of the ingredients, apart from the spinach, and stir thoroughly.
3. Cover and cook on High for 4 hours or Low for 7 hours.
4. Add the spinach to the top of the pot and leave it to wilt, then stir in before serving.
5. Optional: if you like your curry sauce a little thicker, then in a separate container, mix 1 tablespoon of cornflour with 3 tablespoons of water to make a smooth paste. Stir into the slow cooker and leave to complete the cooker cycle.
6. Stir to mix in the wilted spinach and serve with fresh, warmed naan bread.

NUTRITION PER PORTION:
SERVES - 3 | CALORIES - 256KCAL | PROTEIN - 35G | CARBOHYDRATES - 19G | FAT - 5G

CHICKEN AND MUSHROOM PIE (PIE FILLING)
● ●

INGREDIENTS

- 2 tablespoons of plain flour
- 250ml of white wine
- Seasoning to taste
- 300g of fresh mushrooms roughly chopped
- 400g of chicken breast, diced
- 1 chicken stock cube
- 1 teaspoon of thyme

For the pie topping
◆ 20g of butter
◆ 50g of frozen filo pastry sheets

METHOD
1. In a container, whisk together the wine and flour, adding seasoning to taste.
2. Put the chicken and mushrooms into the slow cooker and pour the wine mixture over the top. Add the thyme, then crumble a chicken stock cube into the mixture. Stir thoroughly.
3. Cook on a Low setting for 5 hours or High for 3 hours.

For the filo pie topping
1. Grease a pie dish.
2. Melt the butter and transfer to a shallow bowl or plate.
3. Coat the filo pastry sheets in the butter (either by dipping into the butter on the plate or using a pastry brush) and lay on top of the pie dish containing the pie filling. Ensure the edges are sealed.
4. Cook at gas mark 5 (190C) for 25-30 minutes until the pastry crust is golden brown.

NUTRITION PER PORTION:
SERVES - 2 | CALORIES - 552KCAL | PROTEIN - 51G | CARBOHYDRATES - 32G | FAT - 14G

BEEF

BEEF CHILLI

INGREDIENTS

- 1 tablespoon of rapeseed oil
- 2 garlic cloves, crushed
- 1 large onion, finely chopped
- 2 teaspoons of ground cumin
- 1 ½ teaspoons of sweet smoked paprika
- Optional: 1 teaspoon of mild chilli powder
- 2 carrots, diced
- 1 courgette, diced
- 2 celery sticks, diced
- 1 red pepper, diced
- 400g of lean beef mince
- 3 x 400g cans of chopped tomatoes
- 1 beef stock cube
- 1 tablespoon of tomato purée
- 1 x 400g can of flageolet beans, rinsed through
- 1 x 400g can of green lentils, rinsed through
- To serve: rice or tacos, soured cream, grated cheese and sliced avocado

METHOD

1. Heat the oil in a large frying pan and stir fry the onion for a few minutes until it softens. Add the garlic and spices and cook for a further 1-2 minutes.
2. Transfer to a slow cooker, and add the diced vegetables, mince, chopped tomatoes, stock cube and tomato purée. Give everything a good stir to combine
3. Cover and cook on a Low setting for 6-7 hours.
4. Half an hour before serving stir in the lentils and flageolet beans.
5. Replace the lid and cook for another 30 minutes on Low.
6. Stir and serve with rice or tacos, soured cream, grated cheese and sliced avocado.

NUTRITION PER PORTION:

SERVES - 6 | CALORIES - 251KCAL | PROTEIN - 23G | CARBOHYDRATES - 22G | FAT - 6G

DRUNKEN SLOW-COOKED BEEF

INGREDIENTS

- Vegetable oil for cooking.
- 12 shallots, peeled and left whole
- 500g of diced beef stew meat (large chunks
- 1 tablespoon of plain flour
- 350ml of Irish stout beer (such as Guinness®)
- 2 onions, peeled and sliced
- 1 garlic clove, crushed
- 4 slices of smoked streaky bacon, cut into strips
- 180g of fresh button mushrooms whole or halved
- Seasoning to taste

METHOD

1. Preheat the slow cooker on a Low setting.
2. Heat 2 teaspoons of cooking oil in a frying pan. Cook the shallots for a few minutes until they are browned all over then transfer to the slow cooker.
3. Using the same frying pan, cook the beef chunks until browned on all side. Mix in the flour and pour in the beer.
4. Bring to a boil, stirring continuously, then transfer the beef-beer mixture to the slow cooker.

5. Absorb the moisture from the frying pan with a bit of kitchen roll, heat some more cooking oil, and fry the onion for a few minutes until softened.
6. Add the garlic and bacon, and cook for a further minute, then transfer the cooked onion, garlic and bacon to the slow cooker. Set the frying pan to one side.
7. Tip the mushrooms into the slow cooker, season to taste, then cover and cook for 5 hours on Low. and season to taste. Cover.
8. Cook on Low until meat is cooked through.
9. Serve with rice, or mash and peas.

NUTRITION PER PORTION:
SERVES - 4 | CALORIES - 513KCAL | PROTEIN - 29G | CARBOHYDRATES - 42G | FAT - 24G

BEEF BOURGUIGNON
• •

INGREDIENTS

- 1 ½kg of stewing or braising steak, cut into small chunks
- 3 tablespoons of vegetable oil
- 2 celery stalks, chopped
- 2 large onions, peeled and chopped
- 2 carrots, chopped
- 2 bay leaves
- Fresh thyme
- 3 tablespoons of plain flour
- 1 beef stock cube
- 1 teaspoon of caster sugar
- 750ml bottle red wine
- 2 tablespoons of tomato purée
- 100g of unsmoked bacon lardons
- 6 small shallots, peeled, halved or quartered
- 300g of closed cup mushrooms halved or quartered
- To serve: buttery mashed potatoes or wedges of crusty bread

METHOD

1. Preheat the slow cooker on a Low setting, and lightly spritz with cooking oil.
2. Heat 2 tablespoons of cooking oil in a large frying pan. Season the meat and fast fry for 3-4 minutes until browned all over. Move to a plate and set to one side.
3. Use the same frying pan to fry the onion, carrot, and celery for a few minutes until soft. Add in the herbs and plain flour and cook for another 2 minutes. Add to the slow cooker.
4. Pour some of the wine into the frying pan to absorb the cooking juices and stir in the stock cube, sugar, and tomato purée. Mix to form a smooth paste.
5. Transfer the paste to the slow cooker with the remaining wine and stir in the browned beef. If needed, add a splash of extra water to cover the meat completely.
6. Cover the slow cooker and cook on a Low setting for 8 hours.
7. About 35 minutes before serving, heat the remaining oil in a frying pan. Fry the bacon, shallots, and mushrooms together in the pan for 5-8 minutes until softened and starting to caramelise. Add to the slow cooker and stir through.
8. Recover and cook the stew on High for a further 30 minutes.
9. Serve with mashed potatoes or wedges of fresh crusty bread.

NUTRITION PER PORTION:
SERVES - 6-8 | CALORIES - 497KCAL | PROTEIN - 47G | CARBOHYDRATES - 14G | FAT - 20G

BEEF GOULASH, V1

INGREDIENTS

- 2kg of braising or stewing steak, cut into chunks#
- 3 tablespoons of olive oil
- 3 garlic cloves, crushed
- 4 mixed peppers, cut into 4cm chunks
- 2 large onions, finely chopped
- 2 tablespoons of plain flour
- 2 teaspoons of caraway seeds
- 1 tablespoon of sweet smoked paprika, plus extra to serve
- 2 teaspoons of hot smoked paprika
- 4 large tomatoes, diced
- 4 tablespoons of tomato purée
- 500ml of beef stock (fresh or made from stock cubes)
- 300ml of soured cream
- Fresh parsley, chopped

METHOD

1. Preheat the slow cooker on a low setting. Spritz lightly with cooking oil.
2. Heat 2 tablespoons of oil in a large frying pan. Season the beef, then sear in the pan until thoroughly browned. Move to a plate and set aside.
3. Heat some more oil and fry the onions until softened and golden. Add the garlic and peppers, and fry for a few more minutes.
4. Stir in the flour and all the spices, cooking for about 2 minutes, then transfer the onion mix to the slow cooker.
5. Wash a little beef stock around the frying pan to collect the cooking juices, then add to the slow cooker with the rest of the beef stock.
6. Stir in the tomato purée, tomatoes, and the seared beef.
7. Cover and cook on Low for 7 hours.
8. Season and swirl the soured cream and parsley through the stew, saving a little parsley to scatter over the top.
9. Serve with roast potatoes or brown rice, topped with chopped parsley and a sprinkle of sweet smoked paprika.

NUTRITION PER PORTION:
SERVES - 8 | CALORIES - 581KCAL | PROTEIN - 54G | CARBOHYDRATES - 17G | FAT - 32G

COOK-AND-GO BEEF MADRAS

INGREDIENTS

- 400g of beef, diced into large chunks
- 1 onion, chopped
- 2 tablespoons of tomato puree
- 2 garlic cloves, crushed
- 1 jar of madras paste
- 400g of chopped tomatoes or passata
- 1 beef stock cube

METHOD

1. Either sauté the beef for a few minutes in a hot, oiled frying pan to brown it, or put the beef direction into the bottom of the slow cooker depending on how much time you have.
2. Add the rest of the ingredients to the slow cooker and stir thoroughly to combine.
3. Cover and cook on a Low setting for 8 hours or High for 4 hours.
4. Serve with rice and/or warm fresh naan.

NUTRITION PER PORTION:
SERVES - 8 | CALORIES - 581KCAL | PROTEIN - 54G | CARBOHYDRATES - 17G | FAT - 32G

MEXICAN BEEF STEW

INGREDIENTS

- 2 cans of chopped tomatoes
- 2 tablespoons of chipotle paste (For a milder taste, just use 1 tablespoon)
- Juice of 1 lime
- 1 tablespoon of smoked paprika
- 1 teaspoon of chilli powder
- 2 teaspoons of onion powder
- 1 tablespoon of smoked paprika
- 1 teaspoon of ground cumin
- 2 teaspoons of garlic powder
- 100ml of beef stock
- 500g – 700g of diced beef
- 4 garlic cloves, crushed
- 1 onion, sliced
- Optional: 2 peppers, deseeded and sliced
- Optional: For a spicier stew, add a couple of deseeded and chopped chilli)
- Seasoning to taste

METHOD

1. In a container combine the chopped tomatoes, chipotle paste, lime juice, spices, and beef stock.
2. Add the diced beef to the slow cooker along with the chopped onions, crushed garlic, and seasoning.
3. Pour the stock and tomato mixture over the beef.
4. Optional: stir in the peppers if you are using them.
5. Cover and cook on Low for 8 hours or High for 4 hours.
6. Serve with rice or over a jacket potato.

NUTRITION PER PORTION:

SERVES - 4 | CALORIES - 641KCAL | PROTEIN - 55G | CARBOHYDRATES - 15G | FAT - 40G

BEEF WITH PRUNES

INGREDIENTS

- 2 tablespoons of plain flour
- 900g of diced beef
- 3 tablespoons of olive oil
- 2 onions, chopped
- 2 garlic cloves, chopped
- 2-inch piece of peeled ginger, finely chopped
- 2 teaspoons of cumin powder
- 250ml of red wine
- 250ml of beef stock
- 2 tablespoons of honey
- 150g of pitted prunes
- Optional: 15g of flat leaf parsley, chopped
- Optional: 1 red onion, chopped

METHOD

1. Preheat the slow cooker on a low setting.
2. Heat the oil in a large pan. Season the beef, then sauté in the frying pan until brown on all sides. Remove from the pan and set to one side.
3. Heat the remaining oil in the same frying pan and sauté the onion, garlic and ginger for a few minutes until they soften. Stir in the four and cook for a couple of minutes on a low heat.
4. Put the onion mixture into the slow cooker with the cooked beef pieces, the cumin, honey, prunes and red wine.
5. Wash a little stock around the pan used for frying to collect any meat juices and flavours, then add to the slow cooker with the rest of the stock. Stir well to combine.
6. Cover and cook on High for 4 hours or Low for 8 hours.
7. Serve with mash, sprinkled with a garnish of parsley and red onion.

NUTRITION PER PORTION:

SERVES - 6 | CALORIES - 342KCAL | PROTEIN - 37G | CARBOHYDRATES - 21G | FAT - 10G

BEEF STROGANOFF

INGREDIENTS

- 1kg of stewing beef, fat removed and cut into strips
- 130g of chestnut mushrooms cut into quarters
- 2 onions, thinly sliced
- 1 teaspoon of ground cinnamon
- 2 tablespoons of cornflour
- 1 ½ tablespoons of dijon mustard
- 200ml of rich beef stock (fresh or from stock cubes)
- 60ml of fortified wine (vermouth)
- 200ml of crème fraiche
- Seasoning to taste

METHOD

1. Preheat the slow cooker on a Low setting.
2. In a large bowl, combine the beef with the cornflour, mustard, cinnamon and vermouth and mix well.
3. Add the mixture to the slow cooker with the onions and beef stock.
4. Cover and cook for 3 hours on High or 7 on Low.
5. Remove the lid and stir in the mushrooms creme fraiche, and seasoning. Re-cover and cook for a further 1 hour on the same setting.
6. Serve on a bed of rice.

NUTRITION PER PORTION:

SERVES - 4 | CALORIES - 592KCAL | PROTEIN - 62G | CARBOHYDRATES - 19G | FAT - 30G

SPICY SCANDINAVIAN MEATLOAF

INGREDIENTS

- 1 tablespoon of tomato puree
- 1 tablespoon of olive oil
- 1 onion, chopped
- 1 garlic clove, crushed
- 1 teaspoon of allspice
- A pinch of ground cloves
- 250g of pork mince
- 250g of beef mince
- 90g of smoked bacon lardons
- 2 teaspoons of dijon mustard
- Fresh parsley, chopped
- Fresh dill, chopped
- 1 large egg, lightly beaten

For the glaze

- 80g of tomato ketchup
- 1 tablespoon of Worcestershire sauce
- ½ teaspoon of brown sugar

METHOD

1. Preheat your slow cooker on High.
2. Heat the oil in a pan and sauté the onions briefly, then add the garlic and spices and cook for another few minutes.
3. Transfer to a bowl and leave to cool.
4. Add the remaining ingredients, including the mince, to the container, season, then pour in the beaten egg. Use your hands to mix together, and form into a dense loaf shape.
5. Blend the ketchup, Worcestershire sauce and sugar together to make the glaze.
6. Place the meatloaf in the slow cooker and brush the glaze over the top
7. Cover and cook on a Low setting for 6 hours.
8. Serve with buttered jacket potatoes and braised red cabbage.

NUTRITION PER PORTION:

SERVES - 4 | CALORIES - 367KCAL | PROTEIN - 33G | CARBOHYDRATES - 11G | FAT - 22G

BEEF RAGU

INGREDIENTS

- 40g of dried porcini mushrooms
- 450g lean, diced casserole beef
- ½ tablespoon of plain flour
- 1 tablespoon of olive oil
- 15ml of red wine
- 2 carrots, diced
- 3 shallots, diced
- 2 carrots, diced
- 1 garlic clove, chopped
- 1 celery stick, diced
- 1 bay leaf, fresh or dried
- ½ teaspoon of fresh rosemary, chopped
- 75ml of beef stock
- 200g tin of chopped tomatoes
- 200g dried pappardelle pasta
- 2 teaspoons of parmesan, grated

METHOD

1. Put the porcini mushrooms in a heatproof bowl with enough boiling water to cover them completely. Leave to soak for about 10 minutes. Drain into a jug and keep 75ml of the liquid. Roughly chop the mushrooms and put in the slow cooker.
2. Put the flour in a container, add seasoning, then toss in the beef so that it's well coated.
3. Heat oil in a pan and brown the beef all over. Transfer to the slow cooker.
4. Pour the wine into the pan used to brown the beef, bring to the boil and simmer until it reduces, then transfer to the slow cooker.
5. Now add the chopped vegetables, herbs, stock, chopped tomatoes and the 75ml of mushroom soaking liquid to the slow cooker.
6. Cover and cook for 4 hours on Low until the beef is tender. Remove the lid and shred the beef, then recover and leave to reheat.
7. Meanwhile, cook the pappardelle pasta.
8. Season the beef to taste and serve with the pappardelle sprinkled with freshly grated parmesan.

NUTRITION PER PORTION:

SERVES - 2 | CALORIES - 454KCAL | PROTEIN - 44G | CARBOHYDRATES - 32G | FAT - 9G

BEEF STEW WITH WHOLEMEAL DUMPLINGS

INGREDIENTS

For the stew

- 2 tablespoons of wholemeal plain flour
- 2 tablespoons of olive oil
- 800g of diced beef
- 2 garlic cloves, finely chopped
- 1 large onion, roughly chopped

- 2 tablespoons of olive oil
- 3 carrots, peeled and roughly chopped
- 200g button mushrooms halved
- 3 celery sticks, roughly chopped
- 400g tin of chopped tomatoes

- 1 tablespoon of tomato purée
- 500g of beef
- Fresh thyme or rosemary leaves, chopped
- 2 bay leaves

For the dumplings

- 60g of vegetable suet
- 125g of self-raising wholemeal flour

- Fresh thyme or rosemary, finely chopped
- Splash of skimmed milk

For serving

- 3 tablespoons of finely chopped parsley
- 1 garlic clove, finely chopped

METHOD

1. To make the stew: Put 2 tablespoons of flour in a shallow bowl and season. Toss in the diced beef and coat thoroughly. Fry the beef for a few minutes, turning occasionally until it's browned all over. Transfer to a slow cooker.
2. In the same pan, fry the vegetables, garlic, and mushrooms for 5-10 minutes, until the vegetables begin to soften and brown. Add the herbs, stir in the chopped tomatoes, and tomato purée, and leave to bubble for a couple of minutes. Mix with the beef in the slow cooker.
3. Pour in the stock and stir well.
4. Cover and cook for 4 hours on High or 6 hours on Low.
5. To make the dumplings: Combine the flour, suet and herbs in a container with just enough milk to just bring it together to a soft, slightly wet dough, with your hands.
6. Season with Seasoning to taste and roll into 6-8 evenly sized dough balls.
7. Remove the lid of the slow cooker, remove the bay leaves and give the stew a good stir. Season to taste.
8. Gently drop the dumplings evenly over the surface of the stew.
9. Recover and cook for a further 1 hour with the dumplings.
10. Serve the stew topped with the (optional) chopped parsley and garlic, and thick wedges of fresh, crusty job.

NUTRITIONAL INFORMATION PER SERVING
SERVES - 4 | CALORIES - 732KCAL | PROTEIN - 52G | CARBOHYDRATES - 51G | FAT - 33G

SPAGHETTI BOLOGNESE

INGREDIENTS

- 450g of minced beef
- 1 garlic clove, crushed
- 1 onion, chopped
- 1 beef stock cube
- 100ml of red wine
- 2 tablespoons of olive oil
- 1 celery stick, sliced
- 400g can of chopped tomatoes
- 2 tablespoons of tomato puree
- 300g of dry spaghetti

METHOD

1. Heat some oil in a pan and fry the mince until it's browned all over.
2. Add the garlic and onion and fry until it softens, then crumble and stir in the beef stock cube. Add the contents to the slow cooker.
3. Put all the remaining ingredients into the slow cooker (except the spaghetti) and give it all a good stir until combined.
4. Cover and cook on High for 4 hours or Low for 8 hours.
5. Cook the spaghetti in boiling water for 8-10 minutes until tender then drain.
6. Serve the spaghetti topped with the bolognese sauce and sprinkled with grated parmesan.

NUTRITION PER PORTION:
SERVES - 4 | CALORIES - 550KCAL | PROTEIN - 35G | CARBOHYDRATES - 62G | FAT - 18G

BEEF AND PANCETTA RAGU WITH PAPPARDELLE

INGREDIENTS

- 700g of diced braising steak
- 90g of pancetta cut into cubes
- 1 onion, finely chopped
- 1 tablespoon of olive oil
- 2 sticks of celery, finely sliced
- 2 carrots, diced
- 2 cloves of garlic, sliced
- 175ml of red wine
- 2 x 400g tins of chopped tomatoes
- 1 tablespoon of fresh rosemary, finely chopped
- 500g of dried pappardelle pasta
- Optional: parmesan shavings, to serve

METHOD

1. Heat the olive oil in a pan and fry the beef until browned all over. Take off the heat and set to one side.
2. Use the same pan and add the pancetta. Fry for 2-3 minutes then add the onion, carrots and celery and fry for a little longer until it starts to soften and brown. Finally, add the garlic and fry for 1 minute. Transfer to the slow cooker.
3. Pour the wine into the pan that was used for frying and bring it to the boil. Simmer for a couple of minutes, then add to the slow cooker with the rest of the wine.
4. Stir in the beef and both tins of tomatoes. Cover and cook on Low for 6 ½ hours.
5. Open the slow cooker to add the fresh rosemary and seasoning, then stir, close and cook for a further half an hour.
6. Meanwhile, cook the pasta per the packet directions.
7. Serve the spaghetti topped with ragù, sprinkled with parmesan shavings.

NUTRITION PER PORTION:

SERVES - 4 | CALORIES - 608KCAL | PROTEIN - 39G | CARBOHYDRATES - 57G | FAT - 21G

FESTIVE SPICED BRISKET BEEF WITH CRANBERRIES

INGREDIENTS

- 1 tablespoon of honey mixed with 1 tablespoon of balsamic vinegar
- Zest of 2 clementines
- 1 tablespoon of chopped thyme leaves
- ¼ teaspoon of ground allspice
- ½ teaspoon of paprika
- 1 teaspoon of ground cinnamon
- 1.7kg of rolled beef brisket
- 2 tablespoons of olive oil
- 5 garlic cloves, finely chopped
- 3 celery sticks, finely diced
- 2 red onions, finely sliced
- 300ml of hot beef stock (fresh or from stock cubes)
- 1 tablespoon of red wine vinegar
- 1 star anise
- 1 cinnamon stick
- 300g of fresh or frozen cranberries
- 75g of dark brown muscovado sugar
- Optional: 15g of flat leaf parsley, chopped, to serve

METHOD

1. 24 hours before cooking, combine the honey/balsamic mix, clementine zest, thyme, and ground spices in a container together to create the marinade. Season with black pepper only, no salt.
2. Pat the beef brisket dry, place in the bowl of marinade and turn to coat thoroughly. Cover and set aside in the fridge to marinate overnight.
3. The next day, heat half the oil in a large pan, and gently fry the red onions, celery and garlic for about 10 minutes. Stir in the red wine vinegar, then transfer to the slow cooker. Cover and turn to a Low setting to start heating.

4. Use the same pan to heat the remaining oil. Sear the beef on all sides until brown all over. Place in the slow cooker with any residual marinade, the star anise and cinnamon stick. Use a little stock to wash around the frying pan to collect any juices and flavours left over from frying the meat and onions, then add to the slow cooker with the rest of the stock.
5. Cover and continue cooking on Low for 6 hours.
6. After 6 hours, open the slow cooker, turn the beef over and add the cranberries and sugar. Cover and cook for another 2 hours until the beef is tender.
7. Now, remove the beef from the slow cooker to a plate and cover with foil to keep warm.
8. Use a sieve to strain the stock into a pan (setting the fruit to one side). Bring to a rolling boil and simmer for about 15 minutes until reduced to about 350ml. Season or sweeten according to taste.
9. Shred the beef on a plate using two forks. Remove the whole spices from the sauce/fruit and discard. Stir the shredded beef into the pan of reduced sauce and add the reserved fruit.
10. Serve on a plate scattered with chopped parsley. Perfect for a festive buffet serve with freshly baked crusty rolls or wraps.

NUTRITION PER PORTION:

SERVES - 10 | CALORIES - 396KCAL | PROTEIN - 46G | CARBOHYDRATES - 16G | FAT - 16G

BEEF AND BARLEY STEW WITH LEMON, GARLIC AND HERB GREMOLATA

INGREDIENTS

- 3-4 teaspoons of olive oil
- 900g of lean diced beef
- 2 carrots, quartered
- 1 large onion, finely diced

- 1 litre of hot chicken stock (fresh or from stock cubes)
- 2 bay leaves
- 2 celery stalks, finely diced

- 200g of pearl barley, rinsed
- 250g of chestnut mushrooms halved or quartered

For the gremolata

- 28g of chopped parsley
- Zest of 1 large lemon
- 2 garlic cloves, finely chopped

METHOD

1. Heat 1 teaspoon of oil in a pan and sauté the beef pieces until browned all over. Remove from the pan and set to one side.
2. Use the same pan to heat another teaspoon of oil and add the onion, celery and carrot chunks to the pan. Fry for about 10 minutes until the onions soften and begin to brown.
3. Add the beef and vegetables to the slow cooker with the mushrooms bay leaves and seasoning. Wash a little of the hot stock around the pan to collect any meat juices and flavourings and add to the slow cooker along with the rest of the stock.
4. Stir, cover and cook for 3 hours on a Low setting.
5. Remove the carrots (discard or eat!) and add the pearl barley. Cover and cook for another 4 hours on Low. Add a bit more water if it looks dry.
6. To make the gremolata, mix the ingredients together in a small bowl. Serve the beef and barley and scatter the gremolata over the top.

NUTRITION PER PORTION:

SERVES - 4 | CALORIES - 511KCAL | PROTEIN - 58G | CARBOHYDRATES - 48G | FAT - 16G

BEEF WITH CRISPY GNOCCHI

INGREDIENTS

- 2 tablespoons of plain flour
- 600g of braising steak, diced into 2.5cm pieces
- 100g of smoked pancetta or streaky bacon, chopped
- 5 cloves garlic, crushed
- 2 onions, diced
- 3 celery sticks, diced
- 1 large carrot, diced
- 2 tablespoons of olive oil
- 1 tablespoon of rosemary, finely chopped
- 100ml of semi-skimmed milk
- 2 tablespoons of tomato purée
- 200ml of dry white wine (or 200ml of water if preferred)
- 400ml of beef stock (fresh or made from stock cubes)
- 800g of potato gnocchi
- Optional: 25g of grated parmesan
- Optional: 15g of basil leaves

METHOD

1. Add the flour to a shallow bowl and season with black pepper. Toss in the beef pieces so they are coated thoroughly.
2. Heat 1 tablespoon of olive oil in a pan and fry for 4-5 minutes until golden all over. Remove from the pan and set to one side.
3. Use the same pan to heat a little more oil and stir fry the streaky bacon/pancetta, onions, carrot, celery, garlic and rosemary. Cook for a few minutes until softened.
4. Pour the milk into the pan, bring to the boil, then stir and simmer for a few minutes before stirring in the tomato purée. Cook for another 2 minutes, then pour in the wine and reduce by half.
5. Put the vegetables and beef into the slow cooker. Wash a little stock around the pan used to sauté the beef and vegetables to collect and flavourful juices, then pour into the slow cooker with the rest of the stock. Stir well.
6. Cover and cook on Low for 8 hours. Season to taste.
7. Heat the rest of the oil in a pan and cook the potato gnocchi for 3-4 minutes on each side, until crisp and golden.
8. Spoon the ragu over the crispy gnocchi and serve with a topping of grated parmesan and a basil garnish.

NUTRITION PER PORTION:
SERVES - 6 | CALORIES - 517KCAL | PROTEIN - 18G | CARBOHYDRATES - G | FAT - 17G

BEEF BARBACOA

INGREDIENTS

- 1 red onion, roughly chopped
- 3 tablespoons of chipotle paste
- 100ml of cider vinegar
- 2 garlic cloves, crushed
- A pinch of ground cloves
- Juice of 2 limes
- 3 bay leaves
- 500ml of chicken stock (fresh or from stock cubes)
- 1 bunch coriander, roughly chopped
- 1kg of beef brisket, cut into large chunks

To serve

- 2 crisp lettuces, jalapeño chilli slices and crème fraiche

METHOD

1. Preheat the slow cooker and spritz lightly with cooking oil.
2. Place the chipotle paste, red onion, garlic, cloves, lime juice and cider vinegar into the slow cooker and stir until combined.
3. Add the bay leaves, chicken stock and coriander, then put the beef chunks on top. Turn the meat over a few times to coat in the sauce.

4. Cover the slow cooker with the lid and cook on High for 1 hour and then Low for 8 hours. Shred the meat with two forks and stir thoroughly.
5. Serve in crisp lettuce cups with jalapeño chilles and crème fraiche.

BEEF GHOULASH

INGREDIENTS

- 2kg of braising or stewing steak, cut into chunks
- 2 onions, chopped
- 3 tablespoons of olive oil
- 3 garlic cloves, crushed
- 4 mixed peppers, cut into 4cm chunks
- 2 tablespoons of plain flour
- 2 teaspoons of hot smoked paprika
- 2 teaspoons of caraway seeds
- 1 tablespoon of sweet smoked paprika, and extra to serve
- 4 tablespoons of tomato purée
- 500ml of beef stock (fresh or from stock cubes)
- 4 large tomatoes, diced
- 300ml of soured cream
- Optional: a small bunch of parsley, chopped

METHOD

1. Preheat the slow cooker on Low.
2. In the meantime, heat 2 tablespoons of oil in a pan. Season the beef, and sear in batches until brown on all sides. Transfer to a plate and set to one side.
3. Add the remaining oil to the same pan. Fry the onions for about 8-10 minutes until softened and golden in colour, then add the garlic and peppers. Fry for another few minutes.
4. Stir in the flour and all of the spices. Cook for a further 2 minutes more, then add the tomato purée, tomatoes and the beef stock. Bring to the boil and simmer, then add to the slow cooker.
5. Cover and cook on Low for 6-7 hours until the beef is tender, and the sauce has thickened slightly.
6. Adjust the seasoning to taste and stir in the soured cream and parsley.
7. Serve the goulash with roast potatoes or rice, scattered with the remaining parsley and sweet smoked paprika.

PERUVIAN BEEF STEW

INGREDIENTS

- 850g of braising steak, cut into 2cm chunks
- 2 tablespoons of vegetable oil
- 6 garlic cloves, crushed
- 3 red onions, finely chopped
- 2 x 500ml cans of dark beer (e.g., brown ale, or use beef stock if you prefer)
- 3 bay leaves
- 1 bunch of coriander, chopped
- 2 teaspoons each of fennel seeds, coriander seeds and cumin seeds (dry fry in a pan for 2 minutes to toast)
- 2 teaspoons of pink peppercorns
- 1 bunch of parsley, chopped
- 2 teaspoons of dried muña mint (or use dried mint)
- 1.7 litres of beef stock
- 6 large potatoes, each cut into quarters
- 60g of chipotle paste

To garnish

- 200g of cherry tomatoes, skins removed
- 120g can of cannellini beans, warmed first
- 120g of broad beans, cooked and peeled
- handful of mixed chopped herbs (mint, coriander, and parsley)

NOTE: if you can't find the specialist ingredients, use the alternatives in brackets instead.

METHOD

1. Place the beef chunks in a shallow bowl, season to taste and mix with the chilli paste.
2. Now heat 1 tablespoon of oil in a pan and sear the beef until evenly browned on all sides. Remove to a bowl and set to one side.
3. In the same pan, add another tablespoon of oil and fry the onions and garlic for a few minutes until starting to caramelise.
4. Pour in the beer and stir to collect any flavourings left over from cooking in the pan. Bring to a rolling boil and simmer for a few minutes, then add the pan contents to the slow cooker.
5. Add the beef, bay leaves, spices, chopped herbs and dried mint to the slow cooker and pour in 400ml of the stock. Stir well.
6. Cover and cook for about 6 hours on a Low setting; add a little more stock if it gets too thick.
7. Now add the potatoes and cook for a further hour on a low setting.
8. Check the beef and potatoes are cooked through, then turn off the heat and leave to cool with the lid on.
9. Stir the ají amarillo paste into the stew and top with tomatoes, beans and chopped herbs. Serve with crusty bread.

NUTRITION PER PORTION:

SERVES - 6 | CALORIES - 600KCAL | PROTEIN - 42G | CARBOHYDRATES - 34G | FAT - 31G

TRADITIONAL COTTAGE PIE

INGREDIENTS

- 1¼kg of beef mince
- 3 tablespoons of olive oil
- 3 carrots, chopped
- 2 garlic cloves, finely chopped
- 2 onions, finely chopped

- 3 celery sticks, chopped
- 3 tablespoons of plain flour
- Optional: 250ml of red wine
- 1 tablespoon of tomato purée

- 4 tablespoons of Worcestershire sauce
- 850m of beef stock
- Fresh thyme
- 2 bay leaves

For the mash

- 1.8kg potatoes, peeled, chopped, and rinsed
- 225ml of milk

- 25g of butter
- 200g of extra mature cheddar, grated

- freshly grated nutmeg

METHOD

1. Heat 1 tablespoon of olive oil in a large saucepan and the beef mince until it's browned all over. Add directly to the slow cooker.
2. Stir in the rest of the ingredients with the mince (leave the mash for now) and season to taste.
3. Cover and cook on a High setting for 5 hours, stirring occasionally to break up the mince
4. Meanwhile, make the mash. In a large saucepan, cover the potatoes in salted cold water, bring to the boil and simmer until tender - about 20-25 minutes.
5. Drain well, then mash well with the milk, butter, and about 150g of the cheddar. Season with the nutmeg and adjust the seasoning to taste.

6. Transfer the meat into a heatproof dish. Spread over the mash potato and top with the remaining cheese. Fluff up the mash a little with a fork so it crisps up in the oven.
7. Heat the oven to 220C//gas 7 and cook for 25-30 minutes, or until the topping is golden.

NUTRITION PER PORTION:

SERVES - 10 | CALORIES - 600KCAL | PROTEIN - 37G | CARBOHYDRATES - 40G | FAT - 34G

BRISKET WITH ALE GRAVY AND HORSERADISH MASH

INGREDIENTS

- 1.2kg of brisket, rolled
- 2 tablespoons of vegetable oil (extra for drizzling)
- 2 large onions, sliced
- 4 tablespoons of plain flour
- 500-550ml of golden ale (for example, Kona Big Wave or Badger Tanglefoot)
- 1 tablespoon of yeast or beef extract
- 1 tablespoon of dark brown soft sugar, plus extra to taste
- 1 tablespoon of balsamic vinegar, plus extra to taste
- ½ bunch of thyme
- 2 bay leaves
- 500ml of hot beef stock
- Optional: 2 teaspoons of cornflour

For the horseradish mash

- 2kg of floury potatoes, peeled and chopped
- 4 tablespoons of horseradish
- 100g of butter
- 100g of crème fraiche
- Optional: handful of parsley, chopped

METHOD

1. Season the brisket all over with Seasoning to taste.
2. Heat the vegetable oil in a large pan and sear the beef all over so that it is browned on all sides. Transfer to a plate and set to one side.
3. In the same pan, heat a little more oil and stir fry the onions for a few minutes until golden, then sprinkle over some flour and cook for a few more minutes. Stir the onion and flour together well.
4. Pour in the ale and stir to collect up any browned bits of flavouring from the pan and add to the slow cooker.
5. Add the yeast/beef extract, sugar and vinegar, followed by the cooked beef and herbs.
6. Pour in the stock so the brisket is about ⅔ submerged.
7. Cover and cook on Low for about 8 hours. Remove the meat from the slow c\cooker and cover to keep warm.
8. Transfer the liquid to a saucepan, bring to the boil and simmer for 10-15 minutes until the gravy thickens to your liking. Stir in a little cornflour paste (1 teaspoon of cornflour mixed with water to make a paste) if you want really thick gravy.
9. For the horseradish mash: The potatoes will need about 30-40 minutes preparation time, so ensure you plan the time into your preparations.
10. Cook the potatoes in a pan of boiling (salted) water for about 20-25 minutes until tender. Drain into a colander and allow to steam-dry for a couple of minutes.
11. Add the horseradish, butter and creme fraiche and mash until smooth.
12. Slice and serve the brisket with the horseradish mash, scattered with parsley.

NUTRITION PER PORTION:

SERVES - 6 | CALORIES - 928KCAL | PROTEIN - 45G | CARBOHYDRATES - 74G | FAT - 47G

THAI BEEF CURRY

INGREDIENTS

- 1.2kg of beef braising steak, cut into 4cm chunks
- 4 tablespoons of Thai green curry paste
- 1 tablespoon of olive oil
- 2 tablespoons of fish sauce
- 1 tablespoon of brown sugar
- 1 star anise
- Optional: 2 kaffir lime leaves
- 1 x 400 ml tin of coconut milk
- Juice of 1/2-1 lime, to taste
- Fresh coriander, roughly chopped
- Thai jasmine rice and vegetables to serve (Chinese cabbage/bok choy/baby corn cobs/mange tout)

METHOD

1. Pat the beef with kitchen roll to absorb any excess moisture and season.
2. Heat the oil in a pan and fry until browned all over.
3. Transfer the beef and any meat juices to the slow cooker.
4. Stir the fish sauce, brown sugar and curry paste into the slow cooker.
5. Add the coconut milk, kaffir lime leaves and star anise, then cover and cook on Low for about 8 hours until the beef is tender.
6. Stir the beef and gravy to check its consistency. If you like the gravy a bit thicker, strain through a sieve into a saucepan, bring to the boil and simmer to reduce it. Stir back into the slow cooker with the beef.
7. Add the lime juice to the beef to your liking and stir in the coriander.
8. Serve with Thai jasmine rice and vegetables, and scatter with the remaining chopped coriander.

NUTRITION PER PORTION:
SERVES - 4-6 | CALORIES - 632KCAL | PROTEIN - 54G | CARBOHYDRATES - 9G | FAT - 42G

OXTAIL STEW

INGREDIENTS

- 1.5kg of oxtail, cut into pieces
- 5 garlic cloves, peeled but left whole
- 1-inch piece of ginger, don't peel but slice into 6 pieces
- 1 teaspoon of Szechuan peppercorns, crushed
- 4 star anise
- 1 cinnamon stick
- 4 strips of orange peel, pith removed
- 4 bay leaves
- 2 tablespoons of dark soy sauce
- 175ml of red wine
- ½ teaspoon of black peppercorns

To serve

- 1 tablespoon of toasted sesame seeds
- 4 spring onions, finely sliced
- steamed basmati rice
- steamed pak choi or spinach

METHOD

1. Preheat the slow cooker on a Low setting.
2. Combine all of the ingredients into the slow cooker and pour in enough boiling water to just cover the oxtail (about 750ml). No need to add extra salt as the soy sauce is salty enough for now. Add salt at the end if necessary.
3. Cover and cook on High for 5 hours or Low for 10 hours. The meat should fall easily away from the bone when pulled. Skim off any excess fat with a ladle at intervals and discard.
4. Remove the oxtail pieces to a plate and set aside.
5. Strain the gravy/broth through a sieve into a container discarding the spices, orange peel and ginger.

6. Return the gravy/broth with the oxtail to the slow cooker and season to taste with Seasoning to taste.
7. Serve with rice and pak choi, topped with sliced spring onions and sesame seeds.

NUTRITION PER PORTION:

SERVES - 4 | CALORIES - 693KCAL | PROTEIN - 76G | CARBOHYDRATES - 3G | FAT - 38G

TENDER SLOW-COOKED KOREAN BEEF RIBS

INGREDIENTS

- 8 beef short ribs, each about 8cm long
- 3cm piece of ginger, grated
- 1 bunch spring onions, chopped into fine pieces
- 4 garlic cloves, crushed

- 4 tablespoons of rice wine vinegar
- Juice of 1 lime
- 3 tablespoons of gochujang (a Korean red chilli paste) *
- 1 tablespoon of sesame oil

- 2 tablespoons of soy sauce
- 4 tablespoons of soft brown sugar
- 1 tablespoon of ground sesame seeds
- Cooked Basmati rice

For the pickle

- 4 tablespoons of rice vinegar
- sesame oil

- 2 teaspoons of golden caster sugar
- ½ a red chilli, finely diced

- 1 garlic clove, halved
- ½ a cucumber

*NOTE: you can substitute gochujang paste, if necessary, with a mixture of miso paste with a small amount of cayenne pepper.

METHOD

1. Heat 2 tablespoons of oil in a pan then cook the ribs until they are a good dark brown colour all over. Discard any excess fat from the ribs as you cook.
2. Place the garlic, spring onions and ginger into the slow cooker, add the ribs in a single layer, before adding the remainder of the ingredients. Pour in 400-500ml of water to just cover the ribs completely.
3. Cover and cook on a Low setting for 8 hours, until the ribs are falling apart.
4. Remove the ribs to a plate and cool. Transfer the cooking juices from the slow cooker to a jug and chill until any excess fat hardens and can be scooped off and discarded.
5. To make the pickles, combine the vinegar, 2 tablespoons of oil, sugar, chilli and garlic. Use a peeler to cut some strips off lengthways down the cucumber, then cut into discs. Toss with the liquid and chill (remove the garlic before serving).
6. Finally, once the fat has been removed and discarded from the sauce and ribs, reheat the slow cooker and return them to cook on Low to reheat.
7. Serve with rice and pickles.

NUTRITION PER PORTION:

SERVES - 4 | CALORIES - 717KCAL | PROTEIN - 35G | CARBOHYDRATES - 29G | FAT - 51G

BEEF BRISKET WITH SHALLOT AND RED WINE GRAVY

INGREDIENTS

- 6 cloves of garlic, crushed
- 2 tablespoons of olive oil
- 12 shallots, peeled, remaining whole
- 1.5kg of beef brisket, rolled and tied
- A whole nutmeg, grated
- 2 fresh bay leaves
- 1 stick of cinnamon
- 1 x 400 g tin of chopped tomatoes
- 2 tablespoons of tomato purée
- 250ml of red wine
- 1 teaspoon of dried oregano
- 1 handful of black olives
- Fresh thyme
- 2 tablespoons of red wine vinegar

METHOD

1. Heat the oil in a pan on the hob. Season the beef, then put into the pan, turning every few minutes until it is browned all over, including both ends. Remove to a plate and set aside.
2. Heat a little more oil in the same pan and add the whole shallots and garlic and cook gently for around 10 minutes, or until they start to soften and colour a little. Transfer to the slow cooker.
3. Finely grate a quarter of the nutmeg and add to the slow cooker, along with the remaining ingredients including the brisket. Season well.
4. Cover and cook on High for 4 hours or Low for 8 hours. Once cooked, leave the beef to rest for 10 minutes then shred with two forks. It should come apart easily (you can cook for another hour or so if this is not happening).
5. Stir and adjust seasoning as required, then spoon the shredded beef and sauce over rice.

NUTRITION PER PORTION:

SERVES - 8 | CALORIES - 481KCAL | PROTEIN - 36G | CARBOHYDRATES - 4.4G | FAT - 36G

CUBAN BEEF

INGREDIENTS

- 500g of stewing steak, diced
- 240 ml of beef stock (fresh or made from 2 beef stock cubes)
- 400g tin of chopped tomatoes
- 4 garlic cloves, crushed
- 2 onions, sliced
- 4 mixed peppers, deseeded and sliced into strips
- 2 tablespoons of tomato puree
- 1 teaspoon of ground cumin
- 1 teaspoon of oregano
- ½ teaspoon of turmeric
- 1 wine stock pot
- 1 tablespoon of fresh coriander chopped
- 2 bay leaves
- Cooking oil spray
- 1 tablespoon of white wine vinegar
- Seasoning to taste

METHOD

1. Heat a little oil in a pan. Season the diced beef well with Seasoning to taste, then add the diced beef and cook until browned on all sides.
2. Transfer to the slow cooker.
3. Slosh a little of the stock around the pan to collect the flavours from the meat juices then add to the slow cooker with the rest of the stock and remaining ingredients.
4. Cover and cook on High for 6 hours, or Slow for 8 hours.
5. Shred the meat with 2 forks - it should come apart easily once cooked.
6. If you'd like the sauce a little thicker, remove the lid for a little while and allow to reduce slightly.
7. Serve on a bed of rice, topped with a little extra chopped coriander.

NUTRITION PER PORTION:

SERVES - 4 | CALORIES - 279KCAL | PROTEIN - 33G | CARBOHYDRATES - 17G | FAT - 6G

STEAK AND STILTON PIE (PIE FILLING)

INGREDIENTS

- 1 tablespoon of plain flour
- 400g of lean, diced stewing steak
- 1 garlic clove, peeled and crushed
- 1 onion, peeled and sliced
- ½ teaspoon of dried thyme
- 1 stick of celery, sliced
- 2 carrots, peeled and sliced
- 1 red wine stock pot
- 150g of button mushrooms
- 1 tablespoon of Worcestershire sauce
- 300ml of beef stock (fresh or from a stock cube)
- 75g of stilton cheese, crumbed
- 1 egg, beaten
- Seasoning to taste
- 2 x 40g ready rolled sheets of filo pastry
- Cooking spray

METHOD

1. Heat some oil in a pan. Coat the steak in the flour, season and cook for a few minutes until browned all over.
2. Remove from the pan and add to the slow cooker.
3. Heat a little more oil, add the onions, garlic and thyme and sauté for a further 5 minutes and add to the slow cooker with the carrots, celery, stock pot and Worcestershire sauce.
4. Stir a little of the stock around the pan to collect some of the flavours from the meat juices, then transfer to the slow cooker with the remainder of the stock.
5. Cover and cook for 4 hours on High or 7 hours on Low.
6. Half an hour before the end of cooking time, stir in the mushrooms and cook for the remaining 30 minutes.
7. Toss in the crumbled Stilton and stir until melted. Season again.
8. For the pie filling: Preheat the oven to 180C. Pour the mixture into an ovenproof dish.
9. Cut the filo sheets into strips, lightly scrunch and place on top of the pie to completely cover the filling. Brush a little milk or beaten egg over the top.
10. Place on a baking tray and cook on the middle shelf in the oven for 15-20 minutes, or until the pastry is a lovely golden colour. Serve!

NUTRITION PER PORTION:

SERVES - 4 | CALORIES - 340KCAL | PROTEIN - 33G | CARBOHYDRATES - 23G | FAT - 12G

STEAK AND MUSHROOM PIE (PIE FILLING)

INGREDIENTS

- 450g of lean diced steak
- 2 onions, roughly chopped
- 15 mushrooms quartered
- 2 tablespoons of Worcestershire sauce
- ½ teaspoon of tomato puree
- 1 tablespoon of red wine vinegar
- Olive oil or spray for cooking
- Optional: 1 beef stockpot
- 500ml beef stock (fresh or made from stock cubes)

Pastry Top

- 25g sheet of filo pastry

METHOD

1. Heat some oil in a pan on the stove. Brown the beef steak on all sides, then transfer to the slow cooker.
2. Add the remaining pie filling ingredients, cover and cook on High for 4 hours.
3. If you prefer your sauce a little thicker, then remove the lid and cook until the mixture reduces a little to obtain the thickness you like. Alternatively, make up a little cornflour paste (blend a teaspoon with enough water to blend to a smooth paste) and stir in. Cook until thickened.

ASSEMBLING THE PIE

1. Heat the oven to 180C. Lightly spray an ovenproof dish with cooking oil and pour the pie filling into an ovenproof dish.
2. Take one sheet of filo, lay it out flat and spray generously with low calorie cooking spray.
3. Cut the filo sheets into strips, lightly scrunch and place on top of the pie to completely cover the filling. Brush a little milk or beaten egg over the top.
4. Place on a baking tray and cook on the middle shelf in the oven for 15-20 minutes, or until the pastry turns a lovely golden colour. Serve.

NUTRITION PER PORTION:
SERVES - 2 | CALORIES - 499KCAL | PROTEIN - 64G | CARBOHYDRATES - 25G | FAT - 14G

MEATLOAF
● ●

INGREDIENTS

For the meatloaf

- 500g of beef mince
- 500g of pork mince
- 1 onion, finely grated
- 2 eggs beaten
- 40g of breadcrumbs
- 2 garlic cloves, minced
- 1 beef stock cube
- 50ml milk
- 1½ teaspoons of oregano, dried or fresh
- 1½ teaspoons of basil, dried or fresh
- 1½ teaspoons of paprika
- ½ teaspoons of mild chilli powder
- 15g of fresh chopped flat-leaf parsley
- Seasoning to taste

For the glaze

- 6 tablespoons of tomato ketchup
- 2 teaspoons of brown sugar
- 1 teaspoons of garlic granules, finely ground
- 1½ tablespoons of cider vinegar

METHOD

1. Preheat your slow cooker on High.
2. Heat the oil in a pan and sauté the onions briefly, then add the garlic and spices and cook for another few minutes.
3. Transfer to a bowl and leave to cool.
4. Warm the milk in a jug and crumble in the beef stock cube, stir well until dissolved.
5. Add all the remaining ingredients to the container including the milk/stock mixture and beaten eggs. Season, and mix everything together thoroughly with your hands.
6. Use your hands to form into a dense loaf shape.
7. For the glaze: Blend the ketchup, garlic, cider vinegar and sugar together to make the glaze.
8. Place the meatloaf in the slow cooker and brush the glaze over the top
9. Cover and cook on a Low setting for 6 hours.
10. Allow the meatloaf to rest for a few minutes before slicing and serve with mashed potatoes and freshly cooked vegetables.

NUTRITION PER PORTION:
SERVES - 2 | CALORIES - 619KCAL | PROTEIN - 39G | CARBOHYDRATES - 15G | FAT - 44G

BEEF ENCHILADAS

INGREDIENTS

For the slow cooker

- 1 red pepper, chopped
- 1 red onion, diced
- 300g of beef mince
- Seasoning to taste
- 1 x 400g tin of chopped tomatoes
- 1 tin of cannellini beans
- 1 tablespoon of Mexican spice blend
- Pinch of sugar

For the enchiladas

- 100g grated cheddar cheese
- 5 large flour tortillas

METHOD

1. Sauté the beef in a frying pan of hot oil to brown all over, and place into the slow cooker.
2. Season to taste.
3. Add all the remaining ingredients for the slow cooker.
4. Cook on a High setting for 4 hours or Low for 7 hours.
5. Load the wraps and place them seam side down, on an oiled baking tray or oven dish.
6. Scatter the grated cheese evenly over the top.
7. Cook at 200C//gas mark 6 for 10 minutes until golden brown on the outside.
8. Serve and enjoy!

NUTRITION PER PORTION:

SERVES - 5 ENCHILADAS | CALORIES - 298KCAL | PROTEIN - 29G | CARBOHYDRATES - 18G | FAT - 11G

DURBAN BEEF CURRY

INGREDIENTS

- 2 tablespoons of olive oil
- 3 curry leaves
- 2 garlic cloves, grated
- 1 teaspoon of fresh ginger, finely grated
- 1 onion, sliced into rings
- 1 teaspoon of ground cumin
- 1 teaspoon of masala curry powder
- 1 teaspoon of ground coriander
- ⅓ cinnamon stick
- 3 cardamom pods
- ½ teaspoon of ground turmeric
- 500g of diced beef
- 2 small chillies, finely chopped
- 2 medium tomatoes, chopped
- 200ml of beef stock (fresh or from stock cubes)
- 1 tablespoon of tomato purée
- 3 medium potatoes
- 1 small cauliflower, broken into florets
- Seasoning to taste

METHOD

1. Heat the oil in a pan and fry the onion and curry leaves until the onion softens and the curry leaves are fragrant. Add the garlic, ginger and spices and cook for a couple of minutes. Remove to the slow cooker.
2. Heat a little more oil in the same pan and cook the beef until it is brown all over. Stir in the chillies, add the tomatoes, the tomato puree, and half the stock. Mix well then transfer to the slow cooker.
3. Finally, add the potatoes, cauliflower and the remaining half of the beef stock.
4. Cover and cook on a High setting for 4 hours or Low for 7 hours.
5. Remove the cinnamon, cardamom and curry leaves and discard, and adjust the seasoning if necessary.
6. Serve with rice.

NUTRITION PER PORTION:

SERVES - 6 | CALORIES - 334KCAL | PROTEIN - 30G | CARBOHYDRATES - 29G | FAT - 11G

INDIAN BEEF MEATBALLS

INGREDIENTS

- Olive oil for frying
- 30g of fresh coriander, chopped
- 300g of minced beef
- 3 tomatoes, roughly chopped

- 30g of breadcrumbs
- ¼ teaspoon of cayenne
- 1 teaspoon of cumin
- 1 teaspoon of ground coriander

- 1 teaspoon of turmeric
- 200g of spinach, shredded
- 2 tablespoons of natural yoghurt
- Seasoning to taste

For the rice

- 200g of basmati rice
- 1 garlic clove, peeled and grated

- 25g of fresh ginger, peeled and grated

- 200ml tin of coconut milk

METHOD

1. For the meatballs: Put the beef into a large bowl with the breadcrumbs, garlic, ginger, cumin, ground coriander, 50ml of the coconut milk and ½ the chopped coriander.
2. Add a pinch of cayenne, and season with Seasoning to taste.
3. Use your hands to mix the beef and spices together thoroughly and divide into 12 equal sized balls.
4. Heat 1 tablespoon of oil in a pan and flash fry the meatballs until nicely browned all over.
5. Add the meatballs to the slow cooker along with the tomatoes and stir.
6. Next stir 100mls of water into the frying pan, bring to the boil and pour carefully into the slow cooker (it has collected all the delicious meat juices etc., to add flavour to your food).
7. Cover and cook on a High setting for 3 hours or Low for 6 hours.
8. Open the slow cooker, stir in the yoghurt, and add the spinach leaving it to wilt in the heat.
9. Cover the slow cooker again and cook for a further 1 hour on Low.

   NOTE: For an extra spicy kick to your meatballs, add a little extra cayenne pepper to the slow cooker.
10. For the rice: whisk together the coconut milk garlic and ginger in a jug.
11. Put a kettle on to boil while you rinse the rice thoroughly under cold running water in a sieve.
12. Now, put the rice in a large saucepan with the turmeric, 150ml of the coconut milk, a pinch of salt and 300ml of hot water from the kettle.
13. Bring the rice up to a simmer, cover and cook for 20 minutes until just tender.
14. Leave to sit for 5 minutes at the end. Drain any liquid away before serving.
15. Serve the rice topped with the sauce and meatballs, garnished with the remaining chopped coriander.

NUTRITION PER PORTION:

SERVES - 4 | CALORIES - 551KCAL | PROTEIN - 32G | CARBOHYDRATES - 60G | FAT - 21G

SCOTTISH BEEF STOVIES

INGREDIENTS

- 1 large onion, diced
- Vegetable cooking oil
- 1 carrot, chunky diced
- 1 large onion, diced

- 400g potatoes, peeled and cut into 3cm chunks
- 10g rosemary leaves, finely chopped
- 300g of minced beef

- 1 garlic clove, finely chopped
- 250ml of beef stock (fresh or from stock cubes)
- ¼ teaspoons of allspice
- 1 tablespoon of Worcester sauce

To serve

- ½ Savoy cabbage, washed well, and shredded
- 1 packet of Scottish oatcakes

- Seasoning to taste

METHOD

1. Gently fry the onions and carrots in a little oil heated in a frying pan. Add to the slow cooker.
2. Season the beef with Seasoning to taste. In the same pan, heat up a little more oil and fry the beef until browned. Add the garlic and rosemary and fry gently for another 2-3 minutes.
3. Add the beef, garlic and rosemary to the slow cooker and stir thoroughly.
4. Wash a little of the stock around the used frying pan to collect any meat juices and onion flavours and put into the slow cooker with the rest of the stock. Add the allspice and Worcester sauce and mix again thoroughly.
5. Cover and cook on High for 4 hours or Low for 8 hours.
6. Just before the beef is ready, heat 1 tablespoon of oil in a large pan.
7. Add the washed and shredded cabbage. Cook on a medium heat until it wilts and is tender. Season with Seasoning to taste.
8. Serve the beef and potatoes with a pile of seasoned wilted greens with the oatcakes on the side.

NUTRITION PER PORTION:

SERVES - 2 | CALORIES - 641KCAL | PROTEIN - 56G | CARBOHYDRATES - 67G | FAT - 16G

CASTILIAN BEEF STEW

INGREDIENTS

- 1kg of slow-roast beef
- 1 litre of beef stock (fresh or from beef stock cubes)
- 750g potatoes, diced roughly into 1-inch pieces
- 1 celery stick, chopped
- 2 onions, chopped

- 3 carrots, peeled and chopped
- 2 garlic cloves, crushed
- 1 leek, chopped
- 1 small swede, chopped
- 500g of chickpeas - soaked overnight
- 550g of diced chicken

- 3 cooking chorizo sausages
- Optional: 2 morcilla (Spanish black pudding)
- 500g of green cabbage/chard/kale

METHOD

1. In a saucepan, cover the chickpeas in water and add a ladleful of beef broth. Bring to the boil, skim any froth off the top and simmer until tender. Drain and put the chickpeas to one side. Save the liquid in a small jug.
2. Add the beef joint to the slow cooker with the stock, and enough of the saved chickpea water to just about cover the meat.
3. Tuck in the potatoes, swede, carrots, onions, celery, leek and garlic around the beef and season to taste.
4. Next, add the chicken, chorizo and (optional) morcilla to the slow cooker.
5. Cover and cook on Low for 6 hours.
6. Uncover and stir in the pulses and greens. Cook on Low for another 1 hour.
7. Remove the beef from the slow cooker and serve in thick slices with the sausage and chicken and topped with the broth.

NUTRITION PER PORTION:

SERVES - 10 | CALORIES - 641KCAL | PROTEIN - 63G | CARBOHYDRATES - 54G | FAT - 19G

ITALIAN BEEF ROLLS

INGREDIENTS

Main

- 3 tablespoons of olive oil
- 8 beef frying escalopes
- Juice of 2 lemons
- ½ teaspoon of black pepper
- 250ml of chicken stock (fresh or from stock cubes)

For the stuffing

- 3 garlic cloves, diced
- 3 tablespoons of tomatoes from a 400g can
- 2 tablespoons parmesan, grated
- 3 tablespoons fresh parsley, chopped
- Seasoning to taste

METHOD

1. Lightly tenderise the beef escalopes to a thickness of about 3mm.
2. In a container, blend a marinade of the lemon juice, 2 tablespoons of olive oil and the black pepper. Add the beef steaks to the marinade, cover and put in the fridge for a minimum of 1 hour.
3. Preheat the slow cooker on a low setting and begin heating the remaining olive oil.
4. Pulse the stuffing ingredients in a blender.
5. Lay the marinated escalopes out flat on a clean chopping board. Spoon 1 tablespoon of the stuffing mix in each one. Roll each one up and secure with a skewer or cocktail stick. Ensure its secured lengthways so it lays flat in the slow cooker
6. Put the rolled beef escalopes into the slow cooker and spritz lightly with a little cooking oil.
7. Add the stock and remaining marinade and season to taste.
8. Cover and cook on a Low setting for 5-6 hours. Turn the beef rolls about halfway through cooking.
9. Turn off the heat when cooked through and allow to rest for 10 minutes before removing from the slow cooker.
10. Serve whole or sliced with ladles of sauce over the top.

NUTRITION PER PORTION:

SERVES - 8 | CALORIES - 297KCAL | PROTEIN - 42G | CARBOHYDRATES - 4G | FAT - 13G

LAMB

EASY LAMB AND POTATO STEW

INGREDIENTS

- 1.2 kg lamb of shoulder, diced
- 2 red onions, sliced
- 750g small potatoes
- 4 garlic cloves, peeled and chopped
- 4 tablespoons of red wine vinegar
- 1 teaspoon of ground cinnamon
- 2 celery sticks, chopped
- 3 bay leaves
- 400g tin of chopped tomatoes
- 1 teaspoon of dried oregano
- 3 tablespoons of tomato puree
- 100ml of water
- Optional: lemon zest, chopped parsley or dill to serve

METHOD

1. Put the all the ingredients, including the lamb into the slow.
2. Pour in 100ml water and season with salt and black pepper.
3. Cover and cook on Low for 6 hours or on High for 4 hours.
4. Serve chunks of fresh crusty bread, scattered with chopped parsley, dill or lemon zest.

NUTRITION PER PORTION:

SERVES - 8 | CALORIES - 330KCAL | PROTEIN - 33G | CARBOHYDRATES - 20G | FAT - 12G

LAMB SHANKS

INGREDIENTS

- Oil for frying
- 4 lamb shanks
- 4 garlic cloves, crushed
- 2 bay leaves
- 1 onion, sliced
- 1 teaspoon of mixed herbs
- 2 large carrots, peeled and chopped
- 400g of passata or tinned chopped tomatoes
- 500ml of beef stock (fresh or from stock cubes)
- 1 tablespoon of Worcestershire sauce
- 2 tablespoon of tomato puree

METHOD

1. Heat some oil in a pan and gently fry the lamb shanks until they are brown all over. Place in the slow cooker.
2. Add the carrots, onion, garlic, bay leaves and mixed herbs to the lamb.
3. Pour in the passata or chopped tomatoes over the top and stir in the tomato puree and Worcestershire sauce.
4. Add a little beef stock to the pan used to fry the lamb and stir around to collect the meat juices. Gently pour over the lamb with the rest of the beef stock.
5. Cover and cook on High for 4 hours or Low for 8 hours.
6. Serve with mashed potato or rice.

NUTRITION PER PORTION:

SERVES - 4 | CALORIES - 268KCAL | PROTEIN - 28G | CARBOHYDRATES - 12G | FAT - 12G

LAMB CURRY

INGREDIENTS

- 600g of diced lamb leg
- 2 tablespoons of olive oil
- 2 onions, chopped
- 4 carrots, thickly sliced
- 5cm piece of fresh ginger, grated
- 2 green chillies, deseeded, 1 finely chopped, 1 finely sliced
- 1 teaspoon of cinnamon
- 1 tablespoon of garam masala
- 3 garlic cloves, crushed
- 2 teaspoons of ground cumin
- 400ml of coconut milk
- 15g fresh coriander, finely chopped
- 100ml of lamb stock
- 400g tin of chopped tomatoes
- 125g of spinach
- Optional: rice or naan to serve

METHOD

1. Heat 1 tablespoon of oil in a large pan and add the lamb. Cook all over for a few minutes until browned then season and transfer to the slow cooker.
2. Next, add the remaining oil to the same pan and fry the onions and carrots for 10 minutes until softened. Add the chilli, ginger, garlic, spices and coriander stalks stir fry for another minute until fragrant.
3. Add the onion mixture to the slow cooker.
4. Pour a little beef stock into the pan used to fry the lamb and onions and stir around to collect the meat juices. Gently pour over the lamb with the rest of the beef stock.
5. Add the chopped tomatoes and stir to combine thoroughly.
6. Cover and cook on Low for 6 hours.
7. Finally, stir the coconut milk through the curry and cook for a further 30 minutes on Low. Add the spinach 5 minutes before serving, cover and allow to wilt in the heat.
8. Stir and serve with rice or naan. Scatter with sliced chilli and chopped coriander leaves.

   NOTE: If you don't have much time, using a ready-made curry paste to speed things up is the perfect way to get your curry flavour. Instead of ginger, chopped chilli, garlic, spices and coriander, use a rogan josh curry paste. Pop 4 tablespoons into your slow cooker to follow the onions and carrots. Cook for one minute before transferring to the slow cooker, then continue as normal.

NUTRITION PER PORTION:
SERVES - 4 | CALORIES - 451KCAL | PROTEIN - 36G | CARBOHYDRATES - 21G | FAT - 26G

ITALIAN LAMB OSSO BUCCO

INGREDIENTS

- Flour for dusting
- 800g of lamb shoulder/leg meat cut into pieces
- 4 tablespoons of olive oil
- 1 teaspoon of fresh thyme, chopped
- 2 carrots, diced
- 2 celery stalks, diced
- 2 garlic cloves, chopped
- 2 onions, chopped
- 1 x 400g tin of chopped tomatoes
- 250ml of white wine
- 200ml of beef stock

For the gremolata

- 1 garlic clove, grated
- 15g of parsley, chopped
- zest of 1 lemon, plus garnish

METHOD

1. Preheat the slow cooker.
2. In a shallow bowl, season and dust the lamb pieces with flour and fry in a pan of 2 tablespoons of hot oil until browned all over. Transfer to the slow cooker.

3. Heat the remaining olive oil in the same pan and stir fry the carrots, onions, celery, garlic, thyme and seasoning for about 10 minutes until softened.
4. Pour in the wine, stock and tinned tomatoes. Bring to a rolling boil and then pour it over the meat in the slow cooker.
5. Cover and cook for 4 hours on a High setting or 8 hours on Low.
6. In a separate bowl, combine the parsley, lemon and garlic to make the gremolata.
7. Serve with rice or polenta, sprinkled with the gremolata garnish.

NUTRITION PER PORTION:
SERVES - 4-6 | CALORIES - 456KCAL | PROTEIN - 24G | CARBOHYDRATES - 20G | FAT - 32G

LAMB KLEFTIKO WITH LEMON AND HERB POTATOES

INGREDIENTS

- 2 tablespoons of olive oil
- 10 garlic cloves (or 1 complete garlic head) crushed
- Juice of 2 large lemons
- 1 tablespoon of dried oregano
- 6 fresh bay leaves
- 2 tablespoons of fresh oregano leaves
- 1.5kg waxy potatoes, peeled and chopped into large (6cm) chunks
- 6 large, skinless tomatoes, cut into small chunks
- 200g of feta cheese, crumbled
- 6 lamb hind shanks, small and of even weight
- 100ml of water

METHOD

1. Turn the slow cooker on to a Low setting and add 1 tablespoon of olive oil, the crushed garlic, bay leaves, both fresh and dried oreganos, and the lemon juice, Season and stir.
2. Put the potatoes into the slow cooker along with 150g of feta and the chopped tomatoes. Mix well.
3. Add the lamb shanks down into the potato mixture so that they are coated with the flavours and add 100ml water. Drizzle with the remaining olive oil.
4. Cover the slow cooker and cook for 6 hours on High.
5. Skim any excess fat from the surface, then serve straight from the slow cooker. Scatter with fresh oregano leaves and the remaining 50g of crumbled feta.

NUTRITION PER PORTION:
SERVES - 6 | CALORIES - 751KCAL | PROTEIN - 62G | CARBOHYDRATES - 53G | FAT - 31G

CARROT, CUMIN AND LAMB TAGINE

INGREDIENTS

- 1 x 450g of lean diced lamb
- 2 teaspoon of red wine vinegar
- 1 teaspoon of ground cumin
- ½ teaspoon of ground turmeric
- ¼ teaspoon of ground cinnamon
- 3 teaspoons of cumin seeds
- 1 teaspoon of vegetable oil
- 1 large red onion, finely diced
- 3 dates, pitted and finely chopped
- 500ml hot vegetable stock (fresh or made from stock cubes)
- 2 x 400g tins of chickpeas, rinsed and drained
- 500g of baby carrots, scrubbed
- 15g of fresh coriander, stalks finely chopped, and leaves left whole

METHOD

1. Put the ground spices, 2 teaspoons of cumin seeds, the vinegar and some black pepper into a shallow bowl. Toss in the lamb and coat it thoroughly, then cover and put in the fridge to marinate for an hour.
2. Heat the oil in a pan and sauté the onion for about 15 minutes with a pinch of salt until softened and tender.
3. Now add the lamb to the onion along with the spice marinade, and sauté for 5-10 minutes, until the lamb is brown all over.
4. Add a little vegetable stock to the used frying pan and stir to collect the meat and frying juices. Bring to the boil, simmer for a couple of minutes, then transfer to the slow cooker with the chickpeas and the rest of the stock.
5. Cover and cook for 4 hours on Low.
6. Next, add the carrots, 1 teaspoon of cumin seeds and half the coriander, and cook for a further 1-2 hours until tender. If you like your sauce a little thicker, remove the lid for the last 30 minutes to reduce the sauce.
7. Season the tagine and serve with quinoa or couscous, scattered with the coriander.

NUTRITION PER PORTION:
SERVES - 6 | CALORIES - 468KCAL | PROTEIN - 35G | CARBOHYDRATES - 55G | FAT - 12G

LAMB, OLIVE, AND CAPER RAGU

● ●

INGREDIENTS

- 1.5kg of boneless lamb shoulder, trimmed and diced into 4cm chunks
- 2 onions, chopped
- 2 carrots, finely chopped
- 5 garlic cloves, crushed
- 3 tablespoons of olive oil

- 2 tablespoons of tomato purée
- 2 celery sticks, finely chopped
- 3 bay leaves
- 4 sprigs rosemary, leaves picked and chopped
- 250ml of red wine

- 400ml lamb or chicken stock (fresh or made from stock cubes)
- 2 x 400g tins chopped tomatoes
- 50g of capers, drained
- 100g of pitted black olives, drained
- ½ tablespoon of caster sugar

To serve

- cooked gnocchi or pappardelle pasta
- Optional: grated parmesan

METHOD

1. Season the lamb and sauté in 2 tablespoons of heated oil in a large pan until browned all over. Transfer to a plate and set aside.
2. Using the same pan, heat the remaining tablespoon of oil and sauté the onions, carrots and celery for about 10 minutes until softened and lightly browned.
3. Add the garlic and stir for another 2 minutes. Add in the tomato purée, bay leaves and rosemary and mix thoroughly.
4. Pour in the wine, bring to a rolling boil, then simmer until the liquid reduces by half.
5. Finally, stir in the tomatoes and the stock with some seasoning, then return the lamb to the pan.
6. Transfer the mixture to the slow cooker, cover and cook on High for 3 hours, or Low for 7 hours.
7. Use a slotted spoon to scoop the meat out of the slow cooker into a dish and shred with two forks. Discard the bay leaves.
8. Stir the capers, olives, and sugar into the sauce in the slow cooker and return the shredded meat. Season to taste.
9. Serve the ragu over cooked gnocchi or toss through some pappardelle and top with parmesan.

NUTRITION PER PORTION:
SERVES - 8 | CALORIES - 384KCAL | PROTEIN - 33G | CARBOHYDRATES - 11G | FAT - 19G

MOROCCAN LAMB

INGREDIENTS

- 2 lamb leg steaks
- 1 teaspoon of cornflour
- ½ teaspoon of ground cumin
- 1 teaspoon of ground coriander
- 2 teaspoon of rapeseed oil
- 2 onions, sliced
- 1 cinnamon stick

- 210g tin of butter beans, rinsed through
- 100g of stoned dates
- 2 carrots, sliced
- 100g of green beans, each cut into 3 pieces
- 400ml of lamb stock

- Optional: 2 tablespoons of chopped parsley
- Optional: Seeds of ½ a pomegranate

METHOD

1. Add the cornflour, ground coriander and ground cumin to a shallow bowl and toss in the lamb steaks. Coat thoroughly.
2. Heat 1 teaspoon of rapeseed oil in a pan and fry the lamb until browned. Put the lamb in a slow cooker
3. In the same pan, heat 1 further teaspoon of rapeseed oil to the pan and sauté the carrots and onions for about 10 minutes until they soften and start to colour a little. Add to the slow cooker.
4. Now put in the cinnamon stick, stoned dates and butter beans.
5. Add a little of the stock to the pan used for frying and stir, collecting a little of the meat juices and flavours, then add to the slow cooker with the rest of the lamb stock. Stir thoroughly.
6. Cover and cook on High for 4 hours or Low for 8 hours.
7. 30 minutes before the end of the cooking cycle, stir in the green beans.
8. Top with pomegranate seeds and chopped parsley to serve.

NUTRITION PER PORTION:

SERVES - 4 | CALORIES - 370KCAL | PROTEIN - 34G | CARBOHYDRATES - 39G | FAT - 12G

LAMB'S LIVER AND ONION CASSEROLE

INGREDIENTS

- 750g of lamb's liver
- 3 tablespoons of seasoned flour
- 1 tablespoon of olive oil

- 2 onions, finely sliced
- 125g of smoked pancetta rashers, halved widthways

- A handful of sage leaves, sliced
- 400g of peeled plum tomatoes
- 500m of beef stock

METHOD

1. Toss the liver in seasoned flour, then sauté the lamb until brown all over. Set aside.
2. Add the onions, pancetta, sage, tomatoes, stock and seasoning to the slow cook, then add the liver. Cover and cook for 5 hours on High.
3. Mix well, then replace the lid and cook on high for further 4 hours or until the liver is tender.
4. Serve with mashed potatoes and green beans.

NUTRITION PER PORTION:

SERVES - 4 | CALORIES - 493KCAL | PROTEIN - 50G | CARBOHYDRATES - 17G | FAT - 25G

SHEPHERD'S PIE

INGREDIENTS

- 1 tablespoon of olive oil
- Fresh thyme
- 2 carrots, finely diced
- 250g lean lamb mince
- 1 tablespoon of plain flour
- 1 onion, finely chopped
- 1 teaspoon of Worcestershire sauce
- 1 tablespoon of tomato purée
- 400g can of lentils
- 1 tablespoon of tomato purée

For the topping

- 250g of sweet potatoes, peeled and cut into chunks
- 2 tablespoons of crème fraiche
- 650g of potatoes, peeled and cut into chunks

METHOD

1. Start by preheating the slow cooker on a Low setting.
2. Heat the oil in a large frying pan, add the onions and thyme sprigs and sauté for a few minutes before adding the carrots and frying a little more.
3. When the vegetables start to brown, add the mince and fry until it is no longer pink.
4. Add the flour and cook, stirring continuously, for another 1-2 minutes, then add the tomato purée, lentils, Worcestershire sauce and seasoning. Add a splash of water if it seems too dry.
5. Now transfer all the mixture into the slow cooker.
6. For the mash: cook both lots of potatoes in a pan of simmering water for 12-13 minutes until tender.
7. Drain, allow to steam dry in the colander for a few minutes, then return to the saucepan and mash with the creme fraiche until all the lumps are removed.
8. Spread the mash on top of the mince and rough up the surface a little with a fork.
9. Cover the slow cooker and cook on Low for 5 hours. Crisp up the potato topping under the grill.

NUTRITION PER PORTION:

SERVES - 4 | CALORIES - 438KCAL | PROTEIN - 23G | CARBOHYDRATES - 57G | FAT - 10G

TURKISH-STYLE PILAU RICE WITH LAMB

INGREDIENTS

- A small handful of pine nuts or flaked almonds
- 1 tablespoon of olive oil
- 2 cinnamon sticks, broken in half
- 1 onion, halved and sliced
- 500g of lean lamb neck fillet, cubed
- 250g of basmati rice
- Lamb or vegetable stock (fresh or made from stock cubes)
- 12 ready-to-eat dried apricots
- A handful fresh mint leaves, chopped

METHOD

1. Dry fry the pine nuts or almonds in a large pan until lightly toasted, then tip onto a plate and set to one side.
2. Add the oil to the pan and fry the onion and cinnamon together until they turn golden in colour.
3. Add a little more oil, if necessary, turn up the heat, then fry the lamb until it's brown with no pink showing. Put in the rice and stir continuously for one minute.
4. Add the frying contents to the slow cooker. Add the stock, apricots and seasoning to taste.

5. Cover and cook on Low for 4 hours until the rice is tender, and the water is absorbed.
6. Serve scattered with the pine nuts and fresh mint.

NUTRITION PER PORTION:
SERVES - 4 | CALORIES - 584KCAL | PROTEIN - 32G | CARBOHYDRATES - 65G | FAT - 24G

IRISH STEW
● ●

INGREDIENTS
- 1 tablespoon of sunflower oil
- 200g smoked streaky bacon, trimmed and in chunks
- 900g stewing lamb, large chunks
- 6 potatoes, peeled and cut into chunky pieces
- 5 carrots, chunky pieces
- 3 onions, chunky pieces
- Fresh thyme
- 700ml of lamb stock (fresh or from stock cubes)
- 3 bay leaves
- 85g of pearl barley, rinsed thoroughly and drained
- 1 large leek, washed and cut into chunks
- 20g of butter

METHOD
1. Start by preheating the slow cooker on a Low setting.
2. Heat the oil in a large frying pan and fry the bacon until crisp. Add to the slow cooker.
3. Using the same pan, fry the chunks of lamb until browned all over. Add the rest of the ingredients except the barley and the leek. Add the lamb stock, making sure the lamb is well covered. Add a bit more water if necessary.
4. Cover and cook on Low for 7 hours.
5. Remove the lid and stir the pearl barley and leek into the slow cooker, cover again and this time, cook on High for 1 hour until the pearl barley is cooked.
6. Stir in the butter, adjust the seasoning, and serve with wedges of fresh bread to dip and scoop.

NUTRITION PER PORTION:
SERVES - 6 | CALORIES - 673KCAL | PROTEIN - 40G | CARBOHYDRATES - 40G | FAT - 39G

MEXICAN LAMB BARBACOA
● ●

INGREDIENTS
- 2 dried ancho chillies
- 1 teaspoon of cumin seeds
- 1 teaspoon of dried oregano
- 4 tomatoes, cut into quarters
- 1 garlic bulb, cloves peeled
- 400ml of red wine
- ½ lamb shoulder, bone in (about 1.25kg)
- 50g dark chocolate, broken into squares
- 1 cinnamon stick
- 450g//about 8 large new potatoes
- Optional: white cabbage and radish slaw to serve

METHOD
1. Blitz the tomatoes, garlic and chillies with a blender along with the oregano, cumin and one-third of the wine until smooth. Season to taste.
2. Add the lamb straight to the slow cooker and pour the chilli mix over the top.
3. Add the chocolate into the slow cooker with the remaining wine, the cinnamon stick and whole potatoes.
4. Cover and cook on a Low setting for 7 hours.
5. Before serving, discard bones and skin from the lamb, if any, and pull the meat into chunks using two forks.

6. Skim any fat from the cooking juices.
7. Serve the lamb and potato with the meat juices in bowls topped with slaw.

NUTRITION PER PORTION:

SERVES - 4 | CALORIES - 752KCAL | PROTEIN - 45G | CARBOHYDRATES - 24G | FAT - 43G

TRADITIONAL LANCASHIRE HOTPOT

INGREDIENTS

- 8 carrots, peeled and diced
- 2 onions, peeled and diced
- 800g of diced lamb
- 800g potatoes, peeled and sliced
- 400 ml stock (fresh or made up with a stock cube)
- Seasoning to taste

METHOD

1. Preheat the slow cooker on a low setting and spritz lightly with cooking oil.
2. Add the onions and carrots to the slow cooker, followed by a layer of diced lamb.
3. Arrange the potato slices neatly on top with no gaps between.
4. Pour the stock over the potato slices, then season.
5. Cover and cook on a Low setting for 7 hours. Check the potatoes and lamb are cooked; you can cook for another hour if necessary.
6. Crisp up the potatoes under the grill if you prefer them like that.
7. Serve with pickled beetroot, pickled red cabbage and some pickled mixed veg.

NUTRITION PER PORTION:

SERVES - 4 | CALORIES - 568KCAL | PROTEIN - 63G | CARBOHYDRATES - 43G | FAT - 21G

LAMB MOUSSAKA

INGREDIENTS

- Cooking oil spray
- 500g of lean diced lamb
- 1 large courgettes, diced
- 1 large onion, chopped
- 3 tablespoons of tomato puree
- 2 garlic cloves, chopped
- 1 teaspoon of sugar
- 1 x 400g tin of chopped tomatoes
- 2 tablespoons of red wine vinegar
- 1 bay leaf
- 1 teaspoon of oregano
- ½ teaspoon of cinnamon
- Seasoning to taste
- 3 aubergines, sliced lengthways
- 500g of natural yoghurt
- 2 eggs
- ½ teaspoons of mustard powder
- 120g of grated Cheddar cheese

METHOD

1. Preheat the slow cooker on a low setting and spritz lightly with cooking oil.
2. Add the diced lamb into the slow cooker with all the vegetables except the aubergine.
3. Stir in the garlic, tomato puree, red wine vinegar and sugar.
4. Then add the herbs and spices; the cinnamon, bay leaf, seasoning and oregano, and mix everything together.
5. Cover and cook on a High setting for 4 hours or Low for 7 hours.
6. If you prefer the sauce a little thicker, then remove the lid and cook for a further 30-60 minutes to reduce the liquid.
7. Meanwhile, place the aubergine slices onto a baking tray and spray with cooking oil. Grill gently until they begin to soften, then turn over and repeat.

8. In a separate bowl, whisk the yoghurt with the eggs. Stir in the mustard powder and seasoning, then set to one side.
9. Pre-heat the oven to 180°C//gas 4.
10. Take a large ovenproof dish, spritz with cooking oil, then spread one layer of the cooked lamb mixture evenly over the bottom.
11. Add a layer of the cooked aubergine followed by more lamb mixture.
12. Keep layering, finishing with the aubergine on top. Finally, spread the white sauce evenly over everything, filling in any spaces.
13. Sprinkle with grated cheese.
14. Cook for 35 minutes until the cheese bubbles a little and turns a light brown.
15. Once cooked, take the moussaka out of the oven and leave to rest for about 10 minutes before serving.

NUTRITION PER PORTION:

SERVES - 6 | CALORIES - 295KCAL | PROTEIN - 28G | CARBOHYDRATES - 18G | FAT - 8G

LAMB KEEMA

INGREDIENTS

- 3 garlic cloves, chopped
- 300g of lamb mince
- 1 large onion, peeled and chopped
- 100ml of beef stock
- 28g of butter
- Seasoning to taste
- 2-inch piece of ginger, grated
- 1 teaspoon of turmeric
- 1 teaspoon of mild chilli powder
- 1 1/2 teaspoon of garam masala
- 1/2 teaspoon of ground cumin
- 1/2 teaspoon of cinnamon
- 1 1/2 teaspoons of ground coriander
- 80g of frozen peas

METHOD

1. Fry the onions and garlic in a pan of heated butter until softened.
2. Add all of the remaining ingredients, except the peas, into the frying pan with the onion and garlic, and fry until light brown in colour.
3. Transfer the pan's contents into the slow cooker. Keep the peas to one side.
4. Cover and cook on High for 4 hours, or Low for 7 hours. Open the slow cooker, add the peas, close again and cook for a further hour.
5. Serve with rice.

NUTRITION PER PORTION:

SERVES - 3 | CALORIES - 341KCAL | PROTEIN - 21G | CARBOHYDRATES - 12G | FAT - 24G

LAMB MEATBALLS

INGREDIENTS

- 1 garlic clove, crushed
- Cooking oil
- 10g of fresh rosemary, finely chopped
- 1 onion, peeled and finely diced
- 3 tomatoes, whole with a small crosscut in the based
- 300g of lamb kofta meatballs
- 150g of red lentils
- 300ml of chicken stock
- 2 bay leaves
- 2 courgettes, chopped into 2cm chunks.
- 60g of pitted black olives
- Seasoning to taste

METHOD

1. Heat 2 tablespoons of cooking oil in a large pan, add the onion and fry on a low heat for 10 minutes, until softened. Add the rosemary and garlic cloves.
2. Cut a small cross in the base of the tomatoes and put them in a heatproof basin of boiling water. Leave for 45 seconds, drain and run under cold water so the skins come away when pulled gently. Discard the skins and chop the tomatoes.
3. Heat some more oil in a frying pan and add the meatballs, turning them until they are brown all over.
4. Now add all the ingredients to the slow cooker, including the lentils, meatballs, chicken stock, bay leaves, chopped tomatoes, courgette and olives. Add seasoning and stir thoroughly.
5. Cover the slow cooker and cook on Low for about 7 hours.
6. Season with Seasoning to taste, remove the bay leaves then serve into bowls.

NUTRITION PER PORTION:
SERVES - 2 | CALORIES - 618KCAL | PROTEIN - 39G | CARBOHYDRATES - 80G | FAT - 18G

LAMB AND RED PEPPER RAGU

● ●

INGREDIENTS

- 1 onion, peeled and finely diced
- 1 celery stick, washed and diced
- 1 carrot, peeled and finely diced
- 2 garlic cloves, peel and finely diced

- 200g of minced lamb
- Olive oil for frying
- 75ml of red wine
- 1 red pepper, seeds removed and sliced

- 50ml of passata
- ¼ teaspoon of chilli flakes
- ½ teaspoon of dried mint

For the polenta

- 350ml of milk
- 125g of instant polenta
- 25g of butter

- Optional: grated parmesan cheese
- Seasoning to taste

METHOD

1. Heat 2 tablespoons of oil in a pan and sauté the onion, celery, carrots and pepper for 10 minutes, until they soften. Add the garlic for the last 2 minutes. Transfer to the slow cooker.
2. Heat a little more oil in the same pan, season the lamb mince generously, and fry until brown throughout.
3. Pour the wine into the lamb mixture, bring it to the boil and let it simmer, then add to the slow cooker. Stir in the passata, dried chilli flakes and dried mint.
4. Add enough water to just cover the lamb if necessary, and cook on a Low setting for 6 hours, adding a little more water if it starts to dry out.
5. For the polenta: Add 350ml of milk into a large saucepan and top up with 300ml of water. Season and bring to the boil, turning the heat down to a gentle simmer.
6. Add the polenta and simmer gently for 5 minutes, stirring continuously while it thickens.
7. Remove the polenta from the heat and beat in the butter and cheese. Taste and adjust the seasoning. Add a little more water if the polenta is too thick for you.
8. To serve, add the polenta to bowls, and top with the ragu. Sprinkle a little parmesan cheese over the top.

NUTRITION PER PORTION:
SERVES - 2 | CALORIES - 847KCAL | PROTEIN - 40G | CARBOHYDRATES - 74G | FAT - 42G

LAMB AND TURNIP STEW

INGREDIENTS

- 1 onion, finely diced
- olive oil for frying
- 2 celery sticks, finely diced
- 1 carrot, finely diced
- 2 garlic cloves, finely chopped
- 1kg lamb neck, cut into 4cm chunks
- 500ml of hot chicken stock (fresh or from stock cubes)
- 150ml of dry white wine
- 1 bay leaf
- 4 baby turnips, peeled and cut into thick wedges
- 100g of French beans, topped, tailed and thinly sliced
- 100g of broad beans
- Optional: 2 teaspoons of dijon mustard
- Fresh parsley, chopped
- Fresh mint leaves, chopped
- Juice of ½ lemon
- Seasoning to taste

METHOD

1. Heat some olive oil in a pan and sauté the onion, carrot, celery and garlic for about 15 minutes until it softens. Transfer to the slow cooker.
2. Heat a little more oil in the same pan. Season the lamb and sauté until brown all over. Add the wine, bring to the boil and simmer for a few minutes, stirring thoroughly to collect the flavourings from the meat juices.
3. When the wine has reduced by half, add the pan contents to the slow cooker, pour in the stock and add the bay leaf. The meat should be just about covered by the stock.
4. Season the stew, cover the slow cooker and cook for 6 hours on a Low setting.
5. Add the turnip, and the beans to the slow cooker, cover again and cook for a further hour on the Low setting.
6. Finally, stir in the mustard, mint and parsley, add a squeeze of lemon and serve with wedges of crusty bread.

NUTRITION PER PORTION:

SERVES - 4 | CALORIES - 712KCAL | PROTEIN - 15G | CARBOHYDRATES - 19G | FAT - 44G

KARAHI LAMB CURRY

INGREDIENTS

- 500g of onions, sliced
- 150g of ghee (clarified butter)
- 500g of diced lamb
- 3 tablespoons of masala curry paste
- 1 x 400g tin of chopped tomatoes
- 150ml of water
- 1 teaspoon of salt
- 1 tablespoon of ground coriander
- 1 teaspoon of cayenne pepper
- 1 tablespoon of ground cumin
- 1 tablespoon of paprika
- 1 sweet potato, diced
- 1 tin of chickpeas, rinsed through
- 4 medium green chillies, chopped
- 350g ready-to-cook spinach
- small bunch coriander leaves, chopped
- Optional: ½ teaspoon of ground cumin
- Seasoning to taste

METHOD

1. In a large pan, gently fry the onions in hot clarified butter for about 10 minutes until softened. Remove onions with a slotted spoon. Keep the pan of butter.
2. Now, sauté the lamb in the pan of hot butter until brown all over. Use a slotted spoon to transfer the lamb directly to the slow cooker.
3. In a blender, blitz the cooked onions, masala curry paste, tomatoes and water into a smooth paste and return to the pan with the butter. Stir thoroughly to collect up the meat juices and flavours then transfer to the slow cooker with the lamb.
4. Stir in the cayenne, cumin, coriander and paprika into the slow cooker, then add the diced sweet potato and chickpeas. Cover and cook on a Low setting for 6 hours.

5. Use a blender to blitz the green chillies with little water to a puree. Set aside.
6. Remove the lid from the slow cooker and add the spinach leaves. The spinach leaves will wilt in the heat.
7. Cover again and cook on a Low setting for another hour, then stir in the wilted spinach thoroughly.
8. Stir in the chilli puree to taste. Serve with rice and/or warm naan, garnished with chopped coriander, (optional) ground cumin and seasoning to taste.

NUTRITION PER PORTION:

SERVES - 8 | CALORIES - 384KCAL | PROTEIN - 21G | CARBOHYDRATES - 20G | FAT - 26G

POACHED LAMB SHOULDER AND CAPER SAUCE

INGREDIENTS

Main

- Large sprig of thyme
- 3 bay leaves
- 3 stems of parsley
- 1 onion, peel on, washed thoroughly

- 800g of boneless lamb shoulder
- 1 celery stick, trimmed, cut in half
- 1 carrot, peeled, whole
- 1 teaspoon of whole peppercorns

- Mixed seasonal summer vegetables, chopped (peas, carrots, courgettes etc.)

For the caper sauce

- 40g of butter
- 1 small onion, chopped
- 40g of plain flour
- 350ml of broth from the poached lamb

- 1-2 tablespoons of vinegar taken from the caper jar
- 1 teaspoon of dijon mustard
- 1 teaspoon of redcurrant jelly
- 75ml of double cream

- 1 tablespoon of capers
- 1 tablespoon of parsley, chopped
- Seasoning to taste

METHOD

Main

1. Preheat the slow cooker on a Low setting.
2. Add the lamb to the slow cooker with the onion, celery, carrot, peppercorns and herbs. Add enough hot water to cover the ingredients.
3. Cover and cook for 3 hours on a Low setting.
4. Open the slow cooker and scoop off the scum and fat which will collect on the surface and add a little more water to cover if necessary.
5. Cover and cook for 3 further hours on the Low setting.
6. Open the slow cooker and remove the stock vegetables, celery, carrot and onion. Remove any scum or fat from the surface and add the seasonal summer vegetables to the casserole. Add a splash of water if required. Cover and cook on Low for a further hour, or until the summer vegetables are cooked.
7. Remove the lamb from the slow cooker to a serving plate. Leave to rest while you prepare the caper sauce.
8. Strain the stock from the slow cooker through a sieve into a large jug. Save 350ml and freeze any remaining for future use.

Make the caper sauce

9. In a saucepan, fry the butter and onion gently until translucent, and add the flour. Stir and cook to make a roux then gradually whisk in the 350ml stock until smooth.
10. Add the vinegar, seasoning, mustard and redcurrant jelly. Bring to the boil and simmer for 10 minutes, then sieve out any lumps. Whisk in the cream and add the capers and parsley.

11. Serve slices of the poached lamb and the seasonal summer vegetables with crushed boiled new potatoes and caper sauce.

NUTRITION PER PORTION:

SERVES - 8 | CALORIES - 261KCAL | PROTEIN - 30G | CARBOHYDRATES - 8G | FAT - 11G

MEDITERRANEAN-STYLE LAMB CASSEROLE
• •

INGREDIENTS

- 500g of diced lamb shoulder
- 1 onion, finely sliced
- 2 tablespoons of olive oil
- 2 garlic cloves, finely chopped
- 500ml hot lamb or beef stock (fresh or from stock cubes)
- Fresh rosemary
- 400g tin of haricot beans, rinsed through
- 100g of pitted black olives
- 3 large tomatoes, chopped
- 200g of chard leaves (or use spinach), tough stems removed, chopped
- 100g of crème fraiche
- Seasoning to taste

METHOD

1. Heat the oil in a large pan and fry the lamb until its browned all over. Transfer to the slow cooker.
2. Use the same pan to heat a little more oil and sauté the onion and garlic for a few minutes until it softens. Add to the slow cooker.
3. Now add the rosemary, stock and seasoning to taste, then put in the beans, tomatoes and olives.
4. Cover and cook for 6 hours on a Low setting.
5. Stir through the chard/spinach and crème fraiche and cover and cook on Low for another 1 hour. The chard will wilt in the heat.
6. Give the casserole a stir, adjust seasoning to taste and serve with wedges of crusty bread.

NUTRITION PER PORTION:

SERVES - 4 | CALORIES - 508KCAL | PROTEIN - 47G | CARBOHYDRATES - 21G | FAT - 28G

SEVILLIAN LAMB STEW
• •

INGREDIENTS

- 1kg of diced lamb
- zest and juice of 4 Seville oranges
- zest and juice of 1 lemon
- 1 tablespoon of seasoned flour
- 3 garlic cloves, grated
- olive oil
- 1.25 litres of stock (fresh or from stock cubes)
- 2 large onions, chopped very small
- A handful of greens, finely chopped
- ½ teaspoon of allspice
- ½ teaspoon of cinnamon
- A good pinch of ground cloves
- ½ teaspoon of coriander seed
- 2 tins of chickpeas or butter beans (as preferred), rinsed through
- Optional: 2 tablespoons of parsley or mint, chopped roughly to garnish
- Seasoning to taste

METHOD

1. Add the orange and lemon juice together in a container, add the lamb, cover and marinade overnight.
2. Drain the lamb but keep the juice. In a shallow bowl, toss the lamb into the seasoned flour coating it all over.
3. Heat the oil in a pan and fry the lamb until it's browned all over, then transfer to the slow cooker.
4. Use the same pan to fry and soften the onion and garlic for a few minutes before adding to the slow cooker with the lamb.

5. Add the reserved marinade juice.
6. Put the remaining ingredients and zest into the slow cooker, season to taste and stir thoroughly.
7. Cover and cook on a Low setting for 8 hours.
8. Serve sprinkled with parsley (or mint) accompanied by wedges of crusty bread.

NUTRITION PER PORTION:

SERVES - 4 | CALORIES - 720KCAL | PROTEIN - 76G | CARBOHYDRATES - 28G | FAT - 34G

MUTTON TAGINE

• •

INGREDIENTS

- 2 garlic cloves, crushed and chopped
- 2 tablespoons of olive oil
- 1 teaspoons of saffron strands
- 1 onion, chopped
- 800g of diced mutton or lamb
- 1 cinnamon stick
- 1 teaspoons of ground turmeric
- 1 small red chilli, thinly sliced

- 1 teaspoon of ground cinnamon
- 1 sweet potato, peeled and diced
- 300ml lamb or chicken stock (fresh or from stock cubes)
- 75g of dried apricots
- 2 tablespoons of ground almonds
- 75g of dried prunes
- 1 can of chickpeas, rinsed through

- Juice of 1 lemon
- 50g of flaked almonds
- 375g of couscous, prepared according to packet instructions
- 1 tablespoon of olive oil
- Fresh coriander or mint, chopped
- Seasoning to taste

METHOD

1. Heat the oil in a large pan and sauté the chopped onions, saffron threads and garlic for 5 minutes until they soften.
2. Turn up the heat, and add the mutton, frying until it's brown all over.
3. Add the ground cinnamon, turmeric, very thinly sliced chilli, cinnamon stick and salt to taste. Fry for a couple of minutes before adding the stock.
4. Bring the stock to the boil, simmer for a couple of minutes to collect all the meat juices and flavouring, then transfer to the slow cooker.
5. Stir in the diced sweet potato, dried fruits, chickpeas, almonds, and lemon juice.
6. Cover and cook on a Low setting for 6 hours.
7. Ten minutes before the end of cooking time, dry fry the flaked almonds in a pan for a couple of minutes until golden.
8. Prepare the couscous according to instructions and drain. Stir through some coriander/mint, olive oil, and seasoning to taste.
9. Serve the tagine with couscous. Top with the toasted almonds.

NUTRITION PER PORTION:

SERVES - 4 | CALORIES - 840KCAL | PROTEIN - 65G | CARBOHYDRATES - 81G | FAT - 31G

PORK

PORK CASSEROLE

INGREDIENTS

- 1 tablespoon of vegetable oil
- 1 onion, chopped
- 750g of pork shoulder steaks, cut into large chunks
- 1 leek, chopped
- 1 x Bouquet garni
- 1 chicken stock cube
- 1 carrot, chopped
- 2 teaspoons of dijon mustard
- 1 tablespoon of cider vinegar
- 1 tablespoon of honey
- 2 teaspoons of cornflour

METHOD

1. Preheat your slow cooker and spritz lightly with a little cooking oil spray.
2. Add the oil to a frying pan, season the pork, then fry, turning regularly until it turns a deep brown all over. Transfer the pork to the slow cooker.
3. Use the same pan with a little more oil if necessary to sauté the onion and leeks for a few minutes, until they soften.
4. Pour a little water in the pan and stir to collect any flavours and juices, then transfer to the slow cooker.
5. Next add the carrot and herbs, mustard, vinegar, and crumbled stock cube, along with enough water to cover the ingredients.
6. Stir thoroughly, cover the slow cooker, and cook on Low for 6-8 hours, or High for 5-6 hours.
7. Meanwhile, in a clean pan blend the honey with the cornflour and add 1-2 teaspoons of liquid removed from the slow cooker. Blend to a smooth paste. Add another 100ml liquid from the slow cooker, bring to the boil and simmer until thickened.
8. Stir the cornflour mixture back into the casserole.
9. Serve with mash, topped with fresh chopped thyme leaves.

NUTRITION PER PORTION:

SERVES - 4 | CALORIES - 416KCAL | PROTEIN - 41G | CARBOHYDRATES - 13G | FAT - 21G

PORK LOIN WITH HONEY AND MUSTARD

INGREDIENTS

- 1½ teaspoons of fennel seeds
- 2 garlic cloves
- Fresh thyme leaves
- 2 tablespoons of rapeseed or olive oil
- 1.8kg pork loin, skin removed, and fat well scored
- 300g of shallots (see note 3)
- 1 small celeriac, peeled, quartered, and chopped
- 2 eating apples, cut into wedges, peel and core removed
- 150ml of white wine
- 250ml of chicken or pork stock (fresh or from stock cubes)
- 1 tablespoon of honey
- 1 tablespoon of dijon mustard

METHOD

1. Use a pestle and mortar to lightly crush the fennel, garlic and thyme leaves together. Add 1 tablespoon of oil and season, then mix firmly to a rough paste marinade. Rub the marinade paste all over the pork, cover and refrigerate for a minimum of 2 hours.
2. Preheat the slow cooker on a Low setting.

3. In a heatproof bowl, pour boiling water over the shallots and leave to steep for 2 minutes. Drain and rinse under cold water, then peel and trim.
4. Heat the rest of the oil in a frying pan that will be big enough to contain the pork joint.
5. First, brown the shallots for a few minutes then transfer to the slow cooker.
6. Next, add the celeriac and apples, season well and mix with the onions.
7. Finally, add the pork to the pan and brown all over and transfer to the slow cooker with the fat-side up on top of the vegetable mixture.
8. Pour the wine into the used frying pan and bubble for 1 min. Add the stock, honey and mustard and bubble for another minute, then pour into the slow cooker and over the pork.
9. Cover and cook on Low for 6 hours, turning the meat and stirring the veg halfway through cooking, if you're available.
10. Lift the pork out of the slow cooker, cover and leave to rest for 10 minutes before carving.
11. Serve, cut into thick slices with the cooked vegetables and some greens.

NUTRITION PER PORTION:

SERVES - 6 | CALORIES - 597KCAL | PROTEIN - 42G | CARBOHYDRATES - 9G | FAT - 41G

SHREDDED HAM WITH PINEAPPLE

INGREDIENTS

- 1– 1.5kg of boneless gammon
- 435g tin of pineapple chunks in juice

METHOD

1. Put the gammon into the slow cooker and pour the tin of pineapple chunks along with the juice over the top.
2. Cover and cook on High for 6 hours or Low for 8 hours.
3. Remove the gammon from the slow cooker, discard the pineapple and juice, and shred the meat with 2 forks.
4. Serve hot or cold.

NUTRITION PER PORTION:

SERVES - 6 | CALORIES - 274KCAL | PROTEIN - 32G | CARBOHYDRATES - 32G | FAT - 2G

PORK CACCIATORE

INGREDIENTS

- 1 x 400g can of chopped tomatoes
- 225g of fresh button mushrooms sliced
- 2 green peppers, chopped
- 1 small onion, chopped
- 1 x 6oz can of tomato paste
- 500g of pork tenderloin, cut into 8 equal pieces
- 1 teaspoon of dried oregano
- 400g of penne pasta, uncooked
- 1 tablespoon of cornflour
- 60ml of water
- Optional: 250g of mozzarella cheese
- Optional: 2 tablespoons of grated parmigiano-reggiano

METHOD

1. Blend the canned tomatoes and tomato paste in a slow cooker, then stir in the peppers, mushrooms, and onions.
2. Season the pork pieces with oregano and add to the slow cooker, pressing them into the tomato sauce.
3. Cover and cook on Low for 4½ hours or on High for 3 hours.

4. Prepare the pasta according to the packet instructions and drain when cooked.
5. Move the meat to a plate and cover to keep warm. Keep the sauce in the slow cooker for now.
6. In a small bowl, blend the cornflour and water to a runny paste and add to the tomato sauce in the slow cooker.
7. Turn the setting to High, cover and cook for 6 to 8 minutes until it thickens.
8. Serve the pasta topped with the pork and rich tomato sauce, topped with the cheeses.

NUTRITION PER PORTION:

SERVES - 4 | CALORIES - 659KCAL | PROTEIN - 57G | CARBOHYDRATES - 77G | FAT - 13G

PORK RIBS, BBQ

INGREDIENTS

- 1 kg of pork ribs
- 300ml of barbecue sauce
- 1 tablespoon of smoked paprika
- 3 garlic cloves, crushed
- 1 tablespoon of Worcestershire sauce

METHOD

1. Mix the barbecue sauce, Worcestershire sauce, crushed garlic and smoked paprika in a container together until blended.
2. Put the pork ribs straight into the slow cooker.
3. Pour ¾ of the sauce over the pork ribs, keeping what's left for later use.
4. Close the slow cooker lid and cook on Low for 8 hours, or High for 4 hours.
5. Remove the pork ribs from the slow cooker, transferring them carefully to a baking tray.
6. Mix 3-4 spoonfuls of the liquid from the slow cooker in with the ¼ sauce that was reserved previously (see step 3).
7. Drizzle the sauce over the pork ribs and grill for 5 to 10 minutes or until they start to crisp up.
8. Serve immediately!

NUTRITION PER PORTION:

SERVES - 4 | CALORIES - 813KCAL | PROTEIN - 67G | CARBOHYDRATES - 31G | FAT - 45G

SLOW-COOKED ASIAN ROAST PORK

INGREDIENTS

- 900g of pork leg steaks
- 3 garlic cloves, sliced
- 1 tablespoon of vegetable oil
- 1 inch piece of fresh ginger, peeled and finely chopped
- 2 long red chillies, seeded and sliced
- 3 whole star anise
- 1 tablespoon of honey
- 150ml of hoisin sauce
- 250ml of sherry

METHOD

1. Preheat the slow cooker and spritz lightly with cooking oil.
2. Heat the oil in a frying pan, season the pork legs steaks, then fry on all sides until they are nicely browned all over. Remove from the pan and set to one side.
3. In the same pan with a little more heated oil, if necessary, sauté the garlic and ginger and one of the chillies for 5 minutes (save the other chilli for later).

4. Pour the hoisin sauce, sherry and star anise into the frying pan with the ginger and garlic. Stir to mix well.
5. Put the pork leg steaks into the slow cooker, pour the sauce from the frying pan evenly over the top, and cover with the slow cooker lid.
6. Cook on a Low setting for 8 hours or High for 4 hours.
7. Serve the leg steaks over rice with the remaining sliced red chilli and some chopped spring onions.

NUTRITION PER PORTION:
SERVES - 6 | CALORIES - 312KCAL | PROTEIN - 35G | CARBOHYDRATES - 17G | FAT - 8G

CHINESE BRAISED PORK

INGREDIENTS

- 1 tablespoon of vegetable oil
- 1kg of pork shoulder, cut into 5cm pieces
- 4 tablespoons of soy sauce
- 2-inch piece of fresh ginger, shredded into matchstick-size pieces
- 2 red chillies, sliced
- 2 garlic cloves, sliced
- 4 tablespoons of red wine vinegar
- 200ml of sherry
- 50g of soft brown sugar
- 150ml of water

METHOD

1. Marinate the meat in a container with 1 tablespoon of the soy sauce. Cover and place in the fridge for 2 hours.
2. Heat the oil in a frying pan and sauté the garlic, ginger and half the chilli for 5 minutes until softened.
3. Add the sherry, vinegar, 3 remaining tablespoons of soy sauce, sugar, and water over some heat to dissolve the sugar. Stir continuously.
4. Put the marinated meat into the slow cooker and pour over the sauce.
5. Cover and cook for 4 hours on High or 8 hours on Slow.
6. Remove/soak any excess oil off the top with a spoon or some kitchen roll. Transfer the meat to a serving plate and strain the sauce through a mesh sieve into a jug.
7. Serve the pork pieces on a plate of rice noodles, with the sauce poured over the top, and garnished with chopped spring onions, red chillies, fresh coriander and toasted sesame seeds.

NUTRITION PER PORTION:
SERVES - 4-6 | CALORIES - 294KCAL | PROTEIN - 35G | CARBOHYDRATES - 10G | FAT - 9G

BOOZY PORK SAUSAGE STEW

INGREDIENTS

- 2 tablespoons of olive oil
- 4 pork sausages
- 500g//approx. 4 pork shoulder steaks, cut in half
- 2 tablespoons of plain flour
- 1 onion chopped
- 1 teaspoon of cumin seeds
- 1 tablespoon of grain mustard
- 300ml of cider
- 3 leeks, white part only, chopped

METHOD

1. Preheat the slow cooker and spritz lightly with cooking oil.
2. Heat a frying pan with 1 tablespoon of the oil and sauté the sausages and pork steaks on all sides until they are nicely browned. Remove to a plate and set to one side.

3. Use the same pan, heat the rest of the olive oil and sauté the onions for about 5 minutes until softened. Sprinkle in the flour and sauté for another minute. Stir in the mustard, cumin and seasoning, then stir in the cider. Stir well and pour into the slow cooker along with the meat.
4. Cover and cook for 4 hours on a High setting or 8 hours on Low.
5. Half an hour before the end of the cooking cycle, add the leeks into the slow cooker on top of the meat. Cover and continue cooking for the final 30 minutes of the cooking cycle.
6. Serve as a stew with wedges of crusty bread or serve with mash and freshly chopped flat leaf parsley.

NUTRITION PER PORTION:
SERVES - 4-6 | CALORIES - 276KCAL | PROTEIN - 23G | CARBOHYDRATES - 12G | FAT - 15G

BOOZY SLOW-COOKED HAM WITH A CIDER, CLOVE, AND HONEY GLAZE

INGREDIENTS

- 2.5kg boneless, unsmoked gammon joint
- 5 whole cloves

- 1 onion, sliced
- 10 peppercorns
- 1 bay leaf

- 1.2 litres of cider

For the glaze

- 75g of demerara sugar, plus 1-2 teaspoons extra
- 1½ tablespoons of honey

- ½ tablespoon of black treacle
- 1½ tablespoons of cider vinegar
- 100ml of cider

- a handful of whole cloves
- 2-3 teaspoons of English mustard

METHOD

1. The gammon should be at room temperature before beginning to cook.
2. Put the onion, 5 cloves, bay leaf and peppercorns directly into the slow cooker and sit the gammon on top with the skin-side up.
3. Pour in the cider, secure the lid and cook on a Low setting for 6 hours.
4. When cooked through, remove the gammon to a chopping board and pat dry. Leave to cool slightly for 10 minutes.
5. Preheat the oven to 180°C//gas 6.
6. Remove any string or netting and cut off the skin with a sharp knife. Leave behind the fat covering. Score the fat in a crisscross pattern.
7. To make the glaze: put the sugar, honey, treacle, vinegar, cider and 5 cloves all together in a pan and warm until the sugar has dissolved.
8. Increase the heat slightly and simmer the mixture for about 8-10 minutes until it's reduced and is thick and syrupy: about 8-10 minutes.
9. Take out the cloves and discard. Leave the glaze to cool for a couple of minutes.
10. Put the gammon in a roasting tin lined with foil. Roast in the oven for 5 minutes.
11. Remove the ham from the oven and brush the fat all over with the mustard to coat, then stud with cloves.
12. Brush with about ¾ of the glaze and return to the oven to roast for another 10 minutes.
13. Remove the gammon from the oven, drizzle over the remaining glaze and sprinkle with 1-2 teaspoons of demerara sugar.

14. Again, return to the oven for another 10-15 minutes until the fat is crisp and caramelised, but make sure it doesn't burn.
15. Let the ham rest for at least 15 minutes before carving into slices and serving.

NUTRITION PER PORTION:
SERVES - 12 | CALORIES - 204KCAL | PROTEIN - 21G | CARBOHYDRATES - 5G | FAT - 11G

PORK AND PANCETTA RAGU

INGREDIENTS

- 250g of unsmoked pancetta, diced
- 2 tablespoons of olive oil
- 1kg pork shoulder, diced into 3cm pieces
- 2 carrots, sliced into large chunks
- 2 red onions, halved

- 2 sticks of celery, sliced
- 7 garlic cloves, peeled but left whole
- ¼-½ teaspoon of crushed dried chilli flakes, to taste
- 2 bay leaves
- 1 teaspoon of fennel seeds

- Fresh parsley leaves, chopped
- ½ teaspoon of dried oregano
- 3 tablespoons of tomato purée
- 200ml of white wine
- 400g tin of chopped tomatoes
- 400ml of chicken stock (fresh or from stock cubes)

To serve

- a splash of olive oil
- 450g of pappardelle pasta

- 15g basil, leaves picked and roughly chopped

- 30g of parmesan, finely grated

METHOD

1. Heat a little oil up in a large pan and add the pancetta. Stir for a few minutes until it begins to turn golden, then lift out onto kitchen paper.
2. Add a little more oil and turn up the heat a little. Season the pork and sauté it in the pan for about 10–15 minutes, stirring occasionally until all the liquid comes out and reduces, leaving just oil in the bottom of the pan. Remove the pork with a slotted spoon from the pan and put on the kitchen paper with the pancetta.
3. Use a food processor to blend the carrots, onions, celery and garlic until cut into small pieces, but don't puree.
4. Use the same pan and stir fry the vegetables, chilli flakes, fennel seeds, parsley, bay leaves and oregano for about 6 minutes until the vegetables soften.
5. Return the pork and pancetta to the pan, add the tomato purée and stir so everything is well coated.
6. Keep stirring as you pour in the wine, which will quickly reduce and be absorbed.
7. Finally, add the tomatoes and the chicken stock. Season to taste, bring it all to the boil and simmer for a few minutes.
8. Transfer to a slow cooker and cook on High for 4 hours.
9. About 30 minutes before the end of the cooking cycle, cook the pasta, and drain, reserving one cup of pasta water.
10. Turn off the heat and return the drained pasta to the pan. Ladle in the hot ragù, and gently mix together.
11. Serve and sprinkle with grated parmesan and basil leaves

NUTRITION PER PORTION:
SERVES - 6 | CALORIES - 764KCAL | PROTEIN - 59G | CARBOHYDRATES - 60G | FAT - 28G

SWEET AND SOUR PORK BALLS

INGREDIENTS

- 30g of peeled root ginger
- 6 tablespoons of cornflour
- 1 teaspoon of Chinese 5 spice
- 4 tablespoon of light soy sauce
- 1 x 225g tin sliced water chestnuts, drained
- 1 bunch spring onions, sliced
- 4 garlic cloves, peeled

- 500g of pork mince
- 2 tablespoons of dark brown sugar
- 75g of tomato ketchup
- 1 tablespoon of cider vinegar
- 1 x 435g tin of pineapple chunks in juice
- 1 tablespoon of sesame oil

- 2 large onions, cut into wedges
- 3 mixed peppers, deseeded and roughly chopped
- 500ml chicken stock (fresh or made from stock cubes)

METHOD

1. Make the meatballs: Blend 20g of the ginger, 2 tablespoons of cornflour, the Chinese 5 spice and 1 tablespoon of soy in a food processor. Add half of each of the garlic, spring onions and water chestnuts and blitz again until finely chopped.
2. Tip the mixture into a container with the pork mince, combine thoroughly with your hands and shape into 30 small meatballs (dip your hands in water to stop the mixture from sticking to them). Transfer to a plate. Cover and chill in the fridge for at least 30 minutes.
3. Grate the remaining ginger and garlic and use a jug to combine with the sugar, vinegar and ketchup plus 3 tablespoons of soy. Now add the pineapple juice from the tin to make the sauce and set aside.
4. Heat the sesame oil in a pan and fry the onions on a high heat for 3-4 minutes. Add the peppers, pour in the sauce and the stock, bring to the boil and then allow to simmer.
5. Transfer the onion mixture to the slow cooker and add the meatballs.
6. Cover the slow cooker and cook for 3 hours on Low or 1 1/2 hours on High.
7. Stir in the rest of the water chestnuts and the pineapple.
8. Finally, blend the remaining 4 tablespoons of cornflour in a container with enough cold water to make a paste, and add some of the sweet and sour sauce from the slow cooker. Add the cornflour mixture back to the slow cooker, stirring continuously.
9. Cover and cook on High for another 20-30 minutes to thicken the sauce.
10. Serve with steamed or egg-fried rice, scattered with the rest of the spring onions.

NUTRITION PER PORTION:

SERVES - 6 | CALORIES - 296KCAL | PROTEIN - 20G | CARBOHYDRATES - 37G | FAT - 7G

PORK VINDALOO

INGREDIENTS

- 750g of pork shoulder steaks, diced
- 2 medium onions, chopped
- 1 tablespoon of tomato puree

To make the paste

- 3 cardamom pods
- 1 teaspoon of black peppercorns
- 1 teaspoon of cumin seeds
- 2 teaspoons of chilli powder
- 1 teaspoon of turmeric

- 6 baby potatoes, cut in half
- 3 tablespoons of vegetable oil
- 1 cinnamon stick
- 1 x 400g tin of chopped tomatoes

- 1-inch of ginger root, chopped
- 3 garlic cloves
- 3 tablespoons of cider vinegar

- 100ml of chicken or vegetable stock

METHOD

1. Grind all the spices for the spice paste together in a mortar and pestle.
2. Use a blender to puree together with the ginger, garlic and vinegar.
3. Use a shallow bowl to put the pork pieces in and pour the spice paste over, coating the meat thoroughly. Cover and marinate for 2 hours in the fridge.
4. Put the marinated meat with the potatoes into the slow cooker.
5. Heat some oil in a frying and sauté the onions with a little seasoning for about 10 minutes until it softens.
6. Stir in the tomato purée, chopped tomatoes, cinnamon stick and stock, bring to the boil, and simmer for a minute before pouring the mixture into the slow cooker over the meat and potatoes.
7. Put the lid on and cook for 4 hours on High or 8 hours Low.
8. Serve the pork vindaloo over steamed rice with fresh chopped coriander and red onion, with yoghurt and your favourite chutneys.

NUTRITION PER PORTION:

SERVES - 6 | CALORIES - 250KCAL | PROTEIN - 28G | CARBOHYDRATES - 10G | FAT - 11G

CLASSIC PORK MEDALLIONS WITH APPLE

INGREDIENTS

- ½ tablespoon of rapeseed oil
- 500g of pork medallions
- 1 medium onion, finely chopped
- 1 tablespoon of dijon mustard
- 3 eating apples, cored and cut into quarters
- 150ml of chicken stock (fresh or from stock cubes)
- 4 sage leaves, finely sliced
- 2 tablespoons of crème fraiche

METHOD

1. Preheat the slow cooker and lightly spritz with cooking oil.
2. Heat the oil in a pan and fry the pork medallions so that they are browned all over. Add the onions and sauté until they soften, then add the mustard and stir in the stock. Put the pan contents to the slow cooker.
3. Now add the apple quarters, followed by the sage and season to taste.
4. Cover and cook on Low for 4 hours.
5. Stir in the crème fraiche and serve with rice.

NUTRITION PER PORTION:

SERVES - 6 | CALORIES - 344KCAL | PROTEIN - 33G | CARBOHYDRATES - 18G | FAT - 14G

SEASONED BEAN AND SAUSAGE STEW

INGREDIENTS

- 8 chipolata sausages
- 2 x 420g cans of mixed beans
- 2 x 400g cans of chopped tomatoes
- 1 teaspoon of dried basil
- 2 teaspoons of dried oregano
- 1 tablespoon of sugar

METHOD

1. Heat some cooking oil in a frying pan and fry the sausages for a few minutes until they are browned all over.
2. Place the cooked sausages into the slow cooker and add both cans of beans and one can of tomatoes.
3. Strain and discard the juice from the second can of tomatoes and add just the tomatoes to the slow cooker.
4. Stir in the sugar and herbs and season to taste.

5. Cover and cook on Low for 8 hours.
6. Serve with chunks of crusty bread.

NUTRITION PER PORTION:

SERVES - 4 | CALORIES - 355KCAL | PROTEIN - 20G | CARBOHYDRATES - 37G | FAT - 15G

SMOKEY CHORIZO AND BUTTERNUT STEW

INGREDIENTS

For the stew

- 1 onion, finely sliced
- 2 teaspoons of vegetable oil
- 3 tablespoons of tomato purée
- 1 tablespoon of sweet smoked paprika

- 3 garlic cloves, crushed
- 2 mixed colour peppers, deseeded and sliced
- ½ teaspoon of hot chilli powder (to taste)

- 200g chorizo ring, skinned and sliced
- 500g of butternut squash, diced
- 680g of passata
- 2 teaspoons. dried thyme

To serve

- 60g of soured cream

- Fresh parsley leaves roughly chopped

METHOD

1. Heat the oil in a pan and sauté the onion for 10 minutes until softened. Stir in the garlic, spices and tomato purée and fry for a further 2 minutes.
2. Empty the contents of the bowl into the slow cooker and add the rest of the stew ingredients. Season to taste. Stir thoroughly, cover and cook on Low for 6 hours.
3. Adjust the seasoning to taste and serve garnished with parsley and with a dollop of soured cream.

NUTRITION PER PORTION:

SERVES - 4 | CALORIES - 424KCAL | PROTEIN - 19G | CARBOHYDRATES - 36G | FAT - 21G

RAMEN PORK

INGREDIENTS

- 1 litre of hot chicken stock (fresh or from stock cubes)
- 1 teaspoon of soft dark brown sugar
- 100g of white miso paste
- 4 tablespoons of dark soy sauce
- 1 tablespoon of mirin

- 200g of mixed exotic mushrooms
- 3 garlic cloves, crushed
- 2-inch piece of fresh root ginger, peeled and finely grated
- 600g of pork shoulder steaks
- Juice of 1 lime
- 2 pak choi, halved lengthways

- 250g ramen or other dried noodles
- 2 spring onions, finely sliced
- Optional: 4 soft-boiled eggs, halved

METHOD

1. Whisk up the stock, miso paste, mirin, soy sauce and sugar until the miso and sugar dissolve completely.
2. Next, place the ginger, pork, garlic, and mushrooms in the slow cooker and add the stock mixture. Stir well.
3. Put the lid on and cook on low for 6 hours.
4. Stir in the lime juice, break up any big pork chunks, and adjust seasoning to taste.

5. Follow the pack instructions for cooking the noodles and add the pak choi during the final minute's cooking. Drain the water away.
6. Serve the noodles/pak choi in deep bowls, with the ramen mixture spooned over the top, evenly distributing the pork and mushrooms between the bowls.
7. Top with spring onions, and a halved egg to each bowl and serve.

NUTRITION PER PORTION:

SERVES - 4 | CALORIES - 803KCAL | PROTEIN - 70G | CARBOHYDRATES - 51G | FAT - 3G

HAM AND RED LENTIL STEW

INGREDIENTS

- 2 teaspoons of olive oil
- 2 red onions, finely sliced
- Fresh rosemary, chopped
- 2 x 400g tins chopped tomatoes
- 200g of cooked ham in chunky pieces
- 150g of red lentils, rinsed in cold water
- 300g of mixed roasted vegetables, in large pieces
- 300g of shredded fresh greens
- such as savoy cabbage, spring greens or kale.
- 700ml of hot vegetable stock (fresh or from stock cubes)

METHOD

1. Heat the oil in a large pan and sauté the onions until softened. Add the rosemary and cook for another 2 minutes. Scrape the contents into the slow cooker.
2. Add the rest of the ingredients including the stock, Put the lid on. Cook on High for 4hours.
3. Open the slow cooker and shred the ham with two forks. Now add the fresh greens.
4. Cover again and cook for a further 45 minutes.
5. Remove rosemary sprigs and season to taste.
6. Serve with crusty bread.

NUTRITION PER PORTION:

SERVES - 4 | CALORIES - 379KCAL | PROTEIN - 25G | CARBOHYDRATES - 46G | FAT - 8G

SAUSAGE CASSEROLE

INGREDIENTS

- 1 tablespoons of olive oil
- 8 thick pork sausages
- 2 red onions, sliced
- 2 tablespoons of plain flour
- 400ml of beef stock
- 3 parsnips, peeled and cut into batons
- 3 tablespoons of (Branston) pickle
- 2 garlic cloves, crushed

METHOD

1. Heat half the oil in a large pan and brown the sausages all over - about 10 minutes. Transfer to the slow cooker.
2. Add the remaining oil to the same pan and sauté the onion until soft - about 10 minutes.
3. Stir in the flour and cook for 1 more minute, then pour in the stock, stirring continuously to mix. Transfer to the slow cooker.
4. Stir the garlic, parsnip and pickle into the slow cooker so everything combines.

5. Cover with lid and cook on High for 4 hours.
6. Adjust the seasoning to taste and serve with mashed potato and steamed broccoli.

PORK, APRICOT AND THYME CASSEROLE

INGREDIENTS

- 150g of apricots, halved and without stones
- ½ red onion, sliced
- 500g of baby new potatoes, each cut in half
- 2 garlic cloves, crushed
- 500g of baby new potatoes, each cut in half
- Fresh thyme leaves, chopped
- 2 teaspoons of olive oil
- 1 tablespoon of apricot jam
- 1kg of bone-in pork chops (about 4 of equal weight)
- 200ml of hot chicken stock (fresh or made from stock cubes)
- 200g of crème fraiche
- 1 teaspoons of runny honey
- 1 tablespoon of cornflour

METHOD

1. Add the garlic, onion, apricots, potatoes, thyme leaves and plenty of seasoning into the slow cooker and mix thoroughly.
2. Add oil to a large pan on a high heat. Brush the apricot jam onto both sides of the pork chop and flash fry for 1 minute per side.
3. Transfer to the slow cooker and season to taste.
4. In a large jug, whisk the stock, honey and crème fraiche and honey and add to the pork.
5. Put the lid on and cook on Low for 6 hours.
6. Lift the pork from the slow cooker to a clean board. Throw away any bones. Strain the sauce through a sieve into a clean pan and return the steak to the slow cooker with the potato/onion mixture. Put the lid on to keep warm.
7. Make a smooth paste by mixing the cornflour with 1 teaspoon of water, then add to the pan of strained sauce. Whisk over a High heat until the sauce bubbles and thickens.
8. Serve, topped with the sauce and greens on the side.

SAUSAGE AND BUTTERNUT RISOTTO

INGREDIENTS

- 1 teaspoon of fennel seeds, lightly crushed
- 2 tablespoons of olive oil
- 400g of pork sausage meat, (or 6 thick pork sausages, casing removed)
- 2 sticks of celery, finely diced
- 1 onion, finely chopped
- 3 garlic cloves, crushed
- 1 butternut squash, peeled, deseeded, and diced
- 300g of risotto rice
- 1 litre of hot chicken stock (fresh or made from stock cubes)
- 200ml of white wine
- Fresh rosemary
- 1 tablespoon of mascarpone, plus extra to serve
- 75g of finely grated parmesan, finely grated, plus extra to serve

METHOD

1. Heat the oil in a large pan and when hot, add the sausage meat along with the crushed fennel seeds and fry for 5 minutes until the meat is browned. Stir with a spoon to break up the chunks of sausage meat, the use a slotted spoon to plate up and set aside.
2. Add a little more oil, then cook the onion and celery for 10 minutes until softened. Stir in the diced squash and garlic and cook for another minute.
3. Turn the heat up, stir in the rice and cook for a couple of minutes then pour in the wine and allow it to bubble.
4. Transfer everything to the slow cooker, stir in the hot stock and add the rosemary sprig.
5. Cover and cook on a High setting for 2 ½ hours until all the rice is absorbed.
6. Stir in the mascarpone thoroughly.
7. Serve with a spoonful of extra mascarpone and topped with grated parmesan.

NUTRITION PER PORTION:

SERVES - 6 | CALORIES - 602KCAL | PROTEIN - 22G | CARBOHYDRATES - 59G | FAT - 27G

PORK PIBIL

● ●

INGREDIENTS

- 2 teaspoons of cumin seeds
- 1 tablespoons of allspice berries
- 1 teaspoons of black peppercorns
- 1 onion, roughly chopped
- 4 garlic cloves

- 1 scotch bonnet chilli, deseeded and roughly chopped
- 1 onion, roughly chopped
- 50g of annatto paste (paprika, nutmeg or saffron make a suitable alternative)

- Juice of 4 oranges
- 100m of white wine vinegar
- 1.6kg of boneless pork shoulder, trimmed and cut into 4 evenly sized pieces
- 2 bay leaves

To serve:

- Corn tortillas
- Avocado

- Soured cream
- Avocado

- Fresh coriander, chopped

For the pickled red onions:

- 1/2 teaspoon of salt
- 3 tablespoons of caster sugar

- 1 teaspoons of allspice berries
- 1 bay leaf

- 2 red onions, thinly sliced
- 175ml of white wine vinegar

METHOD

1. In a heated frying pan, dry fry (no oil) the allspice berries, peppercorns and cumin seeds briefly until fragrant. Grind to a powder using a pestle and mortar.
2. Use a blender to finely chop the spice powder, garlic, chilli, onion and annatto paste (or substitute) and blend until finely chopped and fully combined, then mix in the orange juice and vinegar. This is your marinade.
3. Put the pork into a non-metallic bowl, add the bay leaves and pour over the marinade. Cover, and leave in the fridge for at least an hour (but preferably overnight) to marinade.
4. Transfer the pork and marinade to the slow cooker and cook on Low for 8 hours until the meat is tender.
5. If you'd like the sauce a little thicker, then remove the lid and continue cooking until the sauce has reduced a little.
6. Make the pickled onions: Heat all the ingredients except the onions in a small pan until the sugar dissolves. Remove from the heat and stir in the onions. Set aside until the onions have softened – about an hour.
7. Take the bay leaves out of the slow cooker and throw away. Shred the pork into the sauce using two fords.

8. Serve with tortillas accompanied by the soured cream, avocado, coriander and the freshly made pickled onions.

SAUSAGES WITH BLACKBERRIES, BAY LEAVES AND JUNIPER

INGREDIENTS

- 2 tablespoons of olive oil
- 300g of small round shallots
- 4 streaky bacon rashers, roughly chopped
- 2 cloves garlic, finely sliced
- 8 pork sausages
- 1 tablespoon of plain flour
- 200ml of red wine
- 3 bay leaves
- 1 teaspoons of juniper berries, lightly crushed
- 2 tablespoons of blackberry jam or jelly
- 175g of blackberries (fresh or frozen)
- Optional: mashed potato to serve

METHOD

1. Preheat the slow cooker on a Low setting and spritz lightly with cooking oil.
2. Heat the olive oil in a pan and fry the bacon and whole shallots for 5 minutes until coloured, then add the garlic and cook for a further minute. Remove to a plate.
3. Use the same pan with more oil if needed to fry the sausages and cook for 5 minutes until lightly browned.
4. Add the flour to the pan and stir well, scraping as you do to collect all the flavour from the pan. Return the shallots and bacon and mix everything well.
5. Now add the red wine, bay leaves, juniper and 1 tablespoon of the blackberry jam or jelly and bring to the boil. Transfer everything to the slow cooker.
6. Cover and cook for 4 hours on High or 8 hours on Low.
7. Cook the blackberries in a small pan on a high heat with the rest of the blackberry jam and a splash of water until they are softening.
8. Spoon the cooked blackberries over the sausages and serve with mash.

HAM AND PEAS

INGREDIENTS

- 2.3kg of ham hocks (roughly 3 equal pieces)
- 2 fresh bay leaves
- 2 leeks, trimmed and finely sliced
- 1 stick of celery, trimmed and finely sliced
- 3 carrots, trimmed and finely sliced
- olive oil for frying
- 100g of pearl barley
- 1 litre of chicken stock (fresh or from stock cubes)
- 400g of frozen peas
- 1 heaped tablespoon of mint sauce
- Fresh curly parsley

METHOD

1. You will need to plan for this recipe. Start by soaking the ham hocks in a saucepan of cold water overnight.
2. Once soaked overnight, drain the water from the hocks, refill the saucepan with fresh cold water and bring to the boil. Discard the salty water, rinse the hocks, and repeat.
3. Start preheating the slow cooker on a Low setting and spritz generously with olive oil. Add the vegetables and bay leaves to the slow cooker and season well.
4. Add the chicken stock and drained ham hocks, followed by the pearl barley. Cover and cook for 4 hours on High or 8 hours on Low, stirring occasionally.
5. Now transfer the ham hocks to a clean board and trim away any fat/bones. Shred the meat with two forks and return it to the broth. Add the peas and cook for a further hour on Low.
6. Stir in the parsley, and the mint sauce before serving with bread and English mustard.

NUTRITION PER PORTION:

SERVES - 6-8 | CALORIES - 567KCAL | PROTEIN - 17G | CARBOHYDRATES - 85G | FAT - 3G

EASY MULLED PORK

INGREDIENTS

- 1.2kg pork leg joint
- 440ml of apple cider (1 can)
- 1 teaspoon of dried thyme
- 1 large onion - peeled and sliced
- 150ml of chicken stock (fresh or made from cubes)
- 3 garlic cloves, peeled and halved
- 200g of cranberry sauce

METHOD

1. Dissolve the stock cube in the boiling water, and make up to 150ml
2. Put all the ingredients in the slow cooker, with the pork on top, and pour the stock in.
3. Cook for 7 hours on a High setting, or 10 hours on Low.
4. If you want your sauce thicker, add some chicken gravy granules and stir in.
5. Serve in thick slices with mash and seasonal vegetables.

NUTRITION PER PORTION:

SERVES - 4 | CALORIES - 468KCAL | PROTEIN - 72G | CARBOHYDRATES - 23G | FAT - 7G

THAI PORK CURRY

INGREDIENTS

- 600g of diced pork
- 200ml of coconut milk
- 3 medium potatoes peeled and cut into 3cm chunks
- 100mls of beef stock (fresh or made from stock cubes)
- 1 tablespoon of Thai fish sauce
- 1 tablespoon of tamarind paste
- 1 tablespoon of white granulated sugar
- 2 tablespoons of smooth peanut butter
- 5g fresh, torn basil leaves
- Optional: ¼ small red chilli, in thin slices for garnish
- Optional: a few basil leaves, for a garnish

For the curry paste

- 1 onion, peeled and cut into ⅛ pieces
- 3cm piece of root ginger, peeled and thinly sliced
- 1 teaspoon of ground cumin
- ½ teaspoon of dried chilli flakes
- ½ teaspoon of ground cardamom
- 4 garlic cloves, peeled and left whole
- ½ teaspoon of ground cinnamon
- 1 teaspoons of ground coriander
- ½ teaspoon of ground cloves
- 2 lemongrass stalks, woody parts removed and finely chopped
- 3 tablespoons of water
- Cooking oil spray

METHOD

1. To make the curry paste: Heat some oil in a large pan and stir fry the onion, garlic and ginger for 5-10 minutes until it softens and chars a little around the edges. Transfer to a blender and set aside momentarily.
2. Using the same pan, reduce the heat and cook the chilli flakes, cumin, cardamom, coriander, cinnamon and cloves, stirring well for about 30 seconds until fragrant. Careful not to burn the spices and spoil them.
3. Add the toasted spices to the blender with the onions. Add the lemongrass and water, and blitz to form a coarse paste. Set it to one aside.
4. Heat oil in the same frying pan and this time add the pork. Fry for a few minutes to seal and brown all sides. Add the freshly made curry paste and continue to cook for a further 2–3 minutes, stirring well.
5. Transfer the mixture from the frying pan to the slow cooker, adding the coconut milk and potatoes, the beef stock, fish sauce, tamarind paste, sugar and peanut butter. Stir thoroughly to combine.
6. Cover the slow cooker with the lid and cook High setting for 5 hours, stirring halfway through if possible. If the sauce is too thick for you, add a little water to thin it down; but if it is too thin, remove the lid and cook uncovered for a short time to reduce further.
7. Stir in the torn basil leaves and serve with basmati rice, sprinkled with red chilli slices and a few fresh basil leaves on top.

NUTRITION PER PORTION:

SERVES - 4 | CALORIES - 384 KCAL | PROTEIN - 39G | CARBOHYDRATES - 29G | FAT - 12G

PORK AND APPLE MEATBALLS

INGREDIENTS

- 500g of pork mince
- 1 red apple, peeled, cored and grated
- 1 slice of toasted bread, as fine breadcrumbs

- 1 onion, peeled and grated
- 1 egg, beaten
- 2 garlic cloves, crushed
- 2 teaspoons of dried sage
- Seasoning to taste

- 2 tablespoons of oil
- 4 tablespoons of flour

For the sauce

- 2 garlic cloves, crushed
- 1 red pepper, diced
- 350g of tomato passata
- 4 tablespoons of tomato paste
- 1 onion, diced

- 400g can of chopped tomatoes
- 2 teaspoons of dried basil
- 100ml of chicken stock (fresh or from a stock cube)
- Seasoning to taste

- 1 teaspoon of sugar
- 2 tablespoons of flour

To Serve

- Fresh basil chopped

- Pappardelle pasta

METHOD

Meatballs

1. Put the apple, onion and crushed garlic into a mixing bowl with the breadcrumbs, sage, Seasoning to taste.
2. Add the pork mince to the mixing bowl and pour over half of the beaten egg. Use your clean hands to mix it all together thoroughly, and shape into balls approximately 4cm diameter (about 24 meatballs).
3. Put the flour in a separate bowl and roll each meatball in it so that they are evenly coated.
4. Heat some oil in a pan and flash fry the meatballs for about 2 minutes to ensure that they're browned and sealed.

Sauce

1. Add the onion, pepper and garlic to the slow cooker and sprinkle the flour over the vegetables, coating them evenly.
2. Stir in the tomato passata and chopped tomatoes, then the tomato paste, basil, salt, pepper and sugar.
3. Pour the chicken stock into the slow cooker and stir everything together thoroughly.
4. Add the meatballs into the pot and gently push them down so that they are submerged in the sauce.
5. Cover and cook on a High setting for 4 hours, or Low for 7.
6. Serve with cooked pappardelle pasta, sprinkled with chopped basil.

NUTRITIONAL INFORMATION PER SERVING (EXCLUDING PASTA):

SERVES - 6 | CALORIES - 401KCAL | PROTEIN - 19G | CARBOHYDRATES - 29G | FAT - 24G

CHRISTMAS HAM IN CRANBERRY JUICE

INGREDIENTS

- 2 kg gammon joint
- 1.5 litres of cranberry juice
- 1 carrot, roughly chopped

- 3 bay leaves
- 1 onion, peeled and roughly chopped

- 1 tablespoon of mixed spice

For the Gammon Glaze

- 20 cloves
- 1 orange, sliced
- 1 tablespoon of wholegrain mustard

- 3 tablespoons of muscovado sugar
- 3 tablespoons of orange marmalade

- 1 teaspoon of cider vinegar

METHOD

1. Slow Cooking
2. Preheat the slow cooker on a Low setting and spritz with cooking oil.
3. Put the onion, carrot, bay leaves, and mixed spice into the slow cooker. Put the gammon on top and pour over the cranberry juice.
4. Cover and cook on a Low setting for 7 hours or 3.5 hours on High.

Gammon Glaze

1. Heat your oven to 190C/gas mark 5.
2. Mix the mustard, sugar, marmalade and cider vinegar in a jug, and stir until the sugar is dissolved. (Speed it up by warming the mixture gently in the microwave for 5-10 seconds.
3. Remove the excess fat from the gammon and score a diamond pattern into the remaining fat with a sharp knife. Press a clove into each corner of the lattice.
4. Brush the gammon all over in half of the glaze, then add sliced orange on top (use cloves to hold the orange slices in place!)
5. Bake in the oven for 10 minutes, remove to add the remaining half of the glaze then bake for a final 10 minutes.
6. Serve with festive savoury treats.

NUTRITION PER PORTION:

SERVES - 8 | CALORIES - 664KCAL | PROTEIN - 54G | CARBOHYDRATES - 14G | FAT - 42G

FISH

MEDITERRANEAN COD

INGREDIENTS

- 2 garlic cloves, sliced
- 2 teaspoons of olive oil
- 2 red peppers, sliced
- 1 teaspoon of sherry vinegar
- 1 x 400g can of chopped tomatoes
- 15g of fresh basil, chopped, plus extra to serve
- 2 teaspoons of capers, rinsed and drained
- 50g of pitted green olives, roughly chopped
- 250g of skinless, boneless cod fillet, cut into 5cm pieces
- 50g of ciabatta, torn into pieces

METHOD

1. Heat 1 teaspoon of oil in a pan and fry the peppers for about 10 minutes until they soften. Add the garlic and fry for a minute, then add the chopped tomatoes. sherry vinegar and basil. Bring to a bubble and simmer for a minute, then transfer to the slow cooker.
2. Cover and cook on Low for 3 hours until the sauce thickens.
3. Remove and discard the basil sprigs.
4. Now, stir in the capers and olives. Tuck the cod into the sauce, cover and cook on a Low setting for 30 minutes until the cod is cooked and flaky.
5. Meanwhile, use a blender to whizz the bread and remaining basil together and in the same pan as previously, flash fry in the remaining teaspoon of oil for about 5 minutes until toasted. Season to taste.
6. Serve the fish with the sauce and scatter the toasted herby breadcrumbs over the top

   COOK'S TIP - Prepare the sauce 3 days in advance and chill before using.

NUTRITION PER PORTION:
SERVES - 2 | CALORIES - 315KCAL | PROTEIN - 28G | CARBOHYDRATES - 26G | FAT - 10G

CREOLE PRAWN AND CHICKEN GUMBO

INGREDIENTS

For the gumbo

- 30g of plain flour
- 30g of unsalted butter
- 100g of chorizo, diced
- 4 garlic cloves, crushed
- 1 onion, finely diced
- 2 sticks celery, diced
- 1 green pepper, diced
- 1 teaspoon of ground cumin
- 2 bay leaves
- 1 teaspoon of smoked paprika
- 100ml of white wine (or 100ml of extra stock if you prefer)
- 500g of passata
- 200ml of chicken stock (fresh or from stock cubes)
- 4 chicken thighs, no skin or bones
- 200g of raw peeled prawns

To serve

- 3 tablespoons of flat-leaf parsley, finely chopped
- 5 spring onions, shredded
- 4 slices of sourdough bread
- 200g of cooked long-grain white rice
- 60ml of soured cream, sprinkled with smoked paprika

METHOD

1. Melt the butter in a pan on a low heat. Gradually sprinkle in the flour, stirring continuously until it thickens and makes a paste (known as a roux). Cook and continue to stir for about 10-15 minutes until it browns.
2. Add the roux into the slow cooker. Stir in the rest of the ingredients for the gumbo, except the prawns.
3. Cover the slow cooker with the lid and cook on a Low setting for 6 hours.
4. Add the prawns to the mixture, season to taste and, leaving the slow cooker lid ajar, cook for a further 30 minutes.
5. Serve the gumbo with rice, chunks of sourdough bread and dollops of cream, garnished with parsley and spring onions.

NUTRITIONAL INFORMATION PER SERVING (WITHOUT GARNISHES):

SERVES - 6 | CALORIES - 379KCAL | PROTEIN - 26G | CARBOHYDRATES - 14G | FAT - 22G

SALMON AND LENTIL CURRY

INGREDIENTS

- 150g of red lentils, rinsed until water runs clear
- 400ml of coconut milk
- 2 tablespoons of garam masala
- 2 tablespoons of tomato purée

- 6 cardamom pods
- 2 garlic cloves, sliced
- 3cm piece of fresh ginger, grated
- 2 red chillies, finely sliced
- 180g of cherry tomatoes, halved

- 75ml of water
- 3 salmon fillets, skin removed and cut into chunks
- 2 tablespoons of chopped parsley
- Juice of 1 lemon

To serve

- 450g of long grain rice
- Extra parsley to serve
- Lemon wedges to serve

METHOD

1. Preheat the slow cooker on a Low setting and spritz lightly with cooking oil.
2. Add all the ingredients to the slow cooker except the salmon, lemon and parsley. Mix thoroughly.
3. Cover and cook on a High setting for 3 hours.
4. Open the slow cooker, stir in the salmon chunks, cover and cook for a further 1 hour on High.
5. Cook the rice following the pack instructions.
6. Stir the lemon juice and parsley into the curry.
7. Serve the sauce over the cooked rice sprinkled with extra parsley and lemon wedges.

NUTRITION PER PORTION:

SERVES - 6 | CALORIES - 693KCAL | PROTEIN - 32G | CARBOHYDRATES - 84G | FAT - 26G

PRAWN, CHICKEN AND CHORIZO PAELLA

INGREDIENTS

- 2 tablespoons of olive oil
- 4 chicken thighs, no skin or bone, thickly sliced
- 240g chorizo ring, sliced
- 1 onion, sliced
- 1 tablespoon of sweet smoked paprika
- 2 garlic cloves, crushed
- Optional: pinch of saffron
- 150ml of white wine
- 300g of paella rice
- 400g can of chopped tomatoes
- 400ml of chicken stock
- 150g of frozen peas
- 200g fresh or frozen raw king prawns, peeled
- Fresh parsley, finely chopped
- Optional: lemon wedges and crusty bread

METHOD

1. Preheat the slow cooker on a Low setting and spritz lightly with cooking oil.
2. Heat the oil in a pan and fry the chicken and chorizo together for about 7-10 minutes until golden. Transfer to the slow cooker using tongs.
3. Use the same pan to fry the onion first for 5-7 minutes until just softened, and then the garlic, paprika and saffron for 2 minutes.
4. Pour in the wine, bring to a bubble, then simmer until reduced by half. Transfer to the slow cooker with the rice, tomatoes and stock. Season to taste.
5. Cover and cook for 1½ hours on a Low setting.
6. Finally, open the slow cooker and add the peas and prawns. Recover and cook for 30 minutes more.
7. Serve with crusty bread and lemon wedges, with a scattering of parsley.

NUTRITION PER PORTION:
SERVES - 6 | CALORIES - 517KCAL | PROTEIN - 31G | CARBOHYDRATES - 46G | FAT - 21G

SMOKED HADDOCK CHOWDER

INGREDIENTS

- A generous 20g of butter
- 300g of frozen smoked haddock fillets, broken into pieces
- 2 rashers of streaky, pre-grilled bacon, chopped
- 1 onion, peeled, finely chopped
- 350g of potato (about 2 medium), diced
- 140g of frozen sweetcorn
- 500ml of milk
- Optional: cornflour mixed with a little milk from the chowder to form a paste/roux
- Optional: chopped parsley to serve

METHOD

1. Preheat the slow cooker on a Low setting, spritz lightly with oil, then add the butter to melt in the bottom.
2. Add the fish pieces and bacon pieces to the slow cooker, followed by the onion and sweetcorn.
3. Pour over the milk and stir in the diced potatoes.
4. Cover and cook on High for about 4 hours or Low for about 8 hours.
5. If you like the sauce a little thicker, then blend a teaspoon of cornflour with a spoonful of milk/sauce from the slow cooker, blend to a smooth paste and stir into the chowder mixture. Cover and cook for another 1 hour.
6. Serve in bowls, scattered with chopped parsley, with a side of fresh crusty wedges of bread.

NUTRITION PER PORTION:
SERVES - 2 | CALORIES - 550KCAL | PROTEIN - 47G | CARBOHYDRATES - 59G | FAT - 16G

PRAWN, PEA, AND TOMATO CURRY

INGREDIENTS

- 2 onions, roughly chopped
- 1 tablespoon of vegetable oil
- 3 tablespoons of masala curry paste
- 5 ripe tomatoes, roughly chopped plus 1 tomato cut into 8 wedges
- 1-inch of fresh root ginger, finely chopped
- 6 garlic cloves, roughly chopped
- 400g of raw, shelled king prawns
- 250g of frozen peas
- Optional: chopped coriander
- Optional: basmati rice or chapatis, to serve

METHOD

1. Heat the oil in a frying pan and fry the onions for 5-7 minutes until softened and beginning to brown. Set to one side.
2. In a blender, combine the oil, ginger, garlic, curry paste and all but 8 tomato wedges to a paste and spoon into the slow cooker. Add the cooked onions.
3. Cover and cook on High for 3 hours.
4. Add the 8 tomato wedges, frozen peas, and prawns to the slow cooker. Cover and cook for another 1 hour until the prawns are cooked through.
5. Serve with rice or chapatis, scattered with chopped coriander.

NUTRITION PER PORTION:
SERVES - 4 | CALORIES - 236KCAL | PROTEIN - 24G | CARBOHYDRATES - 18G | FAT - 0G

HEALTHY FISH STEW

INGREDIENTS

- 2 celery stalks, finely chopped
- 1 tablespoon of olive oil
- 2 onions peeled and sliced
- Fresh parsley, chopped
- 200g of roasted red pepper, seeds removed, sliced thickly
- 400g can of chopped tomato with garlic
- 2-3 teaspoons of paprika
- 400g white fish fillets in large chunks
- Optional: A few fresh mussels

METHOD

1. Heat the oil in a pan, and gently fry the onions, celery and a bit of salt for about 10 minutes until they have softened.
2. Use a blender to mix the parsley stalks and half the parsley leaves, oil and seasoning.
3. Mix into the pan with the onions, celery, paprika, peppers and tomatoes. Stir to combine then put into the slow cooker.
4. Cover and cook on a Low setting for 8-10 hours.
5. Next, nestle the (optional) mussels into the sauce in the slow cooker, and spread the fish pieces evenly over the top.
6. Re-cover and cook on High for 30 minutes-1 hour.
7. Dispose of any unopened mussels.
8. Stir the stew thoroughly and serve with crusty bread.

NUTRITION PER PORTION:
SERVES - 4 | CALORIES - 200KCAL | PROTEIN - 21G | CARBOHYDRATES - 11G | FAT - 7G

PRAWN AND FENNEL CURRY

INGREDIENTS

- 1 large fennel bulb, thinly sliced, reserving any fronds
- 1 shallot, thinly sliced
- 2 tablespoons of olive oil
- 300g of risotto rice
- 1 garlic clove, crushed
- 150ml of white wine (or extra stock if preferred)
- 1 litre of vegetable stock (fresh or from stock cubes)
- 300g of raw peeled king prawns
- 2 preserved lemons, roughly chopped (seeds discarded)
- 40g of Pecorino cheese, grated

METHOD

1. Heat the oil in a large pan and fry the fennel for 5 minutes until it begins to soften. Stir in the shallot and fry for 5-8 minutes, until cooked through.
2. Next, add the garlic and risotto rice to the pan and fry for a couple of minutes, then add the wine.
3. Bring the mixture to the boil and leave bubbling for 30 seconds before transferring everything in the pan to the slow cooker.
4. Stir in the stock and season to taste.
5. Cover and cook on a High setting for 1 hour and 45 minutes.
6. At the end of the first cooking cycle, add in the lemons and prawns, recover the slow cooker, and cook for another 10-15 minutes until the prawns are cooked.
7. Stir Pecorino cheese through the curry mixture and adjust the seasoning to taste. If the curry sauce is a bit thick, stir in extra stock to thin.
8. Serve over rice, garnished with fennel fronds with a side of warm naan.

NUTRITION PER PORTION:
SERVES - 4 | CALORIES - 502KCAL | PROTEIN - 23G | CARBOHYDRATES - 67G | FAT - 12G

EASY SLOW-COOKER SALMON FILLETS

INGREDIENTS

- 4 salmon fillets of even weight
- 1 unwaxed lemon, sliced
- Seasoning to taste (dried herbs, spices to suit you)
- Optional: 250ml of water (stock, cider, wine, or even a blended mix)

METHOD

1. Turn the slow cooker onto a Low setting and spritz lightly with cooking oil.
2. Optional: covering the base of your slow cooker with baking paper will make it easier to lift the salmon out once it's cooked.
3. Lay the salmon fillets on top of the paper, side by side.
4. Lay sliced lemons equally across each salmon and add your seasoning of choice.
5. Gently pour your liquid of choice down the side of the salmon so as not to wash the seasonings away.
6. Cover and cook on a Low setting for 2 hours.
7. Lift the salmon carefully from the slow cooker using the baking paper.
8. Serve hot or cold with your choice of foods.

NUTRITIONAL INFORMATION PER SERVING (BASED ON STOCK):
SERVES - 4 | CALORIES - 241KCAL | PROTEIN - 35G | CARBOHYDRATES - 1G | FAT - 11G

GOAN-STYLE FISH CURRY

INGREDIENTS

- 2 garlic cloves, finely chopped
- oil for frying
- 1 onion, diced
- ½ teaspoon of dried chilli flakes
- 1 teaspoon of cumin
- 1 teaspoon of turmeric
- 1 teaspoon of coriander

- 1 tablespoon of finely grated ginger
- 1 tablespoon of curry leaves
- 2 tomatoes, roughly chopped
- 1 tablespoon of tamarind paste
- 400g tin of coconut milk
- 100ml of water

- 150g of French beans, topped and tailed
- 300g of diced pollock
- 200g of cooked basmati rice, boiled with 4 cardamom pods and 1 star anise

METHOD

1. Heat 2 tablespoons of oil in a pan and fry the onion for about 8 minutes, until softened. Next add the garlic, chilli flakes, ginger, spices, tomatoes and tamarind and fry for a further 2 minutes, stirring continuously to avoid the spices sticking or burning.
2. Pour in the coconut milk and 100ml of water. Bring to a boil, season to taste and simmer for 1 minute, then transfer to the slow cooker.
3. Next, season the fish pieces and add them to the slow cooker with the French beans.
4. Cover and cook on a Low setting for 8 hours.
5. Before serving your rice, pick out the cardamom pods and star anise.
6. Adjust seasoning as required and serve your curry on a bed of fluffy rice, garnished with chopped coriander.

NUTRITION PER PORTION:

SERVES - 4 | CALORIES - 572KCAL | PROTEIN - 22G | CARBOHYDRATES - 57G | FAT - 30G

SPANISH FISH STEW

INGREDIENTS

- 1 red pepper, deseeded and sliced
- 1 fennel bulb, thinly sliced
- 1 garlic clove, finely chopped
- oil for frying
- 1 bay leaf
- A pinch of saffron
- 1 teaspoon of smoked paprika
- 1 tablespoon of tomato purée

- 100ml of white wine (or stock if you prefer)
- 400g tin of chopped tomatoes
- 150ml of vegetable or fish stock
- Zest and juice of 1 lemon
- small bunch of parsley, finely chopped
- 300g of diced white fish

METHOD

1. Heat 2 tablespoons of oil in a large saucepan. Fry the fennel and pepper for 10 minutes until starting to soften.
2. Next, add the garlic, saffron, bay leaf, paprika and tomato purée to the same pan, and cook for 1 minute before adding the wine. Bring to the boil and allow to simmer for a couple of minutes until it reduces, then transfer to the slow cooker.
3. Add the chopped tomatoes and vegetable stock, and stir thoroughly, then stir in the diced white fish, Season to taste.

4. Cover and cook on a Low setting for 8 hours.
5. Divide the stew between 2 bowls and garnish with the parsley and zest. Serve with lemon wedges for squeezing.

NUTRITION PER PORTION:
SERVES - 2 | CALORIES - 318KCAL | PROTEIN - 37G | CARBOHYDRATES - 27G | FAT - 3G

FISH CURRY WITH GREEN BEANS AND NEW POTATOES

INGREDIENTS

- oil for frying
- 1 onion, peeled and finely diced
- 25g piece of fresh ginger, peeled and finely grated
- 1 fresh chilli, deseeded and finely sliced
- 1 tablespoons tomato purée
- 50g of tikka spice paste (adjust to taste)
- 1 garlic clove, peeled and finely chopped
- 300ml of stock (fresh or made from stock cubes)
- 480g tomatoes, cut in half
- 500g new potatoes, peel-on, washed and sliced into 2-3cm slices
- Handful of green beans, washed, trimmed and cut into 2cm pieces
- 2 ling fish fillets, each cut into 4 chunks (use Whiting or Barramundi as an alternative)
- A handful of coriander, roughly chopped
- 1 lemon
- Seasoning to taste

METHOD

1. Heat 2 tablespoons of oil in a pan. Add the onion sauté for about 10 minutes until it softens.
2. Add the ginger, garlic and chilli, and fry for 1 minute, then stir in the tomato purée and tikka spice paste.
3. Add the stock, bring to the boil stirring continuously, then transfer to the slow cooker and add the tomatoes and potatoes.
4. Cover and cook on a Low setting for 6 hours.
5. Open up the lid of the slow cooker and add the green beans, then sit the fish on top of the curry.
6. Cover again and cook on Low for a further 2 hours.
7. Lift the fish carefully out of the slow cooker and set aside for a moment.
8. Season the curry sauce to taste, stir in the coriander and add the lemon juice.
9. Divide the curry sauce between two bowls with the tomatoes and potatoes shared evenly. Place the fish carefully on the top of the bowls of curry sauce and serve scattered with chopped coriander and a wedge of lemon.

NUTRITION PER PORTION:
SERVES - 2 | CALORIES - 489KCAL | PROTEIN - 36G | CARBOHYDRATES - 64G | FAT - 11G

MEAT-FREE

PANEER CHILLI CON CARNE

INGREDIENTS

- 140g of paneer, cut into small chunks
- 1 teaspoon of rapeseed oil
- 1 tablespoon of smoked paprika
- 2-3 celery sticks, sliced
- 4 garlic cloves, peeled and sliced
- 2 mixed peppers, deseeded and diced
- 1 tablespoon of ground cumin
- 1/2 teaspoon of chilli flakes (optional)
- 2 x 400g cans of red kidney beans, undrained
- 2 x 400g cans of plum tomatoes
- 2 teaspoons of dried oregano
- 2 teaspoons of vegetable bouillon powder
- 120g of quinoa or rice
- 15g coriander, chopped, plus extra to serve

METHOD

1. Toss the paneer in a shallow bowl with 1/2 teaspoon of the paprika. Heat the oil in a large pan and fry the paneer, turning until golden. Set to one side.
2. Use the same pan to fry the peppers, garlic and celery, cumin, remaining paprika and chilli flakes until they soften and add to the slow cooker.
3. Stir in the tomatoes and beans along with their juice, the bouillon powder and oregano. The paneer should be kept to one side still.
4. Cover and cook for 5-6 hours on Low, stirring occasionally.
5. Meanwhile, cook the quinoa following pack instructions, drain and set aside for 10 minutes.
6. Now stir the coriander and saved paneer into the slow cooker mixture, and sprinkle over extra coriander just before serving.
7. Serve with rice or quinoa.

NUTRITION PER PORTION:

SERVES - 4 | CALORIES - 446KCAL | PROTEIN - 26G | CARBOHYDRATES - 47G | FAT - 13G

SPICY ROOT AND LENTIL CASSEROLE

INGREDIENTS

- 3 garlic cloves, crushed
- 2 tablespoons of olive oil
- 500g of parsnips, peeled and cut into 3cm slices
- 3 carrots, peeled and cut into 3cm slices
- 1 onion, finely chopped
- 1 tablespoon of smoked paprika
- 2 tablespoon of mild curry powder
- 150g of red lentils, rinsed
- 600ml of hot vegetable stock (fresh or from stock cubes)
- lemon juice, to serve
- 2 bay leaves

METHOD

1. Preheat the slow cooker on Low and spritz gently with cooking oil.
2. Heat the oil in a pan and cook the onion for 10 minutes until soft and transparent. Add the carrots and parsnips and cook for a further 8-10 minutes more until the vegetables are just turning golden. Stir in the garlic and spices, and fry for another 4-5 minutes until fragrant. Add a splash of water if needed.

3. Transfer the mixture into the slow cooker and stir through the lentils, vegetables stock, bay and seasoning.
4. Put the lid on and cook on Low for 5-6 hours.
5. Finally, adjust the seasoning to taste, stir in the lemon juice to taste and serve with bread, rice, or potatoes as preferred.

NUTRITION PER PORTION:
SERVES - 4 | CALORIES - 333KCAL | PROTEIN - 13G | CARBOHYDRATES - 44G | FAT - 9G

VEGETABLE LASAGNE
• •

INGREDIENTS

- 1 tablespoon of rapeseed oil
- 2 garlic cloves, peeled and chopped
- 2 tablespoons of tomato purée
- 2 mixed peppers, deseeded and roughly sliced
- 2 onions, sliced
- 400g can of chopped tomatoes
- 2 large courgettes, diced
- 2 teaspoons of vegetable bouillon
- 15g of fresh basil, chopped plus a few extra leaves
- 1 aubergine, sliced cut into long slices
- 6 lasagne pasta sheets
- 125g of buffalo mozzarella, torn roughly into pieces

METHOD

1. Heat 1 tablespoon of oil in a large pan and fry the onion and garlic for about 5 minutes until softened.
2. Add the diced courgettes, peppers, chopped tomatoes, tomato purée, vegetable bouillon and chopped basil.
3. Stir well, cover and simmer for 5 minutes.
4. Put half the slices of aubergine in the base of the slow cooker, then the sheets of lasagne, followed by the ratatouille mixture. Repeat until you have no more mixture left.
5. Cover and cook on High for 3 hours, then turn off the slow cooker.
6. Scatter the mozzarella over the vegetables, close the slow cooker and leave for 10 minutes for the cheese to melt.
7. Top with fresh basil and rocket leaves.

NUTRITION PER PORTION:
SERVES - 4 | CALORIES - 325KCAL | PROTEIN - 15G | CARBOHYDRATES - 36G | FAT - 11G

SWEET POTATO AND RED LENTIL CURRY
• •

INGREDIENTS

- 800g of sweet potatoes, peeled and chopped
- 2 garlic cloves, crushed
- 300g of dried red lentils, rinsed
- 1 tablespoon of fresh root ginger, grated
- 1 onion, chopped
- 4 tablespoons of curry paste* - see NOTE below
- 1 teaspoon of ground cumin
- 1 teaspoon of ground turmeric
- 4 tablespoon of tomato puree
- 1 x 400g tin of coconut milk
- 800ml of vegetable stock (fresh or from stock cubes)
- Optional: a handful of baby spinach leaves
- Seasoning to taste

METHOD

1. Preheat the slow cooker on a Low setting and spritz lightly with cooking oil.
2. Add all the ingredients except the spinach to the slow cooker. Season to taste.
3. Cover and cook on Low for 7 hours, or High for 3 to 4 hours.

4. About 20 minutes before the end of the cooking time, add the spinach leaves and stir in.
5. Serve with naan bread, rice or quinoa.

   *NOTE: most curry pastes complement this vegetable dish. Quantities of curry paste can be adapted according to taste.**

NUTRITION PER PORTION:

SERVES - 4 | CALORIES - 521KCAL | PROTEIN - 15G | CARBOHYDRATES - 71G | FAT - 22G

STUFFED PEPPERS

INGREDIENTS

- 4 - 6 whole mixed peppers, trimmed with seeds removed
- 1 onion, finely sliced
- 1 teaspoon of ground cumin
- 1 teaspoon of chilli powder
- 1 teaspoon of ground coriander
- 2 garlic cloves, crushed
- 1 x 400g tin of red kidney beans or black beans, drained
- 1 x 400g tin of chopped tomatoes
- 200g of uncooked quinoa, or cooked brown rice
- 400ml water/stock/passata (depending on preference)

METHOD

1. Preheat the slow cooker on a Low setting and spritz lightly with cooking oil.
2. Clean and prepare the peppers, keeping them whole and intact ready for stuffing.
3. In a container, mix together the rest of the ingredients.
4. Scoop the mixture into the peppers.
5. Add a little tablespoon of water into the base of the slow cooker.
6. Next, position the peppers in the slow cooker in an upright position.
7. Cover and cook on a Low setting for 4 to 5 hours or High for 3 hours.
8. Serve scattered with fresh chopped coriander, a dollop of sour cream, or melted cheese.

NUTRITION PER PORTION:

SERVES - 6 | CALORIES - 250KCAL | PROTEIN - 13G | CARBOHYDRATES - 47G | FAT - 2G

VEGETABLE TAGINE

INGREDIENTS

- 1 red onion, cut into 2cm chunks
- 2 courgettes, trimmed and cut into 3cm chunks
- 1 aubergine, trimmed and cut into 3cm chunks
- 2 garlic cloves, crushed
- 2 tablespoons of olive oil
- 500g of sweet potatoes, peeled and cut into 3cm chunks
- 4 tablespoons of harissa paste
- 1 tablespoon of ground cumin
- 1 tablespoon of ground coriander
- 3 tablespoons of ras el hanout
- 400g tin of chickpeas, rinsed through
- 6 salad tomatoes, cut into wedges
- 75g of dried apricots, roughly chopped
- 3 tablespoons of cornflour
- 900ml of vegetable stock (fresh or made from stock cubes)
- 500g of passata
- Optional: couscous
- Optional: chopped pistachios
- 30g of fresh coriander, chopped

METHOD

1. Preheat the slow cooker on a Low setting and spritz lightly with cooking oil.
2. Add the sweet potatoes, aubergine, onion and courgettes to the slow cooker.

3. Next mix in the garlic, spices, oil and harissa. Toss in the chickpeas and tomatoes with the apricots and mix everything together thoroughly.
4. In a jug, mix a smooth paste with the cornflour and 3 tablespoons of water and set aside.
5. Now pour over the stock, passata and apricots, and stir in the cornflour paste.
6. Cover the slow cooker and cook on a High setting for 4 hours, stirring once during cooking if you can.
7. Serve with couscous and nuts with a garnish of coriander over the top.

NUTRITION PER PORTION:

SERVES - 6 | CALORIES - 324KCAL | PROTEIN - 9G | CARBOHYDRATES - 49G | FAT - 9G

CHICKPEA CURRY

INGREDIENTS

- 1 onion, chopped
- 3 garlic cloves, crushed
- 2 tablespoons of curry powder (or to taste)
- 2 sweet peppers, deseeded and sliced
- 2 x 400g chopped tomatoes
- 2 x 400g chickpeas, rinsed through
- 2 large potatoes, peeled and diced
- Seasoning to taste.

METHOD

1. Preheat the slow cooker on a Low setting and spritz lightly with cooking oil.
2. Combine all the ingredients in the slow cooker. Stir thoroughly.
3. Cover and cook on a Low setting for 6 to 8 hours.
4. Adjust seasoning to taste and serve on a bed of rice with a side of green salad and warm naan.
5. Optional: the sweet potatoes can be replaced with butternut squash if preferred.

NUTRITION PER PORTION:

SERVES - 4 | CALORIES - 544KCAL | PROTEIN - 25G | CARBOHYDRATES - 103G | FAT - 6G

PLANTAIN, SPINACH AND COCONUT CURRY

INGREDIENTS

- Spray cooking oil
- 1 onion, diced
- 3cm piece ginger, peeled and finely chopped
- 2 garlic cloves, finely chopped
- 1 teaspoon of ground allspice
- 1 scotch bonnet, seeds removed and chopped
- 400ml can of coconut milk
- 4 just-ripe plantains, peeled and sliced into 1cm rounds
- 380g of black beans, rinsed through
- 2 mixed peppers, deseeded and sliced
- 1 tablespoon of chopped thyme leaves
- 260g of fresh spinach
- 14g coriander, roughly chopped, to serve

METHOD

1. Preheat the slow cooker on a Low setting and spritz lightly with cooking oil.
2. Heat some oil in a pan and fry the onion for 5 minutes until softened. Add the scotch bonnet, garlic, allspice and ginger and stir fry for 1-2 minutes, until fragrant. Add the coconut milk and bring gently to the boil. Simmer for a couple of minutes, then transfer to the slow cooker.

3. Add some oil to the same pan and fry the plantain slices on each side for a minute until brown. Transfer the plantain to the slow cooker. Mix in the tin of black beans, peppers, the chopped thyme and a little bit of water. Stir thoroughly with the coconut milk mixture.
4. Cover and cook on a High setting for 1 hour. Add the spinach – it will seem a lot, but it will soon wilt and be incorporated into the curry - and cook for a further 1 hour.
5. Serve with rice sprinkled with coriander.

NUTRITION PER PORTION:

SERVES - 4 | CALORIES - 431KCAL | PROTEIN - 11G | CARBOHYDRATES - 70G | FAT - 9G

ITALIAN CAPONATA

INGREDIENTS

- 2 large aubergines, chopped into small pieces
- 1 red onion, finely sliced
- 1 tablespoon of oil

- 5 large vine tomatoes, roughly chopped
- 2 sticks of celery, finely sliced
- 1 tablespoon of brown sugar

- 2 tablespoons of sundried tomato paste
- 3 tablespoons of red wine vinegar
- 1 tablespoon of capers
- 75g of raisins

To serve

- 25g of toasted pine nuts
- 50g of green olives

- Fresh basil leaves

- ½ loaf of sourdough bread slices, toasted

METHOD

1. Preheat the slow cooker on a Low setting and spritz lightly with cooking oil.
2. Heat the oil in a large pan and fry the aubergines for 3-4 minutes, until lightly browned on both sides.
3. Add to the slow cooker with the rest of the ingredients.
4. Cover and cook on High for 2.5 hours.
5. Stir in the pine nuts and olives. Serve on slices of toasted sourdough, garnished with fresh basil.

NUTRITION PER PORTION:

SERVES - 4 | CALORIES - 261KCAL | PROTEIN - 5G | CARBOHYDRATES - 29G | FAT - 12G

PEARL BARLEY RISOTTO WITH SQUASH AND BLUE CHEESE

INGREDIENTS

- 2 tablespoons of olive oil
- 50g of butter plus a little extra
- 3 celery sticks, finely diced
- 3 echalion shallots, chopped
- 4 garlic cloves, grated
- 300g of dried pearl barley

- 200ml of white wine
- 1.2 litres of vegetable stock (fresh or from stock cubes)
- 1 bay leaf
- 2 sprigs of rosemary

- ½ medium butternut squash, peeled and diced
- 75g of Italian-style hard cheese, finely grated
- 2 tablespoons of double cream
- 150g of blue cheese, crumbled

Optional: For the hazelnut topping

- 25g of blanched hazelnuts, roughly chopped
- 40g of breadcrumbs
- Fresh rosemary leaves, chopped

- Zest of 1 lemon
- 2 tablespoons of olive oil
- 25g of Italian-style hard cheese, finely grated

METHOD

1. Preheat the slow cooker on a Low setting and spritz lightly with cooking oil.
2. Heat half each of the oil and butter in a large pan and cook the shallots and celery for 10 minutes until softened.
3. Stir in the garlic and cook for a further minute. Increase the heat and add the pearl barley, stirring for 1 minute.
4. Next, pour in the white wine, bring to the boil and simmer for a couple of minutes until reduced.
5. Transfer to the slow cooker, and stir in the hot stock, bay leaf and rosemary sprigs. Mix together thoroughly.
6. Cover the slow cooker with the lid and cook on Low for 1 hour.
7. Use the same pan to heat the remaining oil and butter. Fry the squash for 6-8 minutes, turning occasionally until golden brown on all sides. Transfer to a plate lined with kitchen paper to absorb the oil and set aside.
8. Stir in the squash and cook for a further 1 hour on Low then turn off the slow cooker. Stir in the grated hard cheese and cream, season well and leave to sit for 5-10 minutes.
9. Make the hazelnut topping: Heat a clean frying pan until hot, add the hazelnuts and cook over a low heat until just toasted. Add the olive oil, breadcrumbs and rosemary and stir-fry until turning golden. Mix in the cheese and lemon zest; season and cook for a further 3-4 minutes, stirring occasionally until crisp and fragrant.
10. Serve the risotto in bowls, topped with the crumbled blue cheese and a sprinkling of nutty hazelnut topping.

NUTRITION PER PORTION:
SERVES - 4 | CALORIES - 261KCAL | PROTEIN - 20G | CARBOHYDRATES - 52G | FAT - 35G

HERBY DUMPLINGS IN JACKFRUIT AND MUSHROOM STEW

INGREDIENTS

- 10g of dried porcini mushrooms
- 1½ tablespoons of sunflower oil
- 6 shallots, peeled and halved
- 1 large onion, thickly sliced
- 2 garlic cloves, crushed

- 200g of mini portobello mushrooms halved
- 1 tablespoon of chopped//or 1 teaspoon of dried thyme
- 4 tablespoons of plain flour
- ½ teaspoon of smoked paprika

- 300ml of vegetable stock (fresh or from stock cubes)
- 1 teaspoon of Marmite
- Optional: ½ tablespoon of relish
- 1 x 560g tin of jackfruit, drained

For the dumplings

- 60g of vegetable suet

- 150g of self-raising flour

- 3 tablespoons of chopped parsley

METHOD

1. Cover the porcini mushrooms with 400ml of boiling water, cover and leave to soak and soften.
2. Heat the oil in a pan and fry the shallots, cut-side down, until browned.
3. Add the leeks and portobello mushrooms season to taste and fry for 2-3 minutes, stirring continuously.
4. Stir in the garlic and thyme and flash fry until fragrant, then add the flour and smoked paprika and cook for another minute.
5. Drain the porcini mushrooms saving the water in a jug and setting it to one side. Roughly chop the porcini and add to the pan, followed by the porcini liquid and the stock. Stir in the Marmite and (optional) relish.
6. Transfer to a slow cooker, add the drained jackfruit. Cover and cook for 2 ½ hours on Low or 1 ½ hours on High.
7. To make the dumplings: sieve the flour into a container and season. Add the suet then rub with the flour between your fingers until the mixture resembles breadcrumbs. Stir in the parsley.
8. Add 2-3 tablespoons of cold water and use a fork to bring the mixture together into a wet dough. With your hands, shape into 12 dumplings.

9. Add the dumplings to the slow cooker, then replace the lid and cook on High for 30-45 minutes or until the dumplings are fluffy and puffed up.
10. Ladle the stew and dumplings into bowls to serve.

NUTRITION PER PORTION:
SERVES - 4-6 | CALORIES - 380KCAL | PROTEIN - 10G | CARBOHYDRATES - 50G | FAT - 14G

MEXICAN CORN CHOWDER

INGREDIENTS

- 2 onions, peeled and chopped
- 400g of frozen sweetcorn
- 2 mixed peppers, seeds removed and chopped
- 2 tablespoons of Mexican style jalapeños

- 1 potato, peeled and diced
- 290g can of borlotti beans, rinsed through
- 1 stalk of celery, chopped
- 1 teaspoon of ground cumin
- 1 tablespoon of chipotle paste

- 1 garlic clove, crushed
- 1 litres of vegetable stock (fresh or made from stock cubes)
- 100ml of single cream

To serve

- 1 large avocado, peeled and diced into small cubes

- 3 spring onions, finely sliced
- 1 jalapeño chilli, finely sliced

- 10g of coriander, finely chopped

METHOD
1. Heat the slow cooker on High and spritz lightly with cooking oil.
2. Add all the ingredients except the cream to the slow cooker and stir well to combine. If the stock doesn't quite cover the vegetables, then top up with a little water.
3. Cover and cook for 8 hours on Low or 4 hours on High.
4. Roughly 10 minutes before serving, give the chowder a good stir to combine everything and to break up the potato into smaller chunks (but don't mush it).
5. Stir in the single cream then reheat on a Low setting for a final 10 minutes to make sure the meal is hot.
6. Serve in bowls. Top with jalapeño chilli, spring onions, avocado, and coriander.

NUTRITION PER PORTION:
SERVES - 6 | CALORIES - 188KCAL | PROTEIN - 7G | CARBOHYDRATES - 29G | FAT - 6G

AUBERGINE LASAGNE - NO PASTA!

INGREDIENTS

- 70g of frozen spinach, thawed
- 2 aubergines, stalks removed, cut lengthways into 1cm-thick slices
- 250g of ricotta cheese

- 1 garlic clove, crushed
- 315g jar of bolognese pasta sauce
- 50g of grated parmesan
- 70g of wild rocket leaves

- Juice of ½ lemon
- Chopped basil leaves, to serve

METHOD
1. Use the back of a spoon to press down on the thawed spinach in a sieve to squeeze out as much moisture as possible.
2. Grill the aubergine slices for 8-10 minutes, turning occasionally, until tinged brown on both sides
3. In a separate bowl, combine the ricotta with the crushed garlic.

4. Tip half the pasta sauce evenly across the bottom of the slow cooker. Top with a layer of aubergine slices - trim to fit where necessary.
5. Dot the spinach in small amounts evenly over the top.
6. Spread over the ricotta mixture and top with the remaining aubergine. Cover with the rest of the pasta sauce and sprinkle over the grated parmesan.
7. Put the lid on and cook on a Low setting for 4 hours until the aubergine slices are tender, and the sauce is bubbling.
8. Serve topped with rocket leaves and drizzled with lemon juice.

NUTRITION PER PORTION:
SERVES - 4 | CALORIES - 270KCAL | PROTEIN - 17G | CARBOHYDRATES - 30G | FAT - 10G

VEGETABLE KORMA
• •

INGREDIENTS

- 6 cloves of garlic
- 2 onions, chopped
- 3cm piece ginger, peeled and chopped
- 2 tablespoons of rapeseed oil
- 6 cardamom pods, bruised
- 2 bay leaves
- 1 cinnamon stick

- 4 cloves
- 2 tablespoons of mild curry powder
- 400ml tin of coconut milk
- 1 tablespoons of tomato purée
- ½ butternut squash, peeled, and diced into 3cm cubes

- 100g of cashew nuts, lightly toasted
- 180g of trimmed fine beans
- 1 aubergine, peeled and cut into 3cm cubes
- 100g of frozen peas
- 100g of tomatoes, halved
- Coriander, to garnish

METHOD

1. Use a blender to mix the onions, ginger and garlic into a paste.
2. Heat the oil in a pan and stir fry the cloves, cardamom, bay leaves and cinnamon for 1 minute until fragrant.
3. Mix the curry powder in and fry for 1 more minute, then add the blended paste and fry for a further 5 minutes, stirring continuously until the mixture darkens.
4. Add the tomato purée and coconut milk and stir it through with a spoon, scraping any tasty bits off the pan to add to the overall flavour. Bring the mixture to the boil.
5. Transfer to the slow cooker, and add the squash, cashews, beans, and aubergine. Cover and cook on Low for 3 hours.
6. Add the peas and tomatoes then cover again and cook for another 30 minutes. Serve garnish with coriander.

NUTRITION PER PORTION:
SERVES - 4 | CALORIES - 592KCAL | PROTEIN - 12G | CARBOHYDRATES - 51G | FAT - 44G

BEAN AND LENTIL CHILLI
• •

INGREDIENTS

- 1 large onion, diced
- 1 tablespoon of olive oil
- 1 green pepper, deseeded and diced
- 1 heaped teaspoon of oregano
- 1 heaped teaspoon of cumin
- 1 tablespoon of tomato purée

- 1 teaspoon of ground cinnamon
- 1 teaspoon of smoked paprika
- 1 teaspoon of chilli powder
- 4 garlic cloves, crushed
- 400g tin of kidney beans, rinsed through
- 250g of ready-to-eat Puy lentils

- 200ml of vegetable stock (fresh or from stock cubes)
- 20g dark chocolate (70% cocoa solids), grated

To serve

- 200g long-grain white rice, cooked to the pack instructions
- Optional: 10g of coriander, torn
- Optional: 50g of cheddar cheese, grated

METHOD

1. Preheat the slow cooker on a low setting and spritz lightly with cooking oil.
2. Put all the ingredients for the chilli sauce into the slow cooker except the chocolate and stir thoroughly.
3. Cover and cook on Low for 6 hours.
4. Add in the chocolate just before serving and stir until it has melted.
5. Serve the chilli over cooked white rice, topped with cheddar and coriander.

NUTRITION PER PORTION:

SERVES - 4 | CALORIES - 256KCAL | PROTEIN - 16G | CARBOHYDRATES - 40G | FAT - 5G

MEXICAN 3-BEAN TACO BOWL WITH SALSA

INGREDIENTS

- 4 garlic cloves, crushed
- 1 tablespoon of olive oil
- 1 onion, diced
- 1 green pepper, deseeded and sliced
- 1 teaspoon of ground coriander
- 2 teaspoons of smoked paprika
- 2 tablespoons of tomato purée
- 1 teaspoon of ground cumin
- 300ml of vegetable stock
- 400g tin of red kidney beans in water, rinsed through
- 400g tin of black beans in water, rinsed through
- 400g tin of cannellini beans in water, rinsed through

For the salsa

- 4 teaspoons of olive oil
- 2 tablespoons of chopped coriander, plus extra to serve
- 200g of baby plum tomatoes, finely diced
- 1 small red onion, diced
- Juice of 1 lime
- Black pepper to season

To serve

- 200g of long-grain white rice, cooked to packet instructions
- 2 wholemeal tortillas, cut into triangles
- 2 avocados, diced

METHOD

1. Preheat the slow cooker on a low setting and spritz lightly with cooking oil.
2. Heat the oil In a frying pan, and fry the green pepper onion, and garlic in the oil for 5 minutes until it softens.
3. Stir in the tomato purée, coriander, paprika, and cumin, and cook for 1 minute. Transfer to the slow cooker.
4. Add all the beans to the slow cooker along with the vegetable stock.
5. Meanwhile, heat the oven to 190C/gas 5 and cook the tortillas on a baking tray for about 10 minutes.
6. Mix everything together for the salsa in a container and season with black pepper.
7. Serve the rice in bowls, topped with the Mexican beans and with tortillas on the side. Eat with salsa, avocados and a sprinkle of coriander.

NUTRITION PER PORTION:

SERVES - 6 | CALORIES - 670KCAL | PROTEIN - 22G | CARBOHYDRATES - 94G | FAT - 25G

SPINACH, SQUASH AND PEPPER BIRYANI

INGREDIENTS

- 300g of basmati rice
- 300g of butternut squash, cut into cubes
- 250g of mixed sliced bell peppers
- 150g of frozen peas
- 2 garlic cloves, crushed
- 2 red onions, sliced
- 1 cinnamon stick
- 2 star anise
- 1 bay leaf
- 1 tablespoon of garam masala
- 25g of raisins
- 600ml of boiling water
- 180g of baby leaf spinach
- Juice of 1 lemon
- 125g of natural yoghurt
- 1 cooked beetroot, grated
- 30g of unsalted cashews, toasted (dry fry for 1-2 minutes in a frying pan)
- 25g of pomegranate seeds

METHOD

1. Prepare the rice by leaving it to soak in a container of boiling water for 15 minutes.
2. Preheat the slow cooker on a High setting and spritz lightly with cooking oil.
3. Add the vegetables, herbs, spices, garlic and raisins into the slow cooker and give it a good stir.
4. Once the rice has soaked for 15 minutes, drain thoroughly and add over the vegetables in the slow cooker.
5. Pour in the boiling water and stir gently to combine
6. Cover and cook for 2 hours on High.
7. Give the slow cooker another good stir, then add the spinach on top.
8. Cover again and cook for a further 10 minutes until the spinach wilts.
9. To make the raita, mix the beetroot, lemon juice and yoghurt thoroughly in a container.
10. Serve the biryani in bowls and sprinkled with toasted cashews and pomegranate seeds. Eat with raita.

NUTRITION PER PORTION:

SERVES - 6 | CALORIES - 327KCAL | PROTEIN - 9G | CARBOHYDRATES - 66G | FAT - 4G

SWEET POTATO, PEANUT AND TOFU CURRY

INGREDIENTS

- 2 onions, chopped
- 2 teaspoons of rapeseed oil
- ½ teaspoon of chilli flakes, crushed
- 1 garlic clove, chopped
- 2 teaspoons of garam masala
- 396g of tofu, drained and cubed
- 125g of crunchy peanut butter
- 50g of tomato purée
- 1 sweet potato, peeled and cubed
- 400ml of coconut milk
- 200ml of vegetable stock (fresh or made from stock cubes)
- 1 tablespoon of cornflour mixed with a little water (see step 7)
- 200g of pak choi, halved
- 300g of straight-to-wok rice noodles
- 30g of unsalted peanuts, chopped
- 1 lime, sliced
- 1 spring onion, shredded
- 1 red chilli, sliced

METHOD

1. Preheat the slow cooker on a Low setting and spritz lightly with cooking oil.
2. Meanwhile, heat the oil in a pan and cook the onions for 5 minutes until softened. Add the garlic and fry for a further minute.
3. Stir in the crushed chillies with the garam masala then add the tofu. Cook over a low heat for 3 minutes, stirring regularly.
4. Finally, add the peanut butter and tomato purée and continue stirring until combined.
5. Add the mixture to the slow cooker, put in the cubed sweet potato, coconut milk vegetable stock and mix to combine.
6. Cover the slow cooker and cook on Low for 4 hours.

7. In a small bowl, combine the cornflour with 2 tablespoons of cold water to make a smooth paste. Stir the cornflower mixture into the curry, then add the pak choi.
8. Stir and cook for a further 40 minutes on Low until thickened.
9. Follow the packet instructions to cook the rice noodles and divide between bowls.
10. Serve the curry over the rice noodles topped with peanuts, spring onion, slices of lime and red chilli.

NUTRITION PER PORTION:

SERVES - 6 | CALORIES - 508KCAL | PROTEIN - 16G | CARBOHYDRATES - 35G | FAT - 37G

VEGETARIAN STEW

INGREDIENTS

- 1 onion, peeled and chopped
- 250g of sweet mini peppers, seeded and halved
- 360g of butternut squash, chopped into chunks
- 400g tin of cannellini beans, rinsed through
- 400g tin of chopped tomatoes
- 400g tin of chickpeas, rinsed through
- 10-12 basil leaves, shredded
- 75g of toasted pine nuts
- 2 tablespoons of olive oil
- Optional: Italian hard cheese or parmesan, shaved

METHOD

1. Preheat the slow cooker on a Low setting and spritz lightly with cooking oil.
2. Add the peppers, beans, chickpeas, onion, and butternut squash to the slow cooker.
3. Pour over the tomatoes and add half the basil. Season to taste.
4. Stir thoroughly so that everything is combined, then set the slow cooker to Low and cook for 4 hours.
5. Serve topped with a drizzle of olive oil, toasted pine nuts, parmesan and the remaining basil leaves.

NUTRITION PER PORTION:

SERVES - 4 | CALORIES - 383KCAL | PROTEIN - 15G | CARBOHYDRATES - 36G | FAT - 21G

CHUNKY VEGETABLE STEW WITH CHEDDAR DUMPLINGS

INGREDIENTS

- 2 tablespoons of olive oil
- 200g baby carrots, scrubbed, trimmed and halved
- 3 leeks, cut into thick slices
- 3 garlic cloves, crushed
- 3 tablespoons of plain flour
- 400ml of vegetable stock (fresh or from stock cubes)
- 2 courgettes, cut into large chunks
- 2 x 400g cans of butter or cannellini beans, rinsed through
- 1 bay leaf
- 4 thyme, rosemary or tarragon sprigs
- 200ml of crème fraiche
- 1 tablespoon of wholegrain mustard
- 200g of broad beans or peas
- 200g of spinach
- Fresh parsley, finely chopped, plus extra to serve

For the dumplings

- 50g of vegetable suet
- 100g of self-raising flour
- 100g of mature cheddar
- Fresh parsley, chopped

METHOD

1. Preheat the slow cooker on a Low setting and spritz lightly with cooking oil.
2. Heat 1 tablespoon of the oil in a pan and fry the carrots for 5 minutes until just golden, then tip into the slow cooker.

3. Heat the remaining oil in the pan and fry the leeks for 5 minutes until soft. Next, add the garlic and stir in the flour.
4. Gradually blend in the stock, stirring continuously making sure there are no lumps. Bring it to the boil, then stir into the slow cooker. Add the courgettes, beans and herbs, topping up with water to cover the veg, if necessary.
5. Cover the slow cooker with the lid and cook for 4 hours on Low.
6. Stir in the crème fraiche, mustard, broad beans or peas and spinach. Turn the slow cooker to high.
7. See step 10.
8. Arrange the dumplings over the stew, then cover and cook for another 1 hour until firm and doubled in size.
9. Scatter with parsley and serve. to the slow cooker and turn it to high.
10. To make the dumplings, add the flour and suet to a clean bowl and rub between your fingertips until the mixture resembles fine breadcrumbs.
11. Stir in the cheese and parsley and season to taste. Add 3-4 tablespoons of cold water and stir with a fork to bring the mixture together. Use your hands to form a soft, slightly sticky dough and roll into 6 evenly sized balls.
12. Return to step 8.

NUTRITION PER PORTION:
SERVES - 6 | CALORIES - 554KCAL | PROTEIN - 18G | CARBOHYDRATES - 40G | FAT - 33G

MAC 'N' CHEESE

INGREDIENTS

- 350g of dried macaroni pasta
- 600ml of whole milk
- 50g of butter, cubed
- 50g of soft cheese
- 100g of mature cheddar, grated, plus extra to serve
- 20g of parmesan cheese, plus extra to serve

METHOD

1. Preheat the slow cooker on a Low setting and spritz lightly with oil.
2. First pour boiling water straight from the kettle over the pasta and drain. Now add the pasta with all the ingredients to the slow cooker and stir well.
3. Season to taste, cover and cook on Low for 1 hour.
4. Stir again, put the lid back on and cook on Low for another 30 minutes until the pasta is cooked and the sauce is coating the macaroni.
5. If the sauce is still a little runny, leave the lid off and continue cooking to reduce the sauce for the last 10 minutes - or alternatively, add a splash more milk and stir to combine.
6. Serve with extra cheese.

NUTRITION PER PORTION:
SERVES - 4 | CALORIES - 666KCAL | PROTEIN - 25G | CARBOHYDRATES - 71G | FAT - 31G

MAC 'N' CHEESE WITH WILD MUSHROOMS

INGREDIENTS

- 25g of dried mushrooms
- 75g of butter
- 200g of chestnut mushrooms sliced
- 50g of plain flour
- 500m of whole milk
- 1 teaspoon of English mustard
- 350g of dried macaroni pasta
- Grated nutmeg to taste
- 150g of extra mature cheddar, grated
- 50g of parmesan, grated
- Optional: 25g of breadcrumbs

METHOD

1. Using a heatproof bowl, soak the dried mushrooms in just enough boiling water to cover them. Set to one side to soak until cool.
2. Meanwhile, heat 25g of the butter in a pan and when it's sizzling, scatter in the chestnut mushrooms. Season and fry for 4-5 minutes until soft and cooked through. Set aside.
3. Once the dried mushrooms have cooled, drain the water over a bowl to catch all the juice from soaking them. Press into a wire mesh sieve or colander with the back of a spoon to squeeze all the liquid out and save. Chop the mushrooms.
4. Heat most of the remaining butter in a large pan until sizzling, then add the rehydrated mushrooms and fry for 2-3 minutes until well browned.
5. Scatter over the flour and stir together to make a paste. Cook for 2 minutes, then gradually pour in the saved liquid from soaking the mushrooms leaving any sediment in the bottom of the bowl.
6. Simmer, stirring continuously until the sauce thickens, then whisk in the milk and the mustard. Season to taste some grated nutmeg, Seasoning to taste. Leave the sauce to cook gently for a few minutes while you pour boiling water straight from the kettle over the dried pasta, then drain.
7. Put everything in a slow cooker and stir well. Season, cover and cook on Low for 45 minutes.
8. Stir again, put the lid back on and cook for another 30 minutes until the pasta is cooked.
9. Sprinkle with cheese and serve.

NUTRITION PER PORTION:
SERVES - 4-5 | CALORIES - 592KCAL | PROTEIN - 23G | CARBOHYDRATES - 62G | FAT - 27G

MUSHROOM RISOTTO

INGREDIENTS

- 1 teaspoon of olive oil
- 1 onion, finely chopped
- 250g of chestnut mushrooms sliced
- 50g of porcini mushrooms
- 1litre of vegetable stock
- 300g of wholegrain rice
- Fresh parsley, chopped
- Grated parmesan cheese

METHOD

1. Preheat the slow cooker on Low and spritz lightly with oil.
2. Heat 1 teaspoon of oil in a pan and fry the onion for about 10 minutes until it is soft.
3. Add the chestnut mushrooms and stir until they soften and release their juice.
4. Meanwhile add the stock and porcini into a saucepan, bring to a simmer, turn off the heat, and leave to soak.
5. Put the onions and mushrooms into the slow cooker and stir in the rice.
6. Pour over the stock and the soaked porcini (leaving any bits of sediment behind in the saucepan).
7. Cook on High for 3 hours, stirring halfway.

8. The rice should now be cooked, but if it does need more liquid, stir in a bit more water.
9. Stir in the parsley, season to taste, and serve sprinkled with grated parmesan.

NUTRITION PER PORTION:
SERVES - 4 | CALORIES - 346KCAL | PROTEIN - 10G | CARBOHYDRATES - 67G | FAT - 3G

SWEET POTATO AND COCONUT CURRY
• •

INGREDIENTS

- 2 large onions, halved and sliced
- 4 tablespoons of olive oil
- 3 garlic cloves, crushed
- 1-inch piece of root ginger, peeled and grated
- ½ teaspoon of cayenne

- 1 teaspoon of paprika
- 2 red peppers, deseeded and sliced
- 2 red chillies, deseeded and sliced
- 250g of red cabbage, shredded
- 400ml of coconut milk

- 1kg of sweet potatoes, peeled and chopped into chunks
- 300g of passata
- 2 tablespoons of peanut butter

To serve

- fresh coriander, chopped
- cooked couscous

METHOD
1. Heat 1 tablespoon of olive oil in a pan, add the onion and fry gently for 10 minutes until soft.
2. Add the garlic, and grated ginger, then stir in the paprika and cayenne. Cook in the pan for another minute.
3. Transfer the spicy onion mix to the slow cooker.
4. Use the same pan to heat another 1 tablespoon of oil and add the chilli, red pepper and shredded cabbage. Cook for 4-5 minutes then add to the onion mixture in the slow cooker.
5. Use the remaining oil to fry the chunks of sweet potato for about 5 minutes until they start to colour at the edges. Add them to the slow cooker too.
6. Now, stir in the coconut milk and passata, mixing everything thoroughly together.
7. Cover the slow cooker with a lid and cook for 8 hours until the sweet potatoes are tender.
8. Stir the peanut butter through the curry, add seasoning to taste, and serve with couscous topped with coriander.

NUTRITION PER PORTION:
SERVES - 6 | CALORIES - 434KCAL | PROTEIN - 6G | CARBOHYDRATES - 47G | FAT - 22G

RATATOUILLE
• •

INGREDIENTS

- 2 tablespoons of olive oil
- 2 garlic cloves
- 1 red onion, sliced
- 2 aubergines, cut into 1.5cm pieces
- 3 mixed peppers, cut into 2cm pieces
- 3 courgettes, halved and cut into 2cm pieces

- 1 tablespoon of tomato purée
- 6 large ripe tomatoes, roughly chopped
- Fresh basil, roughly chopped, plus extra to serve
- Fresh basil
- 400g can of plum tomatoes
- 1 teaspoon of brown sugar
- 1 tablespoon of red wine vinegar

- Optional: sourdough bread to serve

METHOD

1. Preheat the slow cooker on a Low setting and spritz lightly with cooking oil.
2. Heat the oil in a pan and fry the onion for 8 minutes until it softens. Add the garlic and fry for 1 min.
3. Next, turn the heat up, add the aubergines and fry for 5 minutes until golden, then stir in the courgettes and peppers and fry for another 5 minutes until softened.
4. Stir in the rest of the ingredients except the sourdough bread, bring to the boil and simmer gently for 1 minute.
5. Pour the mixture into the slow cooker and cook on Low for 6 hours until the sauce has thickened.
6. Adjust the seasoning to taste, then serve, scattered with extra basil, and a side of sourdough.

NUTRITION PER PORTION:

SERVES - 6 | CALORIES - 162KCAL | PROTEIN - 6G | CARBOHYDRATES - 17G | FAT - 5G

PUMPKIN STEW

• •

INGREDIENTS

- 1 onion, sliced
- 2 garlic cloves, crushed
- 1 -2 red chillies (to taste), deseeded and sliced
- 2.5cm piece fresh root ginger, peeled and grated
- 2 teaspoons of vegetable oil

- 3 tablespoons of tomato purée
- 2 teaspoons of ground cumin
- 2 teaspoons of coriander seeds
- 600g of pumpkin, peeled, deseeded, and cut into 2.5cm pieces
- 200g of coconut milk

- 400g tin of chopped tomatoes
- 1 vegetable stock cube, crumbled
- 250g of ready-to-use puy lentils
- Optional: Fresh coriander, chopped

METHOD

1. Preheat the slow cooker on a Low setting and spritz lightly with cooking oil.
2. Heat the oil in a pan, add the onion and seasoning, then fry for 10 minutes until softened.
3. Next, stir in the chilli(es) and garlic. Fry for 2 minutes, until fragrant.
4. Add the cumin, coriander seeds, ginger and tomato purée and fry for 1 further minute.
5. Transfer to the slow cooker and stir in the remaining ingredients except for the lentils and coriander. Season to taste.
6. Cover and cook on Low for 6 hours.
7. Stir in the lentils, re-cover and cook for 5 more minutes until the lentils are piping hot.
8. Adjust the seasoning to taste, garnish with chopped coriander, and serve with fresh crusty wedges of bread.

NUTRITION PER PORTION:

SERVES - 4 | CALORIES - 268KCAL | PROTEIN - 11G | CARBOHYDRATES - 24G | FAT - 12G

SWEET POTATO AND AUBERGINE JALFREZI

• •

INGREDIENTS

- 1 tablespoon of vegetable oil
- 1 onion, finely chopped
- 1-2 green chillies (to taste), seeds removed and finely chopped
- 1 whole chilli
- 1 ½ teaspoons of ground cumin
- 2 garlic cloves, crushed

- 1 - 2 teaspoons of chilli powder, to taste
- 1 tablespoon of garam masala
- 1 teaspoon of ground coriander
- 2 teaspoons of ground turmeric
- 1 tablespoon of garam masala
- 300g of passata

- 400g tin of chickpeas, rinsed through
- 2 sweet potatoes, peeled and diced
- 1 aubergine, chopped into small pieces
- Optional: Fresh coriander leaves, chopped

METHOD

1. Heat the oil in a pan and fry the onion for 8-10 minutes until softened.
2. Add the chillies (1 or 2 depending on how hot you like your food), garlic and spices to the pan and cook for a few minutes until fragrant.
3. Transfer everything to the slow cooker and add the sweet potatoes, aubergine, the whole chilli and 300ml of water. Season to taste.
4. Cover the slow cooker with the lid and cook on Low for 5 ½ hours.
5. Finally, stir in the chickpeas, re-cover the slow cooker, and cook for another 30 minutes.
6. Remove the whole chilli, adjust the seasoning to taste, and stir through some coriander.
7. Serve with rice and warm naan.

NUTRITION PER PORTION:

SERVES - 4 | CALORIES - 212KCAL | PROTEIN - 7G | CARBOHYDRATES - 31G | FAT - 5G

AUBERGINE PARMIGIANA

INGREDIENTS

- 2 aubergines, cut into ½ cm circles
- 2 teaspoons of vegetable oil
- 3 eggs, lightly beaten
- 40g of plain flour
- 200g of golden breadcrumbs

- 500g of passata
- 3 tablespoons of tomato purée
- 1 onion, chopped
- 500g of passata
- 2 garlic cloves, crushed
- 2 teaspoons of dried oregano

- teaspoons of caster sugar
- 2 teaspoons of dried basil
- 500g mozzarella, drained weight and sliced into ½ cm rounds
- 100g of grated parmesan.
- Optional: Fresh basil leaves

METHOD

1. Lay the aubergine slice on a baking tray lined with kitchen paper. Sprinkle with salt and leave for 20 minutes to absorb excess moisture. Pat dry and set to one side.
2. Prepare three separate shallow bowls, containing each of seasoned flour, eggs and breadcrumbs. Dip the aubergine slices first into the flour, then the egg and finally breadcrumbs. Repeat the process with all the aubergine slices and set to one side.
3. In a separate bowl, mix the passata and tomato purée with garlic, onion, dried herbs, teaspoons of caster sugar and season with Seasoning to taste. Set aside.
4. Turn the slow cooker to Low and spritz lightly with cooking oil.
5. First put a single layer of aubergine slices into the base of the slow cooker and cover with a ¼ of the tomato sauce. Next lay ¼ of the mozzarella slices with the grated hard cheese. Repeat the process 3 more times, ending with a final layer of hard cheese.
6. Close the lid and cook on Low for 6 hours.
7. Serve garnished with basil, if using.

NUTRITION PER PORTION:

SERVES - 6 | CALORIES - 533KCAL | PROTEIN - 31G | CARBOHYDRATES - 40G | FAT - 27G

MEXICAN-INSPIRED VEGETABLE STEW

INGREDIENTS

For the stew

- 200g of cherry tomatoes, cut into halves
- 1 onion, finely chopped
- 2 teaspoons of ground coriander
- 2 teaspoons of garlic granules
- 2 teaspoons of dried oregano
- 1 tablespoons of chipotle paste
- 1 teaspoon of ground cumin
- 1 vegetable stock cube, crumbled
- 2 x 400g tins black beans, rinsed through
- 2 mixed peppers, deseeded and finely sliced
- 1 teaspoon of cornflour
- 4 eggs

To serve

- Optional: corn tortillas/taco wraps
- Optional: Fresh coriander, roughly chopped
- Optional: 1 avocado, sliced
- Optional: extra cherry tomatoes

METHOD

1. Combine all the ingredients except the eggs and garnished, into the slow cooker.
2. Season and mix well.
3. Close the lid and cook on Low for 6 hours.
4. When the cooking cycle is complete, crack the eggs evenly into the stew.
5. Put the lid back on and cook on Low for another 25 minutes. The whites of the eggs should be set but the yolks, still runny.
6. Serve in bowls with a squeeze of lime, cherry tomatoes and feta. Garnish with a topped of coriander and avocado and add a side of tacos.

NUTRITION PER PORTION:
SERVES - 4 | CALORIES - 363KCAL | PROTEIN - 21G | CARBOHYDRATES - 32G | FAT - 14G

JACKET POTATOES

INGREDIENTS

- 1 tablespoon of olive oil
- 4 baking potatoes
- A selection of toppings to taste

METHOD

1. Wash the potatoes thoroughly, leave to dry, then prick all over with a small knife, or fork.
2. Rub olive oil evenly all over the potato skin and add seasoning to taste.
3. Wrap each potato in foil and put into the slow cooker in one layer.
4. Cover and cook on High for 4 hours - for medium potatoes; 5 hours for large potatoes. Turn over halfway through the cooking cycle.
5. Remove the cooked potatoes to plates and unwrap. Cut a cross in the top of each and serve with 20g of butter and your favourite toppings.

NUTRITION PER PORTION:
SERVES - 4 | CALORIES - 224KCAL | PROTEIN - 4G | CARBOHYDRATES - 37G | FAT - 6G

SWEET AND SOUR LENTIL DAHL

INGREDIENTS

- 500g of chana dahl lentils, rinsed until the water is clear
- 1 onion, finely chopped
- 3 tablespoons of dark muscovado sugar
- 50g of butter
- 3 star anise
- 1 teaspoon of dried chilli flakes
- 3 garlic cloves, crushed
- 2 tablespoons of dried curry leaves
- 3 tablespoons of tamarind paste
- 1 tablespoon of garam masala
- 4 large tomatoes, chopped
- Juice of 2 limes

METHOD

1. Add the lentils to a bowl, cover with water and leave soaking for about 30 minutes.
2. Melt the butter in a pan, add the onion and gently fry for about 8-10 minutes until it softens. Add the garam masala, curry leaves, chilli flakes, garlic and mustard to the pan and cook briefly for 1 minute until the spices are fragrant.
3. Transfer the onion mixture to the slow cooker and add in any remaining dahl ingredients and 600ml of water.
4. Cook on a Low setting for 10 hours, or High for 6 hours.
5. Serve the dahl with rice and warm naan bread.

NUTRITION PER PORTION:

SERVES - 4 | CALORIES - 609KCAL | PROTEIN - 30G | CARBOHYDRATES - 90G | FAT - 16G

MUSHROOM AND BEAN HOTPOT

INGREDIENTS

- 3 tablespoons of olive oil
- 700g of chestnut mushrooms roughly chopped
- 1 large onion, finely chopped
- 2 tablespoons of mild curry paste
- 2 tablespoons of plain flour
- 400g tin of chopped tomatoes
- 2 tablespoons of sun-dried tomato paste
- 150ml of dry white wine
- 2 × 400g tins of mixed beans, rinsed through
- 3 tablespoons of mango chutney
- 3 tablespoons of freshly chopped coriander and mint leaves

METHOD

1. Heat the oil in a pan and fry the mushrooms and onion for 8-10 minutes until just softened and golden. Stir in the curry paste with the flour and cook for 2 minutes. Add the wine, chopped tomatoes, tomato paste and beans. Boil and simmer for 1 minute.
2. Now carefully transfer the mixture to a slow cooker. Cover and cook on Low for 3 hours.
3. Mix the mango chutney and chopped herbs in to the hot pot and serve with rice or naan bread.

NUTRITION PER PORTION:

SERVES - 6 | CALORIES - 280KCAL | PROTEIN - 10G | CARBOHYDRATES - 34G | FAT - 10G

CHICKPEAS COOKED WITH DATES, TURMERIC AND ALMONDS

INGREDIENTS

- 2 tablespoons of olive oil, plus extra to serve
- 400g tin of plum tomatoes
- 100g of pitted dates, halved
- 4 garlic cloves, finely chopped
- Fresh coriander, stalks and leaves separated and roughly chopped
- Fresh ginger root finely grated to 1 tablespoon
- 1 teaspoon of ground coriander
- 1 teaspoon of ground turmeric
- 1 teaspoon of ground cumin
- 1 cinnamon stick
- Juice of 1 lemon plus 2 large strips of the zest
- 660g of large chickpeas, rinsed and drained
- 40g flaked almonds, toasted
- 1 orange, cut into wedges to serve
- Couscous

METHOD

1. Preheat the slow cooker on a Low setting and spritz lightly with cooking oil.
2. Put ½ the tomatoes and ½ the dates into a blender and mix to a purée, then tip into the slow cooker with the rest of the tomatoes.
3. Mix in the oil, garlic, ginger, coriander stalks, spices, the lemon zest into the slow cooker, and pour in 100ml water. Season to taste.
4. Cover and cook on High for 2 hours or on Low for 6 hours until the sauce has thickened.
5. Stir in the chickpeas and the remaining dates and cook for another 30 minutes to warm thorough again.
6. Add the lemon juice and adjust the seasoning to taste. Remove the strips of lemon zest.
7. Serve the chickpeas with a drizzle of olive oil, toasted almonds and chopped coriander, with the orange wedges and couscous on the side.

NUTRITION PER PORTION:

SERVES - 4 | CALORIES - 370KCAL | PROTEIN - 14G | CARBOHYDRATES - 40G | FAT - 15G

AUBERGINE DAAL WITH RICE AND CHAPATIS

INGREDIENTS

- 4 tablespoons of rogan josh curry paste
- 2 red onions, peeled and sliced
- groundnut oil
- 1 large aubergine, cut into 2cm chunks
- 10cm piece of ginger, peeled and finely grated
- 4 garlic cloves, peeled and sliced
- 500g of yellow split peas
- 2 litres of hot vegetable stock (fresh or from stock cubes)

For the rice

- 320g of basmati rice

For the temper

- 1 fresh red chilli, finely sliced
- 1 teaspoon of mustard seeds
- 1 handful of fresh curry leaves
- Chapatis to serve

METHOD

1. Preheat the oven to 180°C//gas 4.
2. Loosely mix 4 tablespoons of groundnut oil with 4 tablespoons of curry paste in a high-sided roasting tin and add the aubergine, garlic, onions, and ginger. Toss together until well coated and roast for 25 minutes.
3. Preheat the slow cooker on a Low setting and spritz lightly with cooking oil.
4. Put just half the roasted vegetables into the slow cooker; turn off the oven and return the other half of the vegetable to keep warm.

5. Add the split peas and pour in the vegetable stock. Stir everything well.
6. Cover and cook on a Low setting for about 6 hours, or until the split peas are tender.
7. In a separate pan, place the rice and 650mls of boiling water. Add a bit of salt.
8. Cook on a medium heat with the lid on for about 12 minutes, or until all the liquid is absorbed.
9. To make the temper (or flavoured oil), heat 3-4 tablespoons of groundnut oil in a clean frying pan and fry the chilli, curry leaves and mustard seeds for 1 to 2 minutes, or until crispy.
10. Remember to warm up your chapatis before serving.
11. Serve loaded chapatis fill with rice, daal and some of the roasted vegetables. Drizzle over some oil, roll and serve.

NUTRITION PER PORTION:

SERVES - 6 | CALORIES - 560KCAL | PROTEIN - 19G | CARBOHYDRATES - 98G | FAT - 13G

PUMPKIN, SPINACH AND DRIED FRUIT CURRY
● ●

INGREDIENTS

- 1 onion, slice
- 500g of peeled pumpkin, cut into wedges
- 1 tin o chickpeas
- 3 garlic cloves, crushed
- 3 chillies, deseeded and sliced

- 1 ½ teaspoons of ground ginger
- 1 teaspoon of ground cinnamon
- ½ teaspoon of ground turmeric
- 2 teaspoons of ground cumin
- 2 tins of chopped tomatoes

- 150ml of vegetable stock (fresh or from stock cubes)
- 150g of dried mixed fruit
- 2 handfuls of spinach
- Seasoning to taste

METHOD

1. Heat some oil in a frying pan and cook the onion until it's softened. Add the garlic and chilli and fry for another 2 minutes.
2. Add the garlic and chilli and cook for 2 minutes. Now add the spices and cook for a further 2 minutes.
3. Transfer to a slow cooker and stir in the rest of the ingredients apart from the spinach. Cover and cook on Low for 6 hours.
4. Add the spinach, cover and cook on Low for a further 30 minutes until it wilts, then stir again.
5. Check the seasoning to taste then serve with rice and warmed naan or chapatis.

NUTRITION PER PORTION:

SERVES - 6 | CALORIES - 150KCAL | PROTEIN - 6G | CARBOHYDRATES - 28G | FAT - 1G

LEEK AND LEMON SPAGHETTI
● ●

INGREDIENTS

- 500ml of vegetable stock (fresh or from stock cubes)
- 400g of washed leeks, cut into ribbons about 8-10cms long/1cm wide
- 1 teaspoon of dried rosemary or thyme
- Juice and zest of 1 lemon
- 150g of spaghetti

- 250g of ricotta cheese
- Seasoning to taste

METHOD

1. Preheat the slow cooker on a Low setting and pour in the vegetable stock.
2. Add the prepared leek ribbons to the slow cooker with the lemon zest and herbs.
3. Cover and cook on Low for 4-8 hours.
4. About 15-20 minutes before the cook cycle has completed, add the pasta, cover and cook until al dente - about 10-15 minutes.
5. Once cooked, add your cheese, and the juice of half the lemon. Taste and adjust with more lemon and salt and to taste.
6. Serve in bowls with a generous grind of pepper, and fresh herbs.

NUTRITION PER PORTION:
SERVES - 2 | CALORIES - 536KCAL | PROTEIN - 27G | CARBOHYDRATES - 81G | FAT - 13G

BUTTERNUT RISOTTO
• •

INGREDIENTS

- 800g of butternut squash, deseeded & chopped into 2cm pieces
- 1 leek, sliced into rounds
- 2 garlic cloves, peeled and chopped
- Fresh thyme leaves
- 2 tablespoons of olive oil
- 300g of risotto rice
- 800-1000ml vegetable stock (to cover the rice to about 2-3cm above)
- Optional: 20g of butter
- 50g of grated parmesan, plus more for serving
- small bunch of tarragon, leaves stripped from stalks and chopped
- Seasoning to taste

METHOD

1. Preheat the slow cooker on a Low setting.
2. Add all the ingredients to the slow cooker except the butter, parmesan and tarragon.
3. Cover and cook on Low for 6 hours until the rice is cooked and creamy.
4. Check the stock level during cooking to make sure the risotto doesn't dry out and add a little more stock or water if required.
5. Stir in the (optional) butter, parmesan and tarragon and adjust seasoning to taste.
6. Serve topped with additional cheese.

NUTRITION PER PORTION:
SERVES - 4 | CALORIES - 534KCAL | PROTEIN - 13G | CARBOHYDRATES - 90G | FAT - 15G

VEGETARIAN DAAL
• •

INGREDIENTS

NOTE: Add whatever vegetables you like and/or have at home.
Vegetables like squash, carrots, parsnip, or courgettes can be added at the beginning with the rest of the ingredients. However, leafy vegetables like spinach or kale need to be added about 30 minutes before the end.

- 1 onion, peeled and diced
- 2 garlic cloves, peeled and grated
- 30g ginger, peeled and grated
- 2 teaspoons of cumin seeds
- 2 teaspoons of ground coriander
- 2 teaspoons of black mustard seeds
- 1 teaspoon of curry powder
- ½ teaspoon of chilli flakes
- 1 teaspoon of turmeric
- 200g of chopped tomatoes (fresh or tinned)
- 400g of split red lentils
- 700-900ml of vegetable stock (the lentils should be covered by about 2cm of water)
- Seasoning to taste

METHOD

1. Preheat the slow cooker to high and spritz lightly with cooking oil.
2. Add all the ingredients directly to the slow cooker and stir well.
3. Cover the slow cooker and cook on High for 4 hours, or Low for 8 hours.
4. Check the daal; add more water if it seems too thick or cook with the lid off for 30 minutes if it seems too watery.
5. Serve with rice or naan bread.

NUTRITION PER PORTION (PLUS WHATEVER VEGETABLES YOU CHOOSE TO ADD):
SERVES - 4 | CALORIES - 430KCAL | PROTEIN - 29G | CARBOHYDRATES - 74G | FAT - 3G

POLISH VEGETABLE STEW
● ●

INGREDIENTS

- 8g of dried Porcini mushrooms
- 1 onion, peeled and sliced
- 1 garlic clove, peeled and chopped
- 50g of mushrooms sliced
- 1 bay leaf
- 1 teaspoon of juniper berries or caraway seeds, crushed
- 100ml of red wine
- ½ teaspoon of smoked paprika
- 2 tablespoons of tomato purée
- 3 dried prunes, pitted and chopped
- ½ small Savoy cabbage, finely sliced
- 2 tablespoons of tamarind or soy sauce
- 100g of smoked tofu, cut into small pieces
- 100g of sauerkraut, drained

METHOD

1. Put the dried porcini in a heatproof bowl and add 500ml of boiling water over them. Leave to soak for about 30 minutes.
2. Heat a little olive oil in a pan and gently fry the onion and garlic for about 8-10 minutes until soft and translucent. Add the sliced mushrooms and cook for another 5-8 minutes. Season to taste.
3. Add the bay leaf, juniper berries, and wine and simmer for a couple of minutes before transferring to the slow cooker.
4. Drain the water from the porcini mushrooms through a fine mesh sieve into a jug. Keep the water and slice up the porcini. Discard any grit from the sieve.
5. Now add the smoked paprika, tomato purée, dried prunes, and sliced porcini mushrooms to the slow cooker along with the savoy cabbage.
6. Stir in the porcini mushroom stock and mix well.
7. Cover and cook on a High setting for 4 hours and a Low setting for 8 hours.
8. About 30 minutes before the cooking cycle ends, heat up some oil in a clean pan, drizzle over the tamarind/soy sauce, and cook the tofu until golden and crispy.
9. Stir the tofu and sauerkraut into the slow cooker and adjust seasoning to taste.
10. Cover the slow cooker again and cook for a further 30 minutes on Low.
11. Serve with wedges of fresh crusty bread.

NUTRITION PER PORTION:
SERVES - 6 | CALORIES - 459KCAL | PROTEIN - 19G | CARBOHYDRATES - 82G | FAT - 6G

MUSHROOM AND DILL STROGANOFF

INGREDIENTS

- 1 onion, peeled and finely chopped
- Oil for frying
- 200g of small mushrooms cleaned and sliced

- 200g of Portobello mushrooms cleaned and cut into quarters
- 15g of parsley, chopped roughly
- 15g of dill
- ½ teaspoon of smoked paprika

- 1 teaspoon of paprika
- 60ml of white wine
- 1 teaspoon of dijon mustard
- 3 tablespoons of soured cream
- 1 lemon

To serve

- 150g of brown or white basmati rice, cooked

- 50g of salad leaves, washed and ready to eat

- Seasoning to taste

METHOD

1. Heat 1 tablespoon of oil in a pan, add the onion and gently fry for 10 minutes until it softens.
2. Next, in the same pan, add the mushrooms with a little more oil if necessary and fry for 2-3 minutes. Stir in the paprika and add Seasoning to taste.
3. Add the wine and 2 tablespoons of water, bring to a simmer, then transfer to the slow cooker.
4. Cover and cook on a Low setting for 6-8 hours.
5. About 30 minutes before the end of the cooking cycle, stir in the mustard, a squeeze of lemon juice and the soured cream, then close the lid and cook for another 30 minutes.
6. If the stroganoff becomes too thick, add a splash of water or a little more cream.
7. Adjust the seasoning to taste and stir in the chopped parsley and dill.
8. Serve over cooked rice with the salad leaves on the side, tossed in a little salad dressing.

NUTRITION PER PORTION:

SERVES - 2 | CALORIES - 433KCAL | PROTEIN - 16G | CARBOHYDRATES - 78G | FAT - 7G

MUSHROOM AND CHESTNUT CASSEROLE WITH THYME

INGREDIENTS

- 2 garlic cloves, peeled and finely chopped
- 2 tablespoons of cooking oil
- 1 red onion, peeled and thinly sliced
- 400g of mushrooms quartered

- 15g of thyme, leaves picked off the stalk
- 1½ teaspoons of cornflour
- 1 tablespoon of tomato purée
- 1 tablespoon of Worcester sauce
- 100ml of red wine
- 300ml of water

- ½ tablespoon of bouillon powder
- 180g of cooked chestnuts
- 500g of potatoes, boiled and ready to mash
- 15g of parsley, chopped
- Optional: 2 tablespoons of white miso paste

METHOD

1. Heat 2 tablespoons of oil in a pan and fry the onion gently for about 8 minutes, until softened.
2. Now add the garlic, thyme, mushrooms cornflour and 1 tablespoon of oil to the onion. Turn up the heat a bit and cook for 2-3 minutes, to soften the mushrooms slightly.
3. Stir in the tomato purée, wine, Worcester sauce, bouillon and 300ml of water. Stir in the chestnuts and season. Bring to the boil.
4. Transfer the mixture to the slow cooker and cook on a High setting for 4 hours and a Low setting for 8 hours. Add a splash more water if needed to prevent the gravy from being too thick.
5. Stir through most of the parsley and adjust seasoning if required.

6. Mash the potatoes with the (optional) miso and some olive oil to loosen if needed. Season.
7. Serve the casserole with the mashed (miso-) potatoes and garnish with the remaining parsley.

NUTRITION PER PORTION:

SERVES - 2 | CALORIES - 685KCAL | PROTEIN - 17G | CARBOHYDRATES - 113G | FAT - 18G

COURGETTE PASTA
• •

INGREDIENTS

- 2 garlic cloves, finely chopped
- 2 tablespoons of olive oil
- 500g of courgettes, very finely sliced
- 200g of dried pasta of choice
- Juice of 1 lemon
- Optional: 1 tablespoon of crème fraiche
- Seasoning to taste

To serve

- parmesan or Pecorino cheese

METHOD

1. Preheat the slow cooker on a Low setting and spritz generously with cooking oil.
2. Put the garlic and courgette slices into the slow cooker with 2 tablespoons of olive oil.
3. Season the courgettes with Seasoning to taste and add the lemon juice.
4. Close the lid on the slow cooker and cook on Low for about 4-6 hours.
5. About 15 minutes before the end of the cooking cycle put your pasta on to cook.
6. Now stir through the creme fraiche and a little olive oil and adjust any seasoning to taste.
7. Drain the cooked pasta, saving a little of the water in a jug.
8. Stir the cooked pasta into the slow cooker with the courgette mixture and add in 2 tablespoons of the pasta water to stop it clumping.
9. Close the slow cooker to heat thorough for about 15 minutes if necessary.
10. Serve in bowls with a generous grating of cheese.

NUTRITION PER PORTION:

SERVES - 2 | CALORIES - 560KCAL | PROTEIN - 16G | CARBOHYDRATES - 86G | FAT - 20G

SQUASH NOODLE LAKSA
• •

INGREDIENTS

- 2 tablespoons of red Thai curry paste
- 1 tablespoon of toasted sesame oil
- 1 teaspoon of turmeric
- 1 tablespoon of soy sauce
- 400ml tin of coconut milk
- 1 teaspoon of bouillon powder
- 400g of butternut, peeled and diced
- Seasoning to taste
- 100g of chard, shredded
- 15g of coriander, chopped roughly
- 30g of roasted and salted peanuts, chopped roughly
- 140g of udon noodles
- 1 lime, cut into wedges

METHOD

1. Heat some sesame oil in a pan and gently cook the Thai curry paste, turmeric, and soy sauce for about a minute until it smells fragrant.
2. Add the coconut milk and 300ml water. Bring to a gentle simmer and stir in the bouillon powder.
3. Transfer to the slow cooker and add the diced butternut and season to taste.
4. Cover and cook on a Low setting for about 6 hours.
5. About an hour from the end of the cooking cycle, add the shredded chard, recover and cook for a further hour.
6. Meanwhile, just before serving, cook the noodles according to the packet, drain and divide between deep bowls.
7. Ladle in the laksa sharing the squash and chard equally between the bowls.
8. Serve garnished with chopped peanuts, and coriander and fat wedges of lime for squeezing.

NUTRITION PER PORTION:
SERVES - 3-4 | CALORIES - 723KCAL | PROTEIN - 13G | CARBOHYDRATES - 52G | FAT - 55G

DUCK

DUCK AND PINEAPPLE CURRY

INGREDIENTS

- 6 duck legs
- 4 tablespoons of red Thai curry paste
- 2 tablespoons of fish sauce
- 2 tablespoons of light brown sugar
- 6 kaffir lime leaves
- 1 x 400ml can of coconut milk
- 1 pineapple, peeled and cut into chunks
- Optional: Thai basil leaves
- Optional: 1 red chilli, deseeded and finely sliced

METHOD

1. Use a frying pan over a low heat to dry-fry the duck legs for about 10-15 minutes, turning once so that they're browned all over. Remove from the pan along with any juices and set to one side.
2. Put the browned duck into the slow cooker, adding the sugar, curry paste, coconut milk, fish sauce and lime leaves.
3. Cover and cook for 8 hours on a High setting.
4. Remove the duck legs from the slow cooker and keep warm, then skim any excess fat that's formed on the curry. Stir in the pineapple, half the chilli and the basil. Cover and heat for a further 15-20 minutes.
5. Adjust the seasoning to taste, Seasoning to taste, a little more fish sauce for the salt flavour, or sugar for sweetness.
6. Just before serving stir in half the (optional) sliced chilli and half the (optional) Thai basil leaves.
7. Serve the cooked duck legs on a bed of jasmine rice, pour over the curry sauce and scatter with the remaining (optional) chilli and Thai basil leaves.

NUTRITION PER PORTION:

SERVES - 6 | CALORIES - 659KCAL | PROTEIN - 38G | CARBOHYDRATES - 20G | FAT - 49G

DUCK AND VEGETABLE CURRY

INGREDIENTS

- 2 duck breasts
- 2 tablespoons of cooking oil
- 3 tablespoons of red Thai or massaman curry paste
- 2 teaspoons of light brown soft sugar
- 2 teaspoons of fish sauce
- 1 aubergine, trimmed and cut into wedges
- 2 teaspoons of light brown soft sugar
- 500g small potatoes, peeled and halved
- 400ml can of coconut milk, plus ½ can of water
- Optional: 2 lime leaves
- Juice of ½ a lime
- Cooked rice
- Optional sliced red chillies, chopped coriander leaves, chopped roasted peanuts or cashews, to serve

METHOD

1. In a large frying pan, fry the duck breasts skin-side down in a little hot oil on a low heat for about 10-15 minutes. Transfer the fried duck with its fat and juices to a plate and set aside to cool.
2. Once cooled, slice the duck into thin strips and put the duck, along with all the saved juices from the frying pan, into the slow cooker.
3. Stir in the sugar, curry paste and fish sauce.
4. Add the aubergine, green beans and potatoes to the slow cooker, and stir to coat.
5. Pour in the coconut milk, water, and (optional) lime leaves.
6. Cover the slow cooker and cook for 8 hours on High.
7. Just before serving stir in the lime juice. Adjust the seasoning to taste; add more lime, sugar or fish sauce as required.
8. Serve with cooked rice

NUTRITION PER PORTION:

SERVES - 4 | CALORIES - 573KCAL | PROTEIN - 20G | CARBOHYDRATES - 27G | FAT - 41G

DUCK AND DATE TAGINE

• •

INGREDIENTS

- Oil for frying
- 6 duck legs with skin removed
- 1 red chilli, deseeded
- A 2-inch piece of ginger, peeled
- 1 large onion
- 2 preserved lemons, halved, pulp and pith scooped out and discarded

- 2 garlic cloves
- 200g of dates (as 2 x 100g)
- 200ml of water
- 1 tablespoon of cinnamon
- 1 tablespoon of coriander
- 1 tablespoon cumin
- 1 teaspoon of ground ginger
- 2 preserved lemons, halved,

- pulp and pith scooped out and discarded
- 400ml of passata
- 100g of blanched almonds, chopped roughly
- Optional: Couscous
- Optional: mint leaves

METHOD

1. Heat the slow cooker on a Low setting.
2. In a large frying pan, heat the oil and fry the duck legs all over until they are a golden colour. Remove from the frying pan and set to one side.
3. Meanwhile, blend the onion, spices, chilli, garlic, ginger and preserved lemon to a chunky paste with a food processor. Transfer to the same frying pan and cook for about 5 minutes until it softens a little.
4. Next blend half the dates (100g) and the water in the food processor until smooth. Roughly chop the remaining 100g of dates.
5. Place the cooked duck legs in the slow cooker along with the pastes, the chopped dates, passata and seasoning. Stir and Put the lid on.
6. Cook for 5 hours on a Low setting, stirring occasionally. Just before serving, put the blanched almonds in the tagine and stir to distribute.
7. Serve with couscous, scattered with mint leaves.

NUTRITION PER PORTION:

SERVES - 6 | CALORIES - 527KCAL | PROTEIN - 53G | CARBOHYDRATES - 30G | FAT - 20G

CRISPY DUCK IN MADEIRA GRAVY

INGREDIENTS

For the duck

- 550g of duck legs (2 large or 4 small)
- 25g of sea salt

For the madeira gravy

- 2 shallots, finely chopped
- Generous chunk of butter
- 1 teaspoon of plain flour

- 4 fresh bay leaves
- 2 teaspoons of crushed black peppercorns

- 300ml of chicken stock (either fresh or from stock cubes)
- 30ml of Madeira wine

- 1 teaspoon of fresh thyme leaves
- Groundnut oil for crisping up

- Optional: Fresh thyme leaves for garnishing

METHOD

1. Put your duck legs in a layer in the slow cooker. Don't season them at this stage. Cover and cook on a Low setting for 4-6 hours depending on the size of the duck legs. Remove the duck legs from the slow cooker and discard the fat.
2. Pat the duck legs dry with some kitchen paper to remove as much moisture as possible.
3. In a large shallow bowl, combine the salt, pepper and herbs. Coat the duck thoroughly in the seasoning mixture and rub into the skin.
4. Heat 100ml of groundnut oil in a frying pan. When it's hot lay the duck legs skin side down and cook for a couple of minutes until it crisps up.
5. Turnover and crisp up the other side.
6. For the Madeira gravy: While the duck is cooking, fry the chopped shallots in a pan with the butter until golden.
7. Stir in the flour and cook, stirring continuously, until the flour browns.
8. Add the stock gradually and whisk continuously as it thickens to avoid lumps.
9. Pour in the Madeira wine and cook for another 2 minutes. Remove any lumps by straining the gravy through a sieve.
10. Serve the crispy duck legs, with the Madeira gravy accompanied by roast potatoes and seasonal vegetables and garnished with a sprig of thyme.

NUTRITION PER PORTION:

SERVES - 2 | CALORIES - 529KCAL | PROTEIN - 83G | CARBOHYDRATES - 5G | FAT - 17G

VENETIAN DUCK RAGU

INGREDIENTS

- 1 tablespoon of olive oil
- 4 duck legs
- 2 onions, finely chopped
- 2 teaspoons of plain flour
- 2 teaspoons of ground cinnamon
- 2 garlic cloves, crushed
- 250ml of red wine
- 2 x 400g cans of chopped tomatoes

- 250ml of chicken stock (fresh or from stock cubes)
- Fresh rosemary leaves
- 1 teaspoon of sugar
- 2 x 400g cans of chopped tomatoes
- 2 bay leaves
- 30ml of milk
- 600g of dried pasta (paccheri or pappardelle)

- Grated parmesan

METHOD

1. Heat the olive oil in a large frying pan and sear the duck legs on all sides for about 10 minutes until they are browned. Move to a plate and set to one side.
2. Place the onions and garlic in the same pan and fry a little until softened, then add the cinnamon and flour and cook for another minute.
3. Put the duck in a single layer at the bottom of the slow cooker. Add the tomatoes, stock, herbs, sugar and seasoning. Wash a little of the wine into the frying pan to collect all the flavourings from cooking the duck and onions and add to the slow cooker along with the rest of the wine.
4. Cover the slow cooker and cook on a Low setting for 7 hours.
5. The duck should be falling off the bone. Lift it out carefully onto a plate and use 2 forks to shred the meat. Discard any bones or excess fat.
6. Return the shredded meat to the slow cooker, stir in the milk, and cook for a further hour on Low.
7. When you're ready to serve, cook the pasta according to the packet instructions and serve on a plate topped with the duck ragu and grated parmesan.

NUTRITION PER PORTION:
SERVES - 6 | CALORIES - 505KCAL | PROTEIN - 30G | CARBOHYDRATES - 62G | FAT - 12G

RABBIT

RABBIT WITH BACON AND PRUNES

INGREDIENTS

- plain flour, for dusting
- 140g of prunes
- 50g of soft brown sugar
- 50ml of brandy
- 150ml of red wine
- 2 rabbits, jointed

- Vegetable oil for frying
- 2 carrots, chopped
- 2 celery sticks, chopped
- 3 rashers smoked streaky bacon, thin strips
- 1 garlic clove, crushed

- Fresh thyme
- 1 onion, chopped
- 1 bay leaf
- 250ml of chicken stock
- Optional: chopped parsley

METHOD

1. Before you start cooking, put the prunes to soak in a container of brown sugar and brandy.
2. Heat oil in a large frying pan. Dust the rabbit lightly with flour then put in the pan and fry all over until golden.
3. Set the rabbit to one side along with the meat juices and use a little red wine in the frying pan to collect any remaining meat juices from the pan.
4. Spritz a little oil into the slow cooker and add the bacon, vegetables, garlic and herbs.
5. Stir in the red wine, including the juice collected from the frying pan. Add the chicken stock, prunes and the seared rabbit.
6. Cover and cook on a Low setting for 3-4 hours until the meat is tender. Stir at intervals.
7. Serve with wild rice and sprinkled with chopped parsley.

NUTRITION PER PORTION:

SERVES - 4 | CALORIES - 607KCAL | PROTEIN - 61G | CARBOHYDRATES - 36G | FAT - 21G

SPANISH RABBIT STEW

INGREDIENTS

- 2 small rabbits (or 1 large rabbit), jointed
- Olive oil for frying
- 12 small red onions, peeled and halved
- 3 garlic cloves, peeled and sliced lengthways
- Fresh rosemary
- ½ tablespoon of sweet paprika
- 750ml of Spanish dry white wine (e.g., albariño wine)
- 1 x 250 - 300g jar of roasted red peppers, drained

METHOD

1. Heat oil in a large frying pan and fry the rabbit all over until golden, transfer to a plate with any juices and set aside.
2. Next, fry the garlic and onion and cook until softened, then add the paprika and rosemary. Season to taste and stir well.
3. Add a little wine to the frying pan to collect up the juices that may have stuck to it and transfer the contents to the slow cooker with the rabbit meat, and the rest of the wine.
4. Cover and cook on a Low setting for 3-4 hours until the meat is tender, and the sauce has thickened. Stir at intervals.
5. Drain the peppers and add to the pan for the final 30 minutes of cooking time.
6. If you like a thicker sauce, mix a teaspoon of cornflour or flour with a little water and add to the rabbit stew. Cover and cook for a further 30 minutes, stirring occasionally.
7. Optional: remove the meat, shred it with two forks, and return to the slow cooker, discarding any bones.
8. Serve with wedges of crusty bread.

NUTRITION PER PORTION:
SERVES - 6-8 | CALORIES - 410KCAL | PROTEIN - 37G | CARBOHYDRATES - 7G | FAT - 17G

GOOSE

GOOSE AND CRANBERRY SALSA

INGREDIENTS

- 1 whole goose (about 6kg), trimmed, giblets/excess fat removed

For the spice mix

- 3 star anise
- 8 whole cloves
- Zest of 2 oranges
- 2 chicken stock cubes
- 1 teaspoon of salt
- 2 teaspoons of ground cinnamon

For the salsa

- 2 onions, finely chopped
- 200g of cranberries (fresh or defrosted)
- 2 tablespoons of olive oil
- Juice and zest of 1 orange
- 1 tablespoon of cranberry sauce
- Zest of 2 limes
- 2 green chillies, finely chopped
- 1 teaspoon of picked thyme leaves

METHOD

1. The goose should be at room temperature before cooking.
2. Spritz the slow cooker with cooking oil and preheat on a Low setting.
3. Dry fry the whole spices in a frying pan over a medium heat until aromatic.
4. Grind the toasted spices to a fine powder and mix with the orange zest, stock cubes, and 1 teaspoon each of salt and cinnamon.
5. Put the goose into the slow cooker and with a sharp knife, score the skin all over. Rub in the spice mix, paying particular attention to the cuts.
6. Put the lid on and cook on a High setting for 4 hours.
7. Meanwhile make the salsa. In a frying pan over a medium heat, fry the onions in cooking oil until softened and golden brown. Add the cranberries and fry for a few more minutes. Remove the pan from the heat and stir in the rest of the salsa ingredients. Cover and place in a warm place to enable the flavours to infuse.
8. Carve the goose and serve with the cranberry salsa.

NUTRITION PER PORTION:
SERVES - 6-8 | CALORIES - 638KCAL | PROTEIN - 54G | CARBOHYDRATES - 5G | FAT - 44G

PHEASANT

PHEASANT CASSEROLE

INGREDIENTS

- 2 tablespoons of plain flour (plus extra for dusting)
- 2 pheasants, ready for the oven and divided into four portions
- 50g of butter
- Seasoning to taste
- 4 streaky bacon rashers, cut in half
- 2 sticks of celery, chopped
- 2 1/2 cm piece of fresh root ginger, sliced
- 2 onions, chopped
- 150ml of stock (fresh or from stock cubes)
- 350ml of dry cider
- 1 tablespoon of dried, crushed juniper berries
- 150 of double cream
- 4 peeled eating apples, cored and cut into wedges
- Juice of 1 lemon

METHOD

1. Dust the pheasant portions flour and season to taste.
2. In a hot pan, melt 40g of butter and sear the pheasant portions until they are browned all over.
3. Place the pheasant portions in the slow cooker, but don't turn it on yet.
4. Use the same frying pan to fry the bacon for about 4 minutes, then add the onions, juniper berries, celery, and ginger. Cook for a further 8-10 minutes to soften the vegetables.
5. Add the flour and stir until it begins to thicken, then gradually add the cider and the stock, stirring constantly until it boils.
6. Pour the stock mixture into the slow cooker and over the pheasant. Season, cover and cook on a Low setting for 7 hours.
7. Remove the cooked pheasant to a warm dish and cover to keep warm.
8. Use a sieve to strain the sauce into a pan and stir in the cream.
9. Bring the mixture to a rolling boil for about 10 minutes until it grows syrupy.
10. Melt the rest of the butter in a pan. Add the apple wedges and lemon juice and fry for 2-3 minutes.
11. Serve the pheasant and apple wedges hot on a platter filled with the fresh sauce.

NUTRITION PER PORTION:
SERVES - 8 | CALORIES - 478KCAL | PROTEIN - 32G | CARBOHYDRATES - 12G | FAT - 28G

PIGEON

PIGEON CASSEROLE

INGREDIENTS

- 2 carrots, peeled and chopped
- 2 onions, peeled and chopped
- 2 cloves of garlic, peeled and grated
- Olive oil for frying
- 4 pigeons, each one cut in half
- Fresh parsley, chopped
- 2 tablespoons of plain flour
- 750ml of chicken stock (fresh or from stock cubes)
- 250ml of dry white wine

METHOD

1. Sauté the chopped onion, carrot and garlic until it softens, then add the pigeon halves and sear them for 3-5 minutes until they are brown. Add flour and stir.
2. Transfer the contents of the frying pan to the slow cooker.
3. Pour in the wine, chicken stock and parsley, and season generously.
4. Put the lid on and cook on High for 4 hours.
5. Remove the cooked pigeon to a plate and use two forks to shred the meat and discard any bones. Return the meat to the slow cooker, stir, then serve with potatoes and crusty bread. Be careful of any bones.

NUTRITION PER PORTION:

SERVES - 4 | CALORIES - 430KCAL | PROTEIN - 16G | CARBOHYDRATES - 17G | FAT - 33G

PIGEON RAGU

INGREDIENTS

- Olive oil for frying
- 3 wood pigeons, quartered
- 275ml of red wine
- 1 onion, peeled and finely chopped
- 2 carrots, peeled and finely chopped
- 1 fresh red chilli, sliced lengthways with the bottom intact
- 3 x 400g tins of plum tomatoes
- 2 x 400g tins of water (use the empty tomato tins to measure)
- 1 bunch of fresh basil, chopped roughly
- 500g of spaghetti

METHOD

1. In a large frying pan, heat the oil and sear the pigeon quarters, turning occasionally until browned all over.
2. Add the wine and cook until it evaporates. Add the onion, carrot and chilli, and fry for a few minutes before transferring to the slow cooker.
3. Add the tins of tomatoes and 2 tins full of water. Stir in the basil.
4. Put the lid on and cook for 4 hours on a Low setting, stirring occasionally to break up the tomatoes. Add a little more water if necessary.
5. Follow the packet cooking instructions to prepare the spaghetti and drain. Add a couple of spoonfuls of sauce from the slow cooker and mix well.
6. Serve the spaghetti on warmed plates with the pigeon and sauce ladled over the top.

NUTRITION PER PORTION:

SERVES - 6 | CALORIES - 567KCAL | PROTEIN - 21G | CARBOHYDRATES - 72G | FAT - 17G

GOAT

GOAT RAGU WITH BROCCOLI AND GARLIC MASH

INGREDIENTS

- Olive oil for frying
- 2 onions, peeled and diced
- Fresh rosemary, chopped
- 3 cloves of garlic, peeled and finely grated
- 3 fresh bay leaves
- 1 teaspoon of ground nutmeg
- 1 tablespoon of red chilli flakes
- 1 teaspoon of dried oregano (or mixed herbs)
- 1 teaspoon of sugar
- 450g of kid goat leg meat, diced
- 150ml of red wine
- 2 tablespoons of tomato purée
- 400g tomatoes, diced (fresh or tinned)
- 175ml of beef stock
- 2 carrots, peeled and grated
- 2 heads of broccoli, chopped
- 2 cloves of garlic, peeled and grated
- 25g of butter
- a few sprigs of fresh basil

METHOD

1. Heat the oil in a frying pan and sauté the onions until softened.
2. Add the bay leaves, garlic, chilli flakes, rosemary, nutmeg, oregano and sugar. Fry for another 3 minutes, stirring often.
3. Next stir in the goat meat for a few minutes until browned. Season well with salt and black pepper.
4. Add the red wine and stir to include all the frying juices that are stuck to the pan, then transfer to the slow cooker.
5. Add the tomato purée and tomatoes. Add the stock, season and stir.
6. Cover the slow cooker and cook for 3 ½ hours on a Low setting.
7. Open the slow cooker and stir in the grated carrot. Cover and cook for a further 30-60 minutes. Add more seasoning if required.
8. About 30 minutes before serving, cook the broccoli in boiling water until softened. Drain, add the garlic and butter, and mash well.
9. Serve the ragu garnished with basil leaves, with the mashed broccoli.

NUTRITION PER PORTION:
SERVES - 4 | CALORIES - 407KCAL | PROTEIN - 40G | CARBOHYDRATES - 26G | FAT - 14G

GOAT AND SPINACH STEW

INGREDIENTS

- 450g of boneless goat shoulder, cut into cubes
- 4 garlic cloves, peeled and grated
- Oil for frying
- 2 medium onions, peeled and chopped
- 5cm piece of fresh ginger, peeled and grated
- 400g tin of chopped tomatoes
- 4 fresh Serrano chillies, quartered
- 1 green pepper, deseeded and sliced thinly
- Optional: 1 Scotch bonnet chilli, pierced rather than sliced
- 150ml of beef stock (fresh or from stock cubes)
- 150g of baby spinach
- 3 sprigs of fresh coriander

METHOD

1. Heat a tablespoon of oil in a large pan and sear the goat all over until browned. Transfer to a separate bowl with all the juices and set aside.
2. Add 2 tablespoons of oil to the same frying pan and fry the onion and garlic until softened. Stir in the tomatoes and fresh ginger.
3. Transfer to the slow cooker and add 100ml of water, the Serrano chillies, the (optional) Scotch Bonnet, and sliced pepper. Season with Seasoning to taste as required.
4. Now add the goat meat and meat juices and stir well.
5. Cover and cook on a Low setting for 4 hours.
6. Near the end of the 4 hours cooking time, remove and discard the Scotch Bonnets, and mix in the spinach. Turn off the heat, cover and leave the spinach to wilt. Stir again.
7. Serve with rice and scattered with coriander leaves.

NUTRITION PER PORTION:

SERVES - 4 | CALORIES - 309KCAL | PROTEIN - 32G | CARBOHYDRATES - 14G | FAT - 14G

VENISON

PORT AND VENISON CASSEROLE WITH DUMPLINGS

INGREDIENTS

- 6 baby turnips, trimmed and quartered
- 2 leeks, sliced
- 2 carrots, sliced
- 2 garlic cloves, sliced

- 2 teaspoons of vegetable oil
- 1.2kg venison, cut into chunks
- 200ml of port
- 100g of bacon lardons (ask your butcher if you're not sure!)

- 400ml of beef stock
- 200g of closed cup mushrooms sliced
- 1 bay leaf
- Seasoning to taste

For the dumplings

- ½ teaspoon of salt
- 20g of rolled oats
- 90g of self-raising flour

- 1 teaspoon of mixed dried herbs
- 1 tablespoon of fresh parsley, roughly chopped

- 50g suet

METHOD

1. Preheat your slow cooker on a Low setting and spritz with cooking oil.
2. Add the prepared carrots, garlic, turnip and leeks to the slow cooker.
3. In a large frying pan, heat the vegetable oil and add the venison chunks, a handful at a time until brown and sealed. Add the cooked venison to the slow cooker.
4. Add in the port to the frying pan, turn the heat up so it bubbles, then immediately transfer to the slow cooker with all the flavourful juices it has collected.
5. Add the bacon lardons to the same frying pan and cook until browned. Pour the beef stock in the frying pan with the lardons, give the mixture a stir and pour into the slow cooker. Add the mushrooms and bay leaf.
6. Cover and cook on a High setting for 6 hours, or a Low setting for 8 hours.
7. To make the dumplings: Add all the dry ingredients into a container and combine.
8. Add the suet and pour in just enough cold water to make a soft dough. It shouldn't be too wet. Knead the dough lightly and make 12 small round dumplings.
9. At the end of the cooking cycle, drop the dumplings gently into the slow cooker so that they sit on the surface of the casserole. Cover and cook for another 25-30 minutes until the dumplings have expanded and are light and fluffy.
10. Add any extra seasoning to the casserole and serve with dumplings and crusty bread.

NUTRITION PER PORTION:

SERVES - 6 | CALORIES - 496KCAL | PROTEIN - 52G | CARBOHYDRATES - 36 G | FAT - 10G

VENISON AND RED WINE CASSEROLE

INGREDIENTS

- 2 tablespoons of plain flour
- 900g venison, diced
- Vegetable oil for frying
- 3 carrots, peeled and finely diced
- 1 large onion, finely sliced
- 3 sticks celery, diced

- 3 garlic cloves, finely chopped
- 450ml of red wine
- 200ml of beef stock
- Optional: 10g dried wild mushrooms chopped
- 1 teaspoon of balsamic vinegar

- 10-12 juniper berries, lightly crushed
- 2 tablespoons of redcurrant jelly
- Fresh thyme and rosemary
- 2 bay leaves
- Seasoning to taste

METHOD

1. Prepare a shallow bowl with flour and seasoning and toss in the venison until it's coated.
2. Heat some oil in a frying pan over a medium heat and fry the diced venison until it's browned. Put the cooked venison the slow cooker.
3. In the same frying pan, heat a little more oil and fry the onion, carrots, celery and garlic for a few minutes to soften, then add to the slow cooker with the venison.
4. Wash a little wine around the frying pan to collect all the juices and flavourings from the meat and onions and pour into the slow cooker with the rest of the wine.
5. Stir in the stock, balsamic vinegar and stock with the dried mushrooms juniper berries and herbs and stir. Season to taste with Seasoning to taste.
6. Put the lid on and cook on Low for 8 hours.
7. Serve.

NUTRITION PER PORTION:

SERVES - 4 | CALORIES - 279KCAL | PROTEIN - 35G | CARBOHYDRATES - 14G | FAT - 2G

VENISON, KALE AND MUSHROOM STROGANOFF

INGREDIENTS

- 200g of venison steaks, cut into strips
- oil for frying
- 2 shallots, peeled and finely sliced
- 100-150g of black kale leaves, shredded
- 2 portobello mushrooms thinly sliced
- 1 teaspoon of paprika
- ½ teaspoon of smoked paprika
- 100ml of white wine
- 150ml of crème fraiche
- 1 lemon
- 1 tablespoon of chopped dill leaves
- Seasoning to taste
- 125g basmati rice

METHOD

1. Heat a frying pan of oil on a medium heat. Season the venison with Seasoning to taste and stir-fry the venison briefly until sealed and browned and place in the bottom of the slow cooker.
2. Turn the heat down and add a little more oil to the same frying pan. Stir fry the shallots, kale and mushrooms on a medium heat for about 3 minutes until the mushrooms have softened. Put in the slow cooker with the meat.
3. Wash a little wine around the frying pan to collect the juices and flavourings and add to the slow cooker with the rest of the wine. Stir in both paprikas.
4. Add the crème fraiche, a squeeze of lemon juice and season to taste. Stir in the dill.
5. Cover and cook on a Low heat for 6 hours.
6. When you're ready to serve, prepare the basmati rice according to packet instructions, and drain thoroughly before serving.
7. Serve the venison stroganoff on a bed of rice.

NUTRITION PER PORTION:

SERVES - 2 | CALORIES - 536KCAL | PROTEIN - 37G | CARBOHYDRATES - 15G | FAT - 33G

VENISON AND ALE PIE (PIE FILLING OR CASSEROLE)

INGREDIENTS

- 1 garlic clove, crushed
- 30g of butter
- 1 large onion, thinly sliced
- 650g of venison, diced
- 1 tablespoon of plain flour, seasoned
- 200ml of strong ale
- 100ml beef stock (fresh or from stock cubes)
- 1 tablespoon of brown sugar
- 1 bouquet garni
- 15ml of vinegar
- 1 tablespoon of beer mustard (buy or make your own)
- Optional: pastry for pie crust
- Seasoning to taste

METHOD

1. Heat a frying pan of oil on a medium heat and fry the onion and garlic until it softens. Remove to the slow cooker with a slotted spoon.
2. Put the flour in a shallow dish and season with Seasoning to taste. Add and turn the diced venison in the flour so it's coated then stir fry it in the frying pan using the remaining butter until it's golden brown. Put in the slow cooker with the onions.
3. Wash a little of the ale around the frying pan to collect the meat juices and flavours, then pour into the slow cooker with the rest of the ale, and the stock.
4. Stir in the vinegar, sugar, mustard, and the bouquet garni.
5. Cover the slow cooker and cook for 6 hours on a Low setting. (Note: remove and discard the bouquet garni after 90 minutes)
6. Optional: For a pie, transfer the casserole to an ovenproof dish, top with pastry, and cook in the oven at 180°C/Gas Mark 4 for about 30 minutes until the pastry is cooked.
7. Optional: Serve as a casserole with mash and savoy cabbage.

NUTRITION PER PORTION:
SERVES - 4 | CALORIES - 328KCAL | PROTEIN - 37G | CARBOHYDRATES - 8G | FAT - 8G

VENISON COTTAGE PIE

INGREDIENTS

- 700g of venison mince
- oil for frying
- 2 garlic cloves, finely chopped
- 2 streaky bacon rashers, finely chopped
- 2 tablespoons of tomato purée
- 2 carrots, peeled and diced
- 1 large onion, finely chopped
- 4 mushrooms chopped into small pieces
- 100ml red wine
- 1 tablespoon of Worcestershire sauce
- ½ teaspoons dried thyme
- 200ml beef stock
- 1 heaped teaspoon of cornflour
- Seasoning to taste
- 800g potatoes, peeled and cut into rough pieces
- 400g celeriac, peeled and diced
- Butter for mashing
- Milk for mashing

METHOD

1. Heat the oil in a frying pan and brown the mince. Break up any larger pieces and put in the bottom of the slow cooker.
2. Add a little more oil to the same pan, and stir fry the bacon, onion, garlic and carrot for a few minutes until the onion is soft. Transfer to the slow cooker with the venison and stir in the mushrooms and tomato puree.
3. Wash a little wine around the frying pan to collect the juices and flavourings from the stir fried meat and vegetables, then pour into the slow cooker with the rest of the wine.
4. Add the Worcestershire sauce, thyme and stock to the slow cooker. Season to taste.

5. Cover the slow cooker and cook for 6 hours on a Low setting.
6. About halfway through, make a paste from the cornflour and a little water, and stir into the slow cooker. Leave to cook for the remainder of the 6 hours, stirring occasionally.
7. Boil the potatoes and celeriac in salted water until tender. Drain and mash with a good 20g of butter and a splash of milk. Season well with Seasoning to taste.
8. Spoon the venison mince into an ovenproof dish and spread the mash over the top covering all the meat. Use a fork to fluff up the top a little.
9. Turn the oven to 180C//gas mark 4. Put the cottage pie dish in the oven and bake for 20-30 minutes, until golden and crisp.
10. Serve the cottage pie with seasonal vegetables.

NUTRITION PER PORTION:

SERVES - 5 | CALORIES - 366KCAL | PROTEIN - 38G | CARBOHYDRATES - 41G | FAT - 4G

VENISON RAGU
• •

INGREDIENTS

- 4 tablespoons of olive oil
- 1 celery stick, finely diced
- 1 onion, finely diced
- 350g of minced venison
- 1 carrot, finely diced
- 150ml of red wine
- 1 x 400g tin of chopped tomatoes
- 1 teaspoon of anchovy paste
- ½ teaspoon of hot chilli flakes
- 1 teaspoon of fresh rosemary leaves, chopped
- Seasoning to taste

METHOD

1. Heat the oil in a large pan and fry the onion, carrot and celery until softened and lightly browned. Transfer to the slow cooker.
2. In the same pan, heat a little more oil and stir fry the mince until it is browned, then add to the onion mix in the slow cooker.
3. Wash a little of the wine around the frying pan to collect the meat juices and flavourings and add to the slow cooker with the rest of the wine.
4. Stir in the anchovy paste, chilli flakes, rosemary, and tomatoes.
5. Season to taste.
6. Cover the slow cooker and cook for 6 hours on a Low setting, stirring occasionally. Just add a little beef stock or water if it gets too dry.

NUTRITION PER PORTION:

SERVES - 4 | CALORIES - 293KCAL | PROTEIN - 21G | CARBOHYDRATES - 9G | FAT - 18G

VENISON CHILLI WITH A CHOCOLATE TWIST
• •

INGREDIENTS

- 500g of minced venison
- ½ teaspoon of dried oregano
- ½ teaspoon of ground cumin
- ½ teaspoon of cinnamon
- 1 teaspoon of cumin seeds
- 1 red chilli, deseeded and thinly sliced
- 2 tablespoons of olive oil
- ½ teaspoon of dried coriander
- 3 garlic cloves, crushed
- 1 teaspoon of coriander seeds
- 2 large onions, chopped
- 2 carrots, chopped
- 400g tin of chopped tomatoes
- 100ml of beef stock
- 2x400g tins of kidney beans, drained
- 50g of 85% dark chocolate, grated
- Seasoning to taste

METHOD

1. In a large bowl, use your hands to mix the venison with the oregano, ground cumin, cinnamon, dried coriander and half the garlic and chilli. Cover and leave to marinade for an hour.
2. Heat the oil in a large pan, add the cumin seeds and coriander seeds and stir continuously until they release their aromas.
3. Add the onion, carrot and remaining garlic and stir fry over a low heat to soften. Turn the heat up a little more and add the spicy venison mince. Stir until browned thoroughly, then transfer all of the mixture to the slow cooker.
4. Pour in the chopped tomatoes, beef stock and the remaining chilli.
5. Cover the slow cooker with the lid and cook on Low for 6 hours, stirring at intervals. Add a little more water or stock if it gets too dry.
6. Finally, stir in the kidney beans and the grated chocolate and mix thoroughly.
7. Cook for another 30 minutes on Low and adjust the seasoning to taste. The venison chilli should now be rich, red and thickened.
8. Serve with rice and top with a dollop of soured cream.

NUTRITION PER PORTION:

SERVES - 4 | CALORIES - 632KCAL | PROTEIN - 49G | CARBOHYDRATES - 61G | FAT - 17G

DESSERTS

BANANA BREAD

INGREDIENTS

- 2 teaspoons baking powder
- 200g of strong white flour
- 2 teaspoons cinnamon
- 2 eggs
- 3 ripe bananas (the softer they are, the better they will mash)
- 100ml of vegetable oil
- 1 teaspoon vanilla extract
- 150g of soft brown sugar

METHOD

1. Preheat the slow cooker on a Low setting.
2. Grease a loaf tin making sure it fits in your slow cooker first.
3. Sift the cinnamon and baking powder into the flour into a container together.
4. In a clean bow bowl whisk the eggs until smooth.
5. In a third bowl use a fork to mash the bananas until they are free of lumps.
6. Pour the beaten eggs into the mashed banana and mix well until combined, then stir in the oil, sugar and vanilla extract.
7. Make a well in the bowl containing the dry ingredients, and slowly pour in the egg mixture, stirring gently until everything is blended to a smooth mixture.
8. Pour the cake mixture into the prepared loaf tin and place the filled tin into the slow cooker. Cook for 2-3 hours on a High setting. When it is ready you should be able to insert a skewer into the centre and it come out clean.
9. Leave to cool for about 10-15 minutes before removing the banana bread from the loaf tin; once removed, place on a cooling rack to cool completely.

TIP: Place a tea towel/kitchen roll under the slow cooker's lid during cooking to prevent the condensation dripping back into your cake or bread, making it soggy.

NUTRITION PER PORTION:
SERVES - 8 | CALORIES - 325KCAL | PROTEIN - 5G | CARBOHYDRATES - 49G | FAT - 13G

APPLE CRUMBLE

INGREDIENTS

- 5 peeled, cored eating apples, each cut into 8 wedges
- Zest and juice of 1 orange
- 1 teaspoon of ground cinnamon
- 60g of rolled oats
- 50g of walnut pieces
- ½ teaspoon of ground ginger
- 85g of light muscovado sugar
- 75g of plain flour
- 90g of unsalted butter, melted

METHOD

1. Preheat the slow cooker and spritz lightly with cooking oil spray.
2. Add the apple slices to the slow cooker and mix in the orange zest, 1 tablespoon of orange juice, and the cinnamon.
3. Pulse the oats and walnuts together in a blender until the mixture breaks up and resembles coarse breadcrumbs, then transfer into a clean bowl. Stir in the plain flour, sugar and ginger. Combine the melted butter.
4. Spoon the crumble mixture over the apples, making sure they are well-covered in an even layer.

5. TIP: Put two sheets of kitchen roll between the crumble and the lid of the slow cooker to prevent condensation dripping back and making your pudding soggy.
6. Cover and cook on a Low heat setting for 3½ hours.
7. Remove the kitchen paper and cook for the last 10 minutes with the lid slightly ajar.

NUTRITION PER PORTION:

SERVES - 4 | CALORIES - 519KCAL | PROTEIN - 6G | CARBOHYDRATES - 64G | FAT - 29G

MANGO AND GINGER SLOW-COOKED CHEESECAKE

INGREDIENTS

- 180g of ginger nut biscuits
- 50g of butter, melted
- 70g of caster sugar
- 2 eggs
- 400g of full fat soft cheese
- 100ml of whipping cream
- 1 passion fruit, halved and seeds scooped out
- Juice and zest of 1 lime
- 1-2 fresh mint sprigs, leaves picked, to garnish
- 1 small, firm mango, peeled
- 2 tablespoons of passion fruit coulis, to serve

METHOD

1. Preheat the slow cooker and spritz lightly with cooking oil spray.
2. Prepare your tin/flan dish - but make sure it fits your slow cooker. Ideally, grease a deep 18cm tin/flan dish and line with nonstick baking paper.
3. Crush 180g of gingernut biscuits into fine crumbs. Add the melted butter, stir well, then press firmly and evenly into the bottom of the prepared tin with the back of a spoon.
4. In a container, beat the eggs, caster sugar and soft cheese until thoroughly combined.
5. Whip the whipping cream in a separate bowl until it forms soft peaks. Add the soft cheese mixture, lime zest and juice and fold together gently with a spoon.
6. Stir in the passionfruit seeds and juice and pour the mixture over the biscuit base.
7. Prepare the slow cooker.
   - Find a heatproof plate that fits snugly inside the slow cooker and place it upside-down in the bottom.
   - Pour 400ml boiling water over the plate and into the bottom of the slow cooker.
   - Sit the cake tin on top of the plate.
   - Close the slow cooker lid.
8. Cook on a Low setting for 2 ½ hours. Keep the lid closed during cooking.
9. Turn off the slow cooker and leave the cheesecake to stand, covered with the lid for another 2 ½ hours.
10. Remove the tin from the slow cooker and place in the fridge to chill overnight (or for 2 hours minimum).
11. When you're ready to serve it, very gently loosen and remove the cheesecake from the tin and set on a plate.
12. Use a potato peeler to shave the flesh off the mango and sprinkle the top of the cheesecake with the mango curls.
13. Serve topped with a drizzle of passionfruit coulis and mint leaves.

NUTRITION PER PORTION:

SERVES - 10 | CALORIES - 240KCAL | PROTEIN - 3G | CARBOHYDRATES - 27G | FAT - 14G

LEMON AND PECAN SLOW COOKED CHEESECAKE

INGREDIENTS

- 50g of butter, melted
- 130g of digestive biscuits
- 50g of toasted and chopped pecan nuts
- 400g of full fat soft cheese
- 70g of caster sugar
- 2 eggs
- 100ml of whipping cream
- 3 tablespoons of lemon curd
- Zest of 1 lemon
- 1-2 fresh mint sprigs, leaves picked, to garnish
- 2 tablespoons of warm lemon curd, to serve

METHOD

1. Preheat the slow cooker and spritz lightly with cooking oil spray.
2. Prepare your tin/flan dish - but make sure it fits your slow cooker. Ideally, grease a deep 18cm flan dish and line with nonstick baking paper.
3. Crush 130g of digestive biscuits into fine crumbs. This is best done in a food processor. Add 50g of toasted and chopped pecan nuts and combine.
4. Add the melted butter, stir well, then press firmly and evenly into the base of the prepared dish using the back of a spoon.
5. In a container, beat the caster sugar, 2 eggs and soft cheese until thoroughly combined.
6. In a separate bowl, whip the cream to form soft peaks, then add the soft cheese, 3 tablespoons of lemon curd, and fold together gently with a spoon. Carefully pour the mixture in an even layer over the biscuit crumb base.
7. Prepare the slow cooker.
   - Find a heatproof plate that fits snugly inside the slow cooker and place it upside-down in the bottom.
   - Pour 400ml boiling water over the plate and into the bottom of the slow cooker.
   - Sit the cake tin on top of the plate.
   - Close the lid on the slow cooker
8. Cook on a Low setting for 2 ½ hours. Don't remove the lid during this time.
9. Turn off the slow cooker and leave the cheesecake to stand, covered with the lid for another 2 ½ hours.
10. Remove the tin from the slow cooker and place in the fridge to chill overnight (or for 2 hours minimum).
11. When you're ready to serve it, very gently loosen and remove the cheesecake from the tin and set on a plate.
12. Sprinkle the top of the cheesecake with the lemon zest.
13. Serve topped with fresh mint leaves and a drizzle of warm lemon curd.

NUTRITION PER PORTION:
SERVES - 10 | CALORIES - 265KCAL | PROTEIN - 4G | CARBOHYDRATES - 18G | FAT - 21 G

GINGER AND DOUBLE CHOCOLATE CHEESECAKE

INGREDIENTS

- 50g of butter, melted
- 180g of dark chocolate and ginger cookies
- 2 eggs
- 400g of full fat soft cheese
- 70g of caster sugar
- 100g of white chocolate, melted
- 100ml of whipping cream
- Optional topping: white and dark chocolate shavings
- Fresh raspberries

METHOD

1. Preheat the slow cooker and spritz lightly with cooking oil spray.
2. Prepare your tin/flan dish - but make sure it fits your slow cooker. Ideally, grease a deep 18cm tin/dish and line with nonstick baking paper.
3. Crush 180g of dark chocolate and ginger cookies into fine crumbs. This is best done in a blender.
4. Add the melted butter, stir well, then press firmly and evenly into the bottom of the prepared tin using the back of a spoon.
5. In a container, beat the 2 eggs, caster sugar and soft cheese until thoroughly combined. Fold in 100g of melted white chocolate.
6. In a container, whip the cream to form soft peaks, then add the soft cheese mixture and fold together gently with a spoon. Carefully pour the mixture in an even layer over the biscuit crumb base.
7. Prepare the slow cooker.
   - Find a heatproof plate that fits snugly inside the slow cooker and place it upside-down in the bottom.
   - Pour 400ml boiling water over the plate and into the bottom of the slow cooker.
   - Sit the cake tin on top of the plate.
   - Close the lid on the slow cooker
8. Cook on a Low setting for 2 ½ hours. Don't remove the lid during this time.
9. Turn off the slow cooker and leave the cheesecake to stand, covered with the lid for another 2 ½ hours.
10. Remove the tin from the slow cooker and place in the fridge to chill overnight (or for 2 hours minimum).
11. When you are ready to serve it, very gently loosen and remove the cheesecake from the tin and set on a plate.
12. Use a potato peeler to shave off curls of white and dark chocolate.
13. Serve topped with fresh raspberries and white and dark chocolate curls.

NUTRITION PER PORTION:

SERVES - 10 | CALORIES - 352KCAL | PROTEIN - 5G | CARBOHYDRATES - 26G | FAT - 26G

DELICIOUS BRIOCHE BREAD PUDDING
WITH SALTED CARAMEL SAUCE

INGREDIENTS

- 30g of unsalted butter
- 1 teaspoon of vanilla extract
- 125g salted caramel sauce
- 200ml of double cream
- 2 large egg yolks only

- Optional: 2 tablespoons of dark rum
- 2 large eggs
- 100g of pecan nuts, chopped roughly

- 8 pack of butter brioche rolls, broken into 3cm pieces
- 100g of dark chocolate, chopped roughly

METHOD

1. Preheat the slow cooker dish on a low setting and grease thoroughly with the butter.
2. Prepare the bread pudding mixture by heating the cream with half the caramel sauce over a medium heat. When it bubbles, turn off the heat and stir thoroughly. Allow to cool.
3. Whisk together the eggs, a pinch of salt, the extra egg yolks, the dark rum (if using) and vanilla extract in a separate bowl.
4. Now, pour the cooled warm cream mixture slowly and carefully into the eggs, whisking until everything is combined.
5. Stir in the chocolate, brioche and pecans until everything is mixed through.
6. Leave soaking for 5 minutes, then stir until the brioche is coated all over.
7. Tip the bread pudding mixture into the greased and preheated slow cooker dish, and level it with a spatula.

8. Cover with a lid and cook for on a Low setting for 1 ½ hours. A knife inserted into the centre of the pudding should come out clean when it's cooked, otherwise give it another 30 minutes cooking time.
9. Warm the remaining caramel sauce and serve over the bread pudding with a spoonful of whipped cream.

NUTRITION PER PORTION:

SERVES - 8 | CALORIES - 544KCAL | PROTEIN - 9G | CARBOHYDRATES - 36G | FAT - 41G

PEAR UPSIDE-DOWN CAKE

INGREDIENTS

- 200g of butter
- 3 pears, peeled, cored and halved lengthways
- 50g of light brown sugar
- 250g of caster sugar
- ½ teaspoon of vanilla extract
- 3 medium eggs
- 200g of plain flour
- 1½ teaspoons of baking powder
- ½ teaspoon of ground ginger
- ½ teaspoon of ground cinnamon
- 50g of ground almonds
- 3 tablespoons of semi-skimmed milk

METHOD

1. Grease your slow cooker and line with foil. Grease the inside of the foil and turn the slow cooker to Low.
2. Dot 50g of the butter evenly across the bottom of the slow cooker. Sprinkle with light brown sugar and layer the pears evenly over the top.
3. In a separate bowl, beat the remaining butter spread with the caster sugar until light and fluffy.
4. Gradually add the eggs, mix in well, then beat in the vanilla extract.
5. Now mix in the baking powder and flour, ground cinnamon and ginger and ground almonds, then beat to combine. Fold in the milk.
6. Pour the cake mixture over the pears and level out.
7. Put a length of kitchen rolls in between the cake and the lid to stop condensation dripping down - but make sure the kitchen roll isn't touching the cake.
8. Put the lid on and cook on a Low setting for 3 hours.
9. Turn off the slow cooker. Leave the cake to rest for 30 minutes with the lid closed, then transfer to a wire rack.
10. Remove the foil, and when ready to serve, transfer to a large plate to slice.

NUTRITION PER PORTION:

SERVES - 12 | CALORIES - 284KCAL | PROTEIN - 5G | CARBOHYDRATES - 40G | FAT - 11G

STEAMED STICKY TOFFEE PUDDING

INGREDIENTS

- 2 teaspoons of black treacle
- 225g of soft dark brown sugar
- 300ml of double cream
- 200g of dates, stones removed and roughly chopped
- 300ml of water, boiled
- 1 teaspoon of bicarbonate of soda
- 50g of unsalted butter
- 175g of self-raising flour, sifted
- 2 medium eggs

METHOD

1. Grease a pudding bowl that will fit in your slow cooker.
2. Firstly, make your toffee sauce. In a saucepan over a gentle heat, stir the cream, black treacle and 50g of sugar, until the sugar has dissolved. Bring to a rolling boil for about 2 minutes.

3. Now add the dates to a saucepan with 300ml of cold water and bring to the boil. Turn off the heat and add the bicarbonate of soda. The mixture will fizz briefly, then settle down.
4. In a container, beat the remaining sugar and butter together until light and fluffy. Add the eggs, fold in the flour, and finally stir in the date mixture.
5. Tip half of the toffee sauce into the bottom of the pudding basin and pour in the pudding/cake mixture on top.
6. Secure buttered foil and baking paper over the top of the basin, making a pleat in the centre to allow the pudding to rise. Tie securely with string to prevent moisture getting into the pudding, and place in the slow cooker. Add enough boiling water to reach halfway up the sides of the slow cooker.
7. Put the lid on and cook for 4 hours on High or 8 hours on Low.
8. Once cooked, leave the pudding to cool then transfer to a plate.
9. Serve the pudding hot with warm toffee sauce, cream or ice cream.

NUTRITION PER PORTION:

SERVES - 12 | CALORIES - 284KCAL | PROTEIN - 5G | CARBOHYDRATES - 40G | FAT - 11G

SPICED AND SLICED APPLES WITH BARLEY

INGREDIENTS

- 100g of barley
- 2 eating apples
- ½ teaspoon of cinnamon
- a grating of fresh nutmeg
- Zest of 1 orange, finely grated
- 60g of natural yoghurt

METHOD

1. Preheat the slow cooker on Low and lightly spritz with cooking oil.
2. Add the barley and 750ml of boiling water to the slow cooker.
3. Peel and core the apples, then each one in half.
4. Place the apples onto the barley layer in the slow cooker, with the flat flesh side facing upwards.
5. In a container, mix up the nutmeg, the cinnamon and orange zest, and sprinkle the spiced mixture over the apples.
6. Cover and cook on a Low setting for 2 hours.
7. Serve with whipped cream, natural Greek yoghurt, or ice cream.

NUTRITION PER PORTION:

SERVES - 4 | CALORIES - 168KCAL | PROTEIN - 6G | CARBOHYDRATES - 28G | FAT - 2G

TREACLE SPONGE

INGREDIENTS

- 3 tablespoons of golden syrup, plus extra for drizzling
- Optional: a splash of brandy
- 1 tablespoon of fresh white breadcrumbs
- Zest of 1 lemon
- 175g of golden caster sugar
- 175g of softened unsalted butter
- 3 eggs, beaten
- 175g of self-raising flour
- 15mls of milk
- clotted cream, to serve

METHOD

1. Grease a pudding basin that will fit in your slow cooker.
2. Preheat your slow cooker on a low setting.
3. Meanwhile, in a container, combine the breadcrumbs, syrup, and (optional) brandy, and place the mixture at the bottom of the pudding basin.
4. In a separate clean bowl, beat the butter, sugar and zest until the mixture is light and fluffy, then gradually add the eggs, fold in the flour, and pour in the milk. Transfer the mixture into the pudding basin.
5. Secure buttered foil and baking paper over the top of the basin, making a pleat in the centre to allow the pudding to rise. Tie securely with string to prevent moisture getting into the pudding, and place in the slow cooker. Add enough boiling water to reach halfway up the sides of the slow cooker.
6. Cook for 4 hours on High or 8 hours on Low.
7. Once cooked, leave the pudding to cool for 2 minutes then transfer to a plate.
8. Serve with hot custard, cream and or even drizzle some golden syrup over the top.

NUTRITION PER PORTION:

SERVES - 4 | CALORIES - 763KCAL | PROTEIN - 10G | CARBOHYDRATES - 90G | FAT - 43G

CHOCOLATE FONDANT CAKE
• •

INGREDIENTS

- 100g of golden caster sugar
- 100g of butter
- 50g of light brown soft sugar
- 3 eggs, beaten
- 50g of cocoa powder

- 1 teaspoon of baking powder
- 250g of self-raising flour
- ½ teaspoons of instant espresso powder

- 100g of dark chocolate, chopped (or use dark chocolate chips)
- 100-150ml of milk
- Crème fraiche, whipped cream or vanilla ice cream, to serve

For the sauce

- 200g of light brown soft sugar
- 25g of cocoa powder

- ½ teaspoon of instant espresso powder

- ½ teaspoon of vanilla extract

METHOD

1. Thoroughly grease the bowl of your slow cooker and set to preheat on a Low setting.
2. Meanwhile, beat the butter and both sugars together until pale and fluffy. Gradually stir in the eggs, then fold in the flour, cocoa, baking powder, espresso, a pinch of salt and the chocolate. Add just enough milk so the batter falls easily off the spatula in dollops. It should not be too runny.
3. Transfer the mixture into the slow cooker.
4. In a heatproof bowl, whisk the sauce ingredients with 300mls of boiling water. Carefully pour the sauce over the batter in the slow cooker, then cover and cook on Low for 5-6 hours or High for 3 hours. The cake should be firm to touch, well-risen and spring back when pressed gently.
5. Serve with crème fraiche, whipped cream or vanilla ice cream. Alternatively, it tastes delicious with hot custard.

NUTRITION PER PORTION:

SERVES - 8 | CALORIES - 518KCAL | PROTEIN - 9G | CARBOHYDRATES - 74G | FAT - 20G

FRUIT AND NUT MUSCOVADO CHEESECAKE

INGREDIENTS

- 100g of blanched hazelnuts
- 50g of butter, melted, plus extra for greasing
- 225g of oat biscuits
- 250g of light muscovado sugar

- 60mls of full-fat milk
- 1 teaspoon of vanilla extract
- 750g of full-fat cream cheese
- 3 large eggs
- 2 tablespoons of plain flour

- 3 large eggs
- 200ml pot of soured cream
- Optional: 15mls of hazelnut liqueur

For the topping

- 2 teaspoons of cornflour
- 45g of golden caster sugar
- 200g of blackberries

METHOD

1. Preheat the slow cooker and spritz lightly with cooking oil spray.
2. Meanwhile, crush the oat biscuits and hazelnuts to fine breadcrumbs in a food processor.
3. Add the melted butter, stir well, then press firmly and evenly into the prepared tin. Put in the fridge to chill for about 10-15 minutes.
4. Heat the muscovado and milk in a saucepan over a low heat until the sugar has completely dissolved. Set to one side to cool.
5. In a separate bowl, beat to combine the cream cheese, vanilla extract plain flour, and eggs until you have a smooth mixture.
6. Stir in the soured cream, the (optional) hazelnut liquor, and the cooled milk and muscovado mixture until well combined.
7. Carefully pour the mixture into the tin over the biscuit base and spread evenly.
8. Prepare the slow cooker.
   - Find a heatproof plate that fits snugly inside the slow cooker and place it upside-down in the bottom.
   - Pour 400ml boiling water over the plate and into the bottom of the slow cooker - it should rise about 4cm up the sides.
   - Sit the cake tin on top of the plate.
   - Wrap the lid in a tea towel to prevent condensation from dripping onto the cheesecake and close the slow cooker.
9. Cook on a Low setting for 2 ½ hours. Leave the lid closed during this time.
10. Turn off the slow cooker and leave the cheesecake to stand, covered with the lid for another 2 ½ hours.
11. Remove the tin from the slow cooker and place in the fridge to chill overnight (or for 2 hours minimum).
12. For the topping: Put the cornflour, caster sugar and half of the blackberries in a saucepan heat. Cook for 3-4 minutes, stirring the mixture and gently squashing the blackberries, so they become syrupy. Throw in the rest of the berries, heat thorough, then remove from the heat and leave to cool until ready to serve.
13. Crush the leftover nuts and dry fry in a frying pan to toast.
14. When you're ready to serve the cheesecake, very gently loosen and remove it from the tin and set on a plate.
15. Serve topped with the cooked berry syrup and toasted hazelnuts - and an extra shot of (optional) hazelnut liqueur.

NUTRITION PER PORTION:
SERVES - 10 | CALORIES - 612KCAL | PROTEIN - 10G | CARBOHYDRATES - 52G | FAT - 39G

RICE PUDDING

INGREDIENTS

- 1 teaspoon of butter
- 1 litre of semi-skimmed milk
- 200g of pudding rice
- A little ground nutmeg or cinnamon
- Optional: 1 tablespoon of honey
- Optional: A handful of toasted, flaked almonds and dried fruit

METHOD

1. Preheat the slow cooker on a High setting, and thoroughly grease all over with the butter.
2. In a saucepan, bring the milk to a simmer on a medium heat.
3. Place the pudding rice into the slow cooker, and immediately pour the warm milk over the top.
4. Add ground nutmeg or cinnamon to taste.
5. Cook for 2½ hours on High, stirring at intervals.
6. Serve with a drizzle of honey, and/or sprinkled with flaked almonds and fruit.

NUTRITION PER PORTION:

SERVES - 6 | CALORIES - 200KCAL | PROTEIN - 8G | CARBOHYDRATES - 32G | FAT - 4G

CHRISTMAS PUDDING

INGREDIENTS

- 100g of sultanas
- 30g of mixed candied peel, chopped
- 100g of raisins
- 100g of currants
- 1 small cooking apple, peeled, cored, and chopped into small pieces
- Zest of 2 lemons
- Zest and juice of two oranges (juice of 1 orange only)
- 75ml of brandy, whiskey or rum
- 100ml of stout
- 2 eggs
- 50g of self-raising flour
- 100g of breadcrumbs
- 1 teaspoon of mixed spice
- 1 teaspoon of ground cinnamon
- 100g of shredded suet
- 200g of dark brown soft sugar
- 50g of blanched almonds, chopped
- brandy butter or custard, to serve

METHOD

1. Find the largest bowl you have and add the sultanas, raisins, currants and candied peel. Next, add the apple, orange and lemon zest, the juice of 1 orange, the brandy and stout. Mix it all together thoroughly, cover the bowl and leave to soak overnight.
2. Put all of the remaining ingredients in the bowl with the soaked dried fruit, add ½ teaspoon salt and mix thoroughly to combine.
3. Thoroughly grease a pudding basin with butter and line the base with a circle of parchment paper. (Make sure the basin will fit in your slow cooker!)
4. Preheat your slow cooker on a low setting.
5. Transfer the mixture into the pudding basin and create a small dip in the middle.
6. Secure buttered foil and baking paper over the top of the basin, making a pleat in the centre to allow the pudding to rise. Tie securely with string to prevent moisture getting into the pudding, and place in the slow cooker. Add enough boiling water to reach halfway up the sides of the slow cooker.
7. Cover with the slow cooker lid.
8. Cook on a Low setting for 10 hours. Top up with extra boiling water as necessary so the slow cooker doesn't go dry.
9. Once cooked, remove the basin from the slow cooker to a cooling rack. Leave to cool completely before storing in a cool, dark place for up to six months.

10. When you're ready to serve, set the slow cooker to Low and place the pudding inside. Pour in enough hot water to come halfway up the sides of the slow cooker.
11. Reheat for 4 hours, then transfer to a serving plate.
12. Serve hot, with lashings of brandy butter, clotted cream or custard.

NUTRITION PER PORTION:

SERVES - 10 | CALORIES - 371KCAL | PROTEIN - 5G | CARBOHYDRATES - 52G | FAT - 13G

CLOTTED CREAM FUDGE

INGREDIENTS

- ◆ 300g of golden caster sugar
- ◆ 100g of golden syrup
- ◆ 200g of clotted cream
- ◆ 2 teaspoons of vanilla extract
- ◆ vegetable oil for greasing the tin

METHOD

1. Preheat the slow cooker on a Low setting.
2. Add the caster sugar, golden syrup, clotted cream, vanilla and a pinch of sea salt to the slow cooker and stir until smooth and combined.
3. Turn the setting to High and cook for 4-5 hours, stirring at 30 minutes intervals. The finished fudge mixture should turn golden and glossy.
4. Oil a 20cm baking tin and line with parchment paper.
5. Lift the slow cooker bowl out onto a heatproof mat. Remove the lid and mix vigorously for 10 minutes to break up any large sugar crystals and to speed up cooling. It will thicken and loose its glossy look.
6. Pour the fudge mixture into the prepared greased tin and spread evenly.
7. Sprinkle with a bit of salt and chill for at least an hour in the fridge until it's the fudge is set.
8. Remove from the tin, cut into chunks and store in an airtight container in the fridge for up to 5 days.

NUTRITION PER PORTION:

SERVES - 16 SQUARES | CALORIES - 169KCAL | PROTEIN - 0.2G | CARBOHYDRATES - 24G | FAT - 8G

SLOW-COOKED RHUBARB

INGREDIENTS

- ◆ 800g of rhubarb cut into 2inch pieces
- ◆ Optional: 100ml of dessert wine
- ◆ 300g of caster sugar
- ◆ Zest of 2 oranges, removed in large strips.

METHOD

1. Preheat the slow cooker on a low setting.
2. Put all the rhubarb pieces into the slow cooker, add the zest and scatter the sugar evenly over the top.
3. Optional: Pour the wine over the rhubarb.
4. Cover with a lid and cook on Low for about 1 hour until the rhubarb tenderises.
5. Serve the rhubarb in its own juices, with scoops of ice cream.

NUTRITION PER PORTION:

SERVES - 6 | CALORIES - 371KCAL | PROTEIN - 5G | CARBOHYDRATES - 52G | FAT - 13G

APPLE, PEAR, AND CHERRY COMPOTE

INGREDIENTS

- 4 medium cooking apples, peeled and cut into chunks
- 8 pears, peeled and thickly sliced
- 8 eating apples peeled and cut into chunks
- 85g of sugar, or to taste
- 50mls of water
- 280g of dried sour cherries (dried cranberries are a good alternative)

METHOD

1. Preheat the slow cooker on a Low setting.
2. Add all of the ingredients into the slow cooker and cover with 50mls of water.
3. Give the fruit mixture a good stir.
4. Put the lid on and cook on a Low setting for 8-10 hours.
5. Delicious serve with ice-cream or cream, or even warm custard.

NUTRITIONAL INFORMATION PER SERVING (WITHOUT ACCOMPANIMENT):

SERVES - 12 | CALORIES - 199KCAL | PROTEIN - 1G | CARBOHYDRATES - 51G | FAT - 1G

POACHED APRICOTS WITH ROSEWATER

INGREDIENTS

- 50g of golden caster sugar
- 400g of ripe apricots, halved and stoned
- 100mls of water
- A few drops of rosewater
- Greek yoghurt, to serve
- Optional: chopped pistachios

METHOD

1. Preheat the slow cooker on a Low setting.
2. Add the apricots and sugar to the slow cooker and pour 100ml of water over the top.
3. Put the lid on and cook on Low for 2 hours until the apricots are soft.
4. Turn off the heat and add the rosewater. Leave to cool.
5. Serve in dessert glasses with dollops of yoghurt or whipped cream and sprinkled with nuts.

NUTRITION PER PORTION:

SERVES - 2 | CALORIES - 161KCAL | PROTEIN - 2G | CARBOHYDRATES - 41G | FAT - 0G

APPLE FLAPJACK CRUMBLE

INGREDIENTS

- 3-4 tablespoons of apricot jam
- 1.1kg of eating apples, peeled, cored and sliced thinly
- Juice of 1 large orange

For the crumble topping

- 140g of porridge oats
- 1 teaspoon of ground cinnamon
- 100g of light muscovado sugar
- 100g of butter
- 100g of plain flour
- 1 tablespoon of golden syrup

METHOD

1. Preheat the slow cooker on a low setting.
2. Place the apples, jam and orange juice in your slow cooker and cook on a Low setting for 2-4 hours until the fruit is tender.
3. When the fruit is nearly cooked, mix all the ingredients for the crumble topping in a container together, and tip onto a greased baking tray or shallow cooking tin.
4. Toast the topping mixture under a low-heat grill for 1-2 minutes until crispy and golden. Take care not to burn it!
5. In the meantime, transfer the cooked apples to a dish and sprinkle over the crumble mixture, pressing it down gently. Allow to cool.
6. Delicious served with warm custard, ice-cream or cream.

NUTRITION PER PORTION:
SERVES - 2 | CALORIES - 447KCAL | PROTEIN - 6G | CARBOHYDRATES - 75G | FAT - 16G

SPICY POACHED PEARS IN CHOCOLATE SAUCE

INGREDIENTS

For the pears

- 750g of golden caster sugar
- 500ml of water
- 1 star anise
- 1 cinnamon stick

- 2 strips of lemon zest (use a potato peeler)
- 5 cloves
- 1 vanilla pod, split lengthways

- 2cm piece of fresh root ginger, peeled and thinly sliced
- 4 ripe pears, peeled, but retain the stalk for dipping at the end

For the chocolate sauce

- 200g of good-quality dark chocolate broken into pieces

- 140mls of double cream
- 150mls of full-fat milk

- A pinch ground cinnamon

METHOD

1. Preheat the slow cook on a Low setting.
2. Pour 500mls of water into the slow cooker and add the sugar, cinnamon stick, star anise, lemon zest, vanilla, cloves and ginger. Stir to mix.
3. Put the lid on and cook on High for about 15 minutes until the sugar has completely dissolved.
4. Remove the lid to add the pears to the slow cooker. Cover again, turn the heat to Low and cook for 2-3 hours until tender.
5. To make the chocolate sauce: In a saucepan over a medium heat, combine the cream, milk and cinnamon and bring to the boil, stirring continuously.
6. Put the dark chocolate pieces into a heatproof bowl and melt over a saucepan of water, or in the microwave. Add to the cream, milk and cinnamon and stir.
7. When the pears are cook, drain, hold the stems, then dip each one in the chocolate sauce so they are completely covered.
8. Serve each pear with a generous scoop of vanilla ice cream or clotted cream.

NUTRITION PER PORTION:
SERVES - 4 | CALORIES - 642KCAL | PROTEIN - 6G | CARBOHYDRATES - 66G | FAT - 41G

BANANA UPSIDE DOWN CAKE

INGREDIENTS

For the banana

- 3 tablespoons of dark rum
- 6 bananas cut in half, lengthways
- 30g of unsalted butter, plus more for greasing
- 150g of dark brown sugar

For the cake

- 100g of plain flour
- ¼ teaspoons of ground nutmeg
- 1/2 teaspoon of ground cinnamon
- 3/4 teaspoon of baking powder
- ¼ teaspoon of fine salt
- 60g of softened, unsalted butter
- 130g of sugar
- 1 large egg
- 1 egg yolk only
- 30ml of whole milk at room temperature
- Ice cream to serve

METHOD

1. Grease the inside of the slow cooker with butter and line completely with buttered foil.
2. Preheat the slow cooker on a High setting. Position the butter, rum and brown sugar evenly at the bottom of the slow cooker, then add the halved bananas, pushing the cut (flat) side down into the sugar.
3. In a container, sift the flour together with the cinnamon, baking powder, nutmeg, and salt so they combine evenly.
4. In a separate bowl, beat the butter and sugar until light and fluffy.
5. Beat in the egg until it's combined, then beat in the yolk.
6. Alternate folding in the flour and the milk and beat briefly until combined into a smooth cake batter.
7. Pour the cake mixture over the bananas and level out.
8. Lay a paper towel over the top of the slow cooker to stop the condensation falling into the cake mixture, but not so it's touching the cake, and close the lid firmly.
9. Cook on a High setting for about 3 ½ hours.
10. Turn off the slow cooker, and leave in the slow cooker, lid remaining closed, for a further 20 minutes.
11. Lift the cake from the slow cooker and leave to cool on a cooling rack for about 30 minutes.
12. Remove the foil and turn the cake out directly onto a plate so that the bananas are on top.
13. Serve in slices with cream or ice cream.

NUTRITION PER PORTION:

SERVES - 6 | CALORIES - 491KCAL | PROTEIN - 5G | CARBOHYDRATES - 87G | FAT - 15G

CHOCOLATE FONDUE

INGREDIENTS

- 340g of milk chocolate pieces
- 112g of dark chocolate pieces
- 235mls of double cream
- 1 teaspoon of vanilla extract
- 120mls of milk
- ¼ teaspoon of salt
- Optional: 30mls of bourbon, or orange, coffee or hazelnut liqueur
- Fondue dippers: pretzels, cake, crisp bacon, crisps, strawberries, waffles and cookies for example

METHOD

1. Use a large heatproof bowl - check it will fit in your slow cooker - and add the milk chocolate, dark chocolate, cream, milk, vanilla and salt.
2. Cover and cook on a Low setting for 45 minutes.
3. Remove the lid and stir the chocolate mixture until smooth.

4. Optional: Stir in the bourbon or liqueur now if using.
5. Cover again and continue to cook on Low for a further 15 to 30 minutes until all the chocolate pieces are melted.
6. Uncover the slow cooker and whisk the fondue until it's smooth and velvety.
7. Turn the slow cooker setting to keep warm and serve the chocolate fondue direct from it. Arrange the dippers around the side of the cooker for easy access.

Note: When removing the lid to stir the fondue, wipe off the condensation so it doesn't drip into the fondue and spoil it.

NUTRITIONAL INFORMATION PER SERVING (FONDUE ONLY):
SERVES - 12 | CALORIES - 292KCAL | PROTEIN - 4G | CARBOHYDRATES - 21G | FAT - 23G

UPSIDE DOWN PINEAPPLE CAKE

INGREDIENTS

- 142g of softened, unsalted butter
- 85g of light brown sugar
- 30mls of dark rum
- 1/2 a medium pineapple, peeled, cored, and cut into rings
- 3/4 teaspoon of baking powder
- 125g of plain flour

- 1/4 teaspoon of freshly grated nutmeg
- 63g of pecans, toasted and finely chopped
- 133g of granulated sugar
- 1/2 teaspoon of ground cinnamon
- A pinch of salt
- 1 teaspoon of vanilla extract

- 2 large eggs
- 30mls of whole milk
- 120mls of double cream
- 1 tablespoon of icing sugar
- 1 tablespoon of chopped maraschino cherries
- Whole cherries for garnish

METHOD

1. Grease your slow cooker thoroughly with a little butter, then line with buttered foil. Preheat your slow cooker on a Low setting.
2. Cut 60g of butter into small cubes and scatter in the slow cooker with the rum and brown sugar.
3. Arrange the pineapple rings in overlapping circles so they completely cover the bottom of the insert; press lightly into the sugar mixture.
4. In a separate bowl mix flour, baking powder, cinnamon, pecans, salt and nutmeg, until combined.
5. Beat the remaining butter and granulated sugar together until the mixture is light and fluffy. Add the eggs and vanilla extract.
6. Fold in the flour mixture and add the milk, finally beating the cake batter until it's smooth.
7. Spread the batter over the pineapples and spread out evenly.
8. Add a layer of kitchen roll between the lid and the slow cooker (without touching the cake) to prevent condensation from dripping from the cover onto the cake.
9. Close the lid firmly and cook on Low for 3-4 hours.
10. Turn off the slow cooker and leave the cake to rest for 20 minutes before lifting it onto a cooling rack.
11. Turn the cake out onto a plate and remove the foil, so that the pineapples are at the top.
12. Whip the cream and carefully stir icing sugar and cherries.
13. Serve the cake in slices with the cherries and cream. Pop a whole cherry on top!

NUTRITION PER PORTION:
SERVES - 8 | CALORIES - 521KCAL | PROTEIN - 5G | CARBOHYDRATES - 51G | FAT - 34G

BERRY COBBLER

INGREDIENTS

For the Berry Filling

- Unsalted butter, for greasing
- 30g of cornflour
- Juice of 1 lemon
- 700g of frozen mixed berries
- 135g of granulated sugar

For the Biscuit Topping

- 1 teaspoon of baking powder
- 160g of plain flour
- ¼ teaspoon of salt
- 45g of granulated sugar
- 60g of chilled, unsalted butter, diced
- 180mls of milk
- 1/4 teaspoon of ground cinnamon

For the Whipped Sour Cream Topping

- 120mls of double cream
- 60mls of sour cream
- 15g of icing sugar

METHOD

1. Grease your slow cooker thoroughly with a little butter. Preheat your slow cooker on a Low setting.
2. Whisk the cornflour, lemon juice and about 30mls of water in a small bowl. Add the mixture to the slow cooker, then toss in the frozen berries and granulated sugar. Mix.
3. For the biscuit topping: In a separate bowl, combine the plain flour with 25g of granulated sugar, baking powder and salt. Add the butter and rub the mixture between your fingers until it resembles breadcrumbs.
4. Gradually add the milk and stir in with a fork until you have a wet dough.
5. Use a spoon to scoop out the dough and drop spoonfuls evenly over the berry mixture.
6. Combine the remaining sugar and the cinnamon in a small bowl and sprinkle it evenly over the top of dough.
7. Cover the slow cooker with the lid and cook on High for 3 ½ hours. Add an extra 30 minutes if it isn't cooked.
8. Turn off the slow cooker and allow to cool before removing onto a cooling rack.
9. For the sour cream topping: Beat the double cream, icing sugar and sour cream together in a container.
10. Serve the cobbler warm, topped with cream.

NUTRITION PER PORTION:

SERVES - 6 | CALORIES - 507KCAL | PROTEIN - 6G | CARBOHYDRATES - 74G | FAT - 22G

PEACH COBBLER

INGREDIENTS

For the peach filling

- Unsalted butter, for greasing insert
- 30g of cornflour
- 30mls of orange juice
- 700g of frozen peaches
- 135g of granulated sugar

For the biscuit topping

- 1 teaspoon of baking powder
- 160g of plain flour
- ¼ teaspoon of salt
- 45g of granulated sugar
- 60g of unsalted butter, chilled and diced
- 1/4 teaspoon of ground cinnamon
- 180mls of milk
- 1/4 teaspoon ground ginger
- Optional: 1/4 to 1/2 teaspoon almond extract

For the topping

- 120mls of double cream
- 60mls of sour cream
- 15g of icing sugar

METHOD

1. Grease your slow cooker thoroughly with a little butter. Preheat your slow cooker on a Low setting.
2. Whisk the cornflour, orange juice and about 30mls of water in a small bowl. Add the mixture to the slow cooker, then toss in the frozen peaches and granulated sugar. Mix.
3. For the biscuit topping: In a separate bowl, combine the plain flour with 25g of granulated sugar, baking powder and salt. Add the butter and rub the mixture between your fingers until it resembles breadcrumbs.
4. Gradually add the milk with the (optional) almond extract and stir in with a fork until you have a wet dough.
5. Use a spoon to scoop out the dough and drop spoonfuls evenly over the peach mixture.
6. Combine the remaining sugar, ginger and the cinnamon in a small bowl and sprinkle it evenly over the top of dough.
7. Cover the slow cooker with the lid and cook on High for 3 ½ hours. Add an extra 30 minutes if it isn't cooked.
8. Turn off the slow cooker and allow to cool before removing onto a cooling rack.
9. For the sour cream topping: Meanwhile, mix the sour cream with the double cream and icing sugar in a container whisk until it creates soft peaks.
10. Serve topped with the cream topping.

NUTRITION PER PORTION:

SERVES - 6 | CALORIES - 522KCAL | PROTEIN - 7G | CARBOHYDRATES - 79G | FAT - 29G

BROWNIE CAKE

INGREDIENTS

- 170g of unsalted butter, melted
- 300g of sugar
- 3 large eggs, lightly beaten
- 67g of unsweetened cocoa powder
- 1 teaspoon of vanilla extract
- 42g of plain flour
- ¼ teaspoon of salt
- 80g of large milk chocolate chips

METHOD

1. Grease your slow cooker thoroughly with a little butter, then line with buttered foil. Preheat your slow cooker on a Low setting.
2. In a container, whisk to combine all the ingredients together.
3. Put the mixture into the slow cooker and lightly spread in an even layer.
4. Put the lid on and cook on a Low setting for 3 hours until the cake is set around the edges and gooey in the centre.
5. Delicious served as warm slices with a scoop of ice cream, or dollop of double cream.

NUTRITION PER PORTION:

SERVES - 6 | CALORIES - 561KCAL | PROTEIN - 8G | CARBOHYDRATES - 72G | FAT - 32G

APPLES STUFFED WITH WALNUTS AND CRANBERRIES

INGREDIENTS

- 75g of walnuts, toasted and chopped
- 65g of chopped dried cranberries
- 56g of packed light brown sugar
- 52g of rolled oats
- 43g of unsalted butter, cut into small pieces
- 1/2 teaspoon of ground cinnamon
- 15mls of fresh lemon juice
- 6 firm cooking apples, washed and cored – see step 2 below
- Pinch of salt
- 230mls of apple cider
- Optional: Vanilla ice cream
- Optional: Maple syrup

METHOD

1. Mix the nuts, oats, cranberries, sugar, salt, cinnamon, butter and lemon juice all together in a container. The final mixture should be wet and grainy in texture.
2. Remove the core carefully from the apples. You shouldn't go right through the bottom or collapse the sides. Stuff each apple with some of the cranberry-walnut mixture.
3. Preheat the slow cooker on a Low setting and lightly spritz with cooking oil.
4. Put the apples in the slow cooker and pour in the apple cider.
5. Put the lid on the slow cooker and cook on a Low setting for 3-4 hours until the apples are tender but still firm.
   NOTE: Cooking time will depend on the size and type of apple, so if your apples are on the smaller size, check after 2 hours.
6. Serve each apple with ice cream and maple syrup.

NUTRITION PER PORTION:
SERVES - 4 | CALORIES - 454KCAL | PROTEIN - 7G | CARBOHYDRATES - 61G | FAT - 23G

CHOCOLATE LAVA CAKE
• •

INGREDIENTS

- 250g of self-raising flour
- 200g of granulated sugar
- 60g of cocoa powder
- Pinch of salt
- 200mls of milk
- 150g of butter, melted
- 2 teaspoons of vanilla extract
- 50g of light brown sugar
- 300mls of hot water

METHOD

1. Preheat the slow cooker and lightly spritz with cooking oil.
2. In a container, blend the flour, granulated sugar, 40g of the cocoa powder and a pinch of salt.
3. Add the butter, milk and vanilla extract to the flour mixture and whisk to a smooth batter.
4. Pour the batter into the slow cooker.
5. Sprinkle the brown sugar evenly over the cake batter in the slow cooker, followed by the remaining cocoa powder.
6. Finally, pour the hot water over the top of everything - but don't stir the mixture.
7. Close the lid of the slow cooker and cook on High for 3 hours, or Low for 5 hours.
8. Serve warm topped with vanilla ice cream, and a drizzle of chocolate syrup.

NUTRITION PER PORTION:
SERVES - 6 | CALORIES - 538KCAL | PROTEIN - 8G | CARBOHYDRATES - 81G | FAT - 23G

BREAD AND BUTTER PUDDING
• •

INGREDIENTS

- 8 slices of thick-sliced white bread
- 70g of butter
- 60g of sugar
- 60g of sultanas
- 450mls of milk
- 250mls of double cream
- 3 medium eggs
- 3 teaspoons of mixed spice

METHOD

1. Grease the slow cooker thoroughly with a little butter and preheat on a Low setting.
2. Butter both sides of each slice of bread, then cut each slice into six pieces. Layer the slices in the slow cooker, sprinkling the sultanas evenly among the layers.
3. Whisk the eggs then beat in 50g of the sugar, milk, cream, and mixed spice.
4. Pour the egg mixture evenly over the bread in the slow cooker so all of the bread is soaked through. The top layer should be just about peeping through the egg mixture, not entirely covered.
5. Scatter the remaining sugar evenly on the top of the pudding.
6. Place clean kitchen roll under the lid of the pot to absorb any excess moisture, then close it firmly.
7. Cook for on a Low setting for 3½ hours or for 2 hours on High.
8. Serve hot or cold with your favourite accompaniment.

NUTRITION PER PORTION:
SERVES - 6 | CALORIES - 465CAL | PROTEIN - 10G | CARBOHYDRATES - 40 G | FAT - 31G

GINGERBREAD CAKE

• •

INGREDIENTS

- 85g of black treacle
- 150g of salted butter
- 100g of golden syrup
- 125g of soft brown muscovado sugar
- 2 large eggs, beaten
- 225g of plain flour

- 2½ teaspoons of ground cinnamon
- 3 level tablespoons of ground ginger
- 1½ teaspoons of fresh ginger, finely crushed
- 1½ teaspoons of baking powder

- Juice from ½ a lime
- 60mls of milk, warmed slightly
- Optional: icing sugar to dust over the top of the cake

METHOD

1. Grease the slow cooker all over with butter and line the bottom with a circle of parchment paper. Preheat the slow cooker on a low setting.
2. Put the sugar, butter, treacle and syrup together into a saucepan over a low heat and stir. Don't allow it to come to the boil, but once the ingredients have mixed into a liquid take off the heat, set aside and allow to cool for a few minutes.
3. In a separate bowl, whisk the eggs. Once treacle mixture has cooled to a warm (rather than hot) temperature, whisk in with the eggs.
4. Now stir in the flour, baking powder, spices (ginger and cinnamon) and lime juice. Finally, pour in the warmed milk and mix thoroughly.
5. Pour the cake mixture into the slow cooker and spread evenly with a spatula. Place a later of kitchen roll inside the lid to stop any condensation dropping into the cake.
6. Cook on a High setting for 2 hours. Once cooked, turn off the heat and leave to stand for 10 minutes in the slow cooker.
7. Once it's cool enough to touch, you can remove the cake from the slow cooker to a cooling rack.
8. Once cold and ready to eat, drizzle with (optional) icing or simply slice and serve!

NUTRITION PER PORTION:
SERVES - 8 | CALORIES - 398CAL | PROTEIN - 5G | CARBOHYDRATES - 57G | FAT - 27G

VANILLA AND BLUEBERRY RICE PUDDING

INGREDIENTS

- 120g of pudding rice
- 800mls of milk
- 200mls of water
- 4 tablespoons of maple syrup
- 1 teaspoon of vanilla paste
- A handful of fresh blueberries
- 1 ripe banana, sliced

METHOD

1. Preheat the slow cooker on a High setting, and grease all over with a little butter.
2. Put the milk, 200ml of water, half the maple syrup and the vanilla into a big pan and bring to a simmer.
3. Add the pudding rice into the slow cooker and pour the warm milk mixture on top.
4. Cook for 2½ hours on High, stirring at intervals.
5. Serve the rice pudding scattered with the blueberries and banana and the remaining maple syrup or honey drizzled on top.

NUTRITION PER PORTION:

SERVES - 4-6 | CALORIES - 224CAL | PROTEIN - 5G | CARBOHYDRATES - 57G | FAT - 27G

'GROWN-UP' RICE PUDDING WITH A BOOZY SAUCE

INGREDIENTS

For the sauce and topping

- 50mls of vodka
- 150g of mixed dried fruit
- 6 teaspoons of crème fraiche
- 150g of fresh redcurrants

For the rice pudding

- 1.5 litres of semi-skimmed milk
- 3 tablespoons of runny honey
- 500mls of single cream
- 1 vanilla pod
- 1 cinnamon stick
- 300g of pudding rice

METHOD

1. Combine the vodka and dried fruit in a pan together enough water to about cover. Simmer for 10 minutes.
2. Transfer to a blender with 75mls of cold water and pulse until smooth.
3. Grease the slow cooker all over with a little butter then preheat on a High setting.
4. Put the milk, cream, honey, and cinnamon stick into another pan. Open the vanilla pod lengthways, scrape the seeds out, and put them in the pan. Bring it all to a simmer.
5. Add all the pudding rice to the slow cooker and pour the warm milk mixture on top.
6. Cook for 2½ hours on High, stirring at intervals.
7. Transfer the cooked pudding to a serving bowl, stir through with the (boozy) fruit sauce and serve topped with crème fraiche and a scattering of fresh redcurrants.

NUTRITION PER PORTION:

SERVES - 6 | CALORIES - 604KCAL | PROTEIN - 5G | CARBOHYDRATES - 57G | FAT - 23G

TANGERINE AND POMEGRANATE CHEESECAKE

INGREDIENTS

- Butter to grease
- 8 sponge/trifle fingers
- 500g of full fat cream cheese
- 80g of caster sugar

- 3 eggs
- 100mls of double cream
- 30mls of freshly squeezed lemon juice

- 2 teaspoons of vanilla extract
- 1 teaspoon of fresh grated lemon zest

For the topping

- 3 tangerines, clementines or satsumas peeled and sliced

- 2-3 tablespoons of pomegranate seeds

- Optional: icing sugar
- Optional: a few mint leaves

METHOD

1. Use a little butter to thoroughly grease a 15cm diameter straight-sided baking dish, then line it with baking paper.
2. Arrange the sponge fingers over the base of the dish.
3. In a large bowl, beat the cream cheese to soften it, add the caster sugar and beat again until you have a smooth mixture.
4. In a separate bowl, beat the eggs, cream and vanilla together and gradually mix into the cream cheese and sugar. Stir in lemon zest and juice.
5. Tip into the prepared dish, covering the sponge fingers, and spread evenly.
6. Cover tightly with a piece of buttered foil.
7. Prepare the slow cooker.
   - Find a heatproof plate that fits snugly inside the slow cooker and place it upside-down in the bottom.
   - Pour 400ml boiling water over the plate and into the bottom of the slow cooker - it should rise about 4cm up the sides.
   - Sit the cake tin on top of the plate.
   - Wrap the slow cooker lid in a tea towel to prevent condensation from dripping onto the cheesecake and close the lid.
8. Cook on High for 2-2½ hours, until set.
9. Remove the cooked cheesecake from the slow cooker and leave to cool for 2 hours, then refrigerate overnight.
10. Serve decorated with slices of satsuma or clementine and scattered with pomegranate seeds.

NUTRITION PER PORTION:
SERVES - 6 | CALORIES - 425KCAL | PROTEIN - 13G | CARBOHYDRATES - 33G | FAT - 30G

CHRISTMAS MINCEMEAT SPONGE PUD

INGREDIENTS

- Butter to grease
- 30g of golden syrup
- 75g of mincemeat
- 30ml of brandy or rum
- 125g of butter

- 125g of caster sugar
- Zest of 1 orange
- Zest of 1 lemon
- 2 large eggs
- 125g of self-raising flour

- 1 tablespoon of milk
- Pinch of salt
- Optional: single cream, custard, whipped cream or brandy butter to serve

METHOD

1. Preheat your slow cooker on a low setting.
2. Thoroughly grease a pudding basin with butter.

3. Measure the golden syrup into the pudding basin first, then in a separate bowl, combine the mincemeat and brandy/rum and put half of it onto the syrup in the basin.
4. In another bowl, beat the butter and sugar together until the mixture is light and fluffy. Gently mix in the eggs, followed by the orange zest, lemon zest and the rest of the mincemeat mix.
5. Fold the flour and salt carefully into the beaten cake mixture then stir in the milk.
6. Pour the finished pudding mixture into the basin on top of the syrup and mincemeat. Use a spatula to level the surface and cover tightly with buttered foil.
7. Prepare the slow cooker.
   - Find a heatproof plate that fits snugly inside the slow cooker and place it upside-down in the bottom.
   - Pour 400ml boiling water over the plate and into the bottom of the slow cooker - it should rise about 4cm up the sides.
   - Sit the pudding basin on top of the plate.
   - Wrap the slow cooker lid in a tea towel to prevent condensation from dripping onto the pudding and close the lid.
8. Cover and cook on High for 3-3½ hours.
9. When cooked, remove the pudding basin from the slow cooker and allow to cool for 20 minutes. Loosen the pudding with a knife slipped around the edge of the basin and turn onto a plate.
10. Serve hot in bowls, covered with cream, custard or brandy butter.

NUTRITION PER PORTION:
SERVES - 6 | CALORIES - 385KCAL | PROTEIN - 5G | CARBOHYDRATES - 48G | FAT - 19G

CHOCOLATE ORANGE SPONGE PUDDING

INGREDIENTS

- 125g of butter plus extra for greasing
- 125g of light soft brown sugar
- 2 eggs
- zest of 1 orange
- 125g of light soft brown sugar

- 1 teaspoon of orange extract (vanilla is a good substitute)
- 2 tablespoons of fine-shred orange marmalade
- 110g of self-raising flour
- 1/4 teaspoon of baking powder
- 15g of cocoa powder

- ¼ teaspoon of salt
- 30mls of milk
- 42g pack of Galaxy Minstrels
- Optional: crème fraiche or whipped cream and orange zest to serve

METHOD
1. Preheat your slow cooker on a low setting; and butter a pudding basin.
2. Gently mix in the eggs, followed by the orange zest, orange (or vanilla) extract and marmalade.
3. Combine the sugar, flour, salt, baking powder and cocoa powder together, then fold into the pudding mixture. Add the milk and Minstrels.
4. Pour the mixture into the pudding basin and cover tightly with a piece of buttered foil.
5. Prepare the slow cooker.
   - Find a heatproof plate that fits snugly inside the slow cooker and place it upside-down in the bottom.
   - Pour 400ml boiling water over the plate and into the bottom of the slow cooker - it should rise about 4cm up the sides.
   - Sit the pudding basin on top of the plate.
   - Wrap the slow cooker lid in a tea towel to prevent condensation from dripping onto the pudding and close the lid.
6. Close the lid and cook on High for 3-3½ hours.

7. When cooked, remove the pudding basin from the slow cooker and allow to cool for 20 minutes. Loosen the pudding with a knife slipped around the edge of the basin and turn onto a plate.
8. Serve hot in bowls, covered with cream, custard or ice cream. Sprinkle with chips of Minstrels.

NUTRITION PER PORTION:
SERVES - 6 | CALORIES - 388KCAL | PROTEIN - 6G | CARBOHYDRATES - 47G | FAT - 22G

CHAI RICE PUDDING - VEGAN

INGREDIENTS

- 1 litre of unsweetened almond milk
- 2 chai teabags
- ¼ teaspoon of vanilla extract
- 150g pudding rice, rinsed
- 6 teaspoons sweetener
- Optional: ground cinnamon

METHOD
1. Thoroughly grease the slow cooker with butter and preheat on a Low setting.
2. Heat the milk, teabags and vanilla extract over a medium heat and simmer for 10 minutes, but don't let it boil.
3. Take off the heat and set to one side of 15 minutes so the teabags can infuse the milk. Now, squeeze, remove and discard the teabags
4. Put the rice into the slow cooker and pour the warmed chai milk over the top.
5. Turn the slow cooker setting to High and cook for 3 hours stirring at intervals. The rice should have absorbed most of the liquid and have a creamy consistency.
6. Add the sweetener to taste and stir in. Serve sprinkled with a little ground cinnamon.

NUTRITION PER PORTION:
SERVES - 6 | CALORIES - 136KCAL | PROTEIN - 3G | CARBOHYDRATES - 30G | FAT - 2G

BASIC CHOCOLATE CAKE WITH CHOCOLATE GLAZE

INGREDIENTS

- 275g of caster sugar
- 2 large eggs
- 150mls of oil
- 150mls of water
- 50mls of milk
- 1 teaspoon of vanilla essence
- 300g of self raising flour
- 1½ teaspoons of baking powder
- 70g of cocoa

For the Chocolate Glaze

- 65g of cocoa powder (sieved),
- 100g of icing sugar (sieved),
- 1 tablespoon of butter,
- 90ml of milk
- ½ teaspoon of vanilla essence

METHOD
1. Grease the slow cooker thoroughly with a little butter and line with one large piece of foil pressed neatly into the slow cooker so that it reaches halfway up the sides.
2. Next, line over the foil with baking parchment using one large piece pressed neatly into the pot and flattened against the sides of the cooker.
3. Preheat the slow cooker on a high setting while you prepare the cake mixture.
4. Beat the eggs with the oil, water, milk and sugar in a large bowl, then gradually fold in the sifted flour, cocoa, baking powder and vanilla.
5. Next, pour the cake batter into the slow cooker over the foil and parchment linings.

6. Trap some kitchen roll between the lid and the slow cooker as you close it. This will absorb any condensation and stop it dripping onto the cake.
7. Cook on a High setting for 2 hours.
8. When cooked, lift the cake from the slow cooker using the edges of the foil/parchment and leave to cool on a cooling rack.
9. Once cool, remove the paper from the cake and discard.
10. For the glaze: Heat all the ingredients in a saucepan over a medium heat. Bring to a rolling boil for 2 minutes, stirring continuously. Allow to cool for 20 minutes before stirring in the icing sugar. Pour into the middle of the cake and allow to run and drip over the sides.
11. Serve in slices.

NUTRITION PER PORTION:

SERVES - 8 | CALORIES - 480KCAL | PROTEIN - 7G | CARBOHYDRATES - 70G | FAT - 20G

PEAR AND ALMOND SPONGE

INGREDIENTS

- 400g of tinned pears, cut into 1cm slices
- 140g of self-raising flour self
- 1 teaspoon of baking powder
- 30g of almond flour
- 170g of butter
- 140g of sugar
- 3 medium eggs
- 45mls of milk
- 25g of flaked almonds
- 8 tablespoons of golden syrup
- 2 teaspoons of almond essence
- ½ teaspoon of vanilla essence

METHOD

1. Thoroughly grease the slow cooker with butter and line the bottom with a sheet of baking parchment. Preheat the slow cooker on a Low setting.
2. Beat the sugar and the butter together in a container until they are creamy and fluffy, then stir in the eggs. Gradually fold in the self-raising flour, the almond flour and the baking powder with a metal spoon.
3. Stir in the milk along with the almond and vanilla essence and set the cake batter to one side for a while.
4. To create the cake topping: pour the syrup over the parchment lining the bottom of the slow cooker, then scatter the flaked almonds evenly over the syrup. Arrange the pear slices evenly over the flaked almonds and syrup.
5. Finally, pour the cake mixture over the pears, almonds, and level it out with a spatula.
6. Place some kitchen roll between the cake mixture and the slow cooker lid and close the lid to secure it. This will stop any condensation dripping onto the cake and spoiling it.
7. Cook on High for 2 hours.
8. Once baked, remove carefully from the slow cooker and turn the cake onto a plate so that the pears are on the top. Remove the parchment to reveal a delicious golden almond and pear topped sponge cake.
9. Serve hot with cream or custard or, cool in traditional slices.

NUTRITION PER PORTION:

SERVES - 6 | CALORIES - 599KCAL | PROTEIN - 8G | CARBOHYDRATES - 75G | FAT - 31G

PLUM AND CARDAMOM CHEESECAKE

INGREDIENTS

For the topping

- 400g of plums, halved & stones removed
- 80g of caster sugar
- Seeds of 3 cardamom pods, crushed

For the biscuit base

- 150g of gingernut biscuits
- 60g of butter

For the cheesecake

- 2 eggs
- 400g of cream cheese
- 70g of caster sugar
- 100ml of whipping cream

METHOD

1. Preheat the slow cooker and spritz lightly with cooking oil spray.
2. Prepare your container - but make sure it fits your slow cooker. Ideally, grease a deep 18cm tin/flan dish and line with nonstick baking paper.
3. Cook the plums in a pan until they soften. Add some water if necessary.
4. Add the caster sugar and crushed cardamom and cook until the mixture becomes syrupy. Pour into a blender and mix until smooth. Set to one side.
5. Put the gingernut biscuits in a blender and pulse until the mixture resembles fine breadcrumbs. Place in a container with the melted butter and combine well.
6. Press the biscuit mixture into the lined flan dish and place in the refrigerator for about 30 minutes.
7. Meanwhile, in a separate bowl beat the eggs, caster sugar and full fat soft cheese until thoroughly combined.
8. In a separate bowl, whip the cream to soft peaks, then add the soft cheese and combine. Swirl 100g of the plum coulis through.
9. Spread the cheesecake mixture over the chilled biscuit base and spread evenly.
10. Prepare the slow cooker.
    - Find a heatproof plate that fits snugly inside the slow cooker and place it upside-down in the bottom.
    - Pour 400ml boiling water over the plate and into the bottom of the slow cooker.
    - Sit the flan dish/tin on top of the plate.
    - Close the lid on the slow cooker
11. Cook on a Low setting for 2 ½ hours. Don't open the lid while cooking.
12. Turn off the slow cooker and leave the cheesecake to stand, covered with the lid for another 2 ½ hours.
13. Remove from the slow cooker and place in the fridge to chill overnight (or for 2 hours minimum).
14. When you're ready to serve it, very gently loosen and remove the cheesecake from the container and set on a plate, then pour the remaining plum coulis on top, creating an even layer.
15. Serve with cream.

NUTRITION PER PORTION:
SERVES - 8 | CALORIES - 563KCAL | PROTEIN - 8G | CARBOHYDRATES - 67G | FAT - 32G

DAMSON SPONGE PUDDING

INGREDIENTS

- 400g of damsons, halved with stones discarded
- 40g of light muscovado sugar
- 3 large eggs
- 100g of caster sugar
- 100g of self-raising flour
- 100g of butter
- ½ teaspoon of baking powder
- 30mls of milk

METHOD

1. Place the stoned damsons and sugar in a pan and cook gently until the fruit softens. Add a little more sugar if required.
2. Grease a pudding basin with butter. Place the cooked damsons in the bottom of the basin, cover and refrigerate.
3. Beat the butter and sugar together until the mixture is light and fluffy. Mix in the eggs, flour and baking powder gently until everything is combined then add the milk.
4. Pour the pudding mix into the basin, covering the damsons and seal with a pleated sheet of baking parchment, followed by a sheet of foil, secured to the rim with string.
5. Prepare the slow cooker.
   - Find a heatproof plate that fits snugly inside the slow cooker and place it upside-down in the bottom.
   - Pour 400ml boiling water over the plate and into the bottom of the slow cooker - it should rise about 4cm up the sides.
   - Sit the pudding basin on top of the plate.
   - Wrap the slow cooker lid in a tea towel to prevent condensation from dripping onto the pudding and close the lid.
6. Close the lid and cook on High for 3-3½ hours.
7. When cooked, remove the pudding basin from the slow cooker and allow to cool for 20 minutes. Loosen the pudding with a knife slipped around the edge of the basin and turn onto a plate.
8. Leave the pudding to sit for 20 minutes before removing it from the dish.
9. Serve warm with lashings of custard or double cream.

NUTRITION PER PORTION:

SERVES - 4 | CALORIES - 518KCAL | PROTEIN - 9G | CARBOHYDRATES - 65G | FAT - 30G

DAMSON AND APPLE UPSIDE DOWN CAKE

INGREDIENTS

- 250g of unsalted butter, softened
- 50g of demerara sugar
- 400g of damsons, halved with stones removed
- 150g of soft dark brown sugar
- 2 eggs
- 1½ teaspoons of mixed spice
- 225g of self-raising flour
- 3 apples, peeled, cored, and grated

METHOD

1. Grease the inside of the slow cooker with butter and line completely with a large piece of buttered foil.
2. Preheat the slow cooker on a High setting.
3. Cut 50g of the butter up into small pieces and sprinkle evenly in the base of the slow cooker. Repeat with the demerara sugar.
4. Now place the damsons evenly over the butter and sugar, cut-side down
5. In a separate bowl, beat the sugar and remaining butter together until light and fluffy, and stir in the eggs.
6. Fold in the flour, spices, and grated apple with a metal spoon until combined.
7. Pour the cake mixture over the damsons even the surface out with a spatula.
8. Lay a paper towel over the top of the slow cooker to stop the condensation falling into the cake mixture, but not so it's touching the cake, and close the lid firmly.
9. Cook on a High setting for about 3 ½ hours.
10. Turn off the slow cooker, and leave in the slow cooker, lid remaining closed, for a further 20 minutes.
11. Lift the cake from the slow cooker and leave to cool on a cooling rack for about 30 minutes.
12. Remove the foil and turn the cake out directly onto a plate so that the damsons are on top.
13. Serve in slices with cream or ice cream.

NUTRITION PER PORTION:

SERVES - 12 | CALORIES - 333KCAL | PROTEIN - 3G | CARBOHYDRATES - 41G | FAT - 18G

Disclaimer

EXCLUSIVE BONUS

40 Weight Loss Recipes

&

14 Days Meal Plan

Scan the QR-Code and receive
the FREE download:

Printed in Great Britain
by Amazon

16404716R00112